ALLSENSORS 2020

The Fifth International Conference on Advances in Sensors, Actuators, Metering and Sensing

November 21 – 25, 2020

Valencia, Spain

ALLSENSORS 2020 Editors

Jaime Lloret Mauri, Polytechnic University of Valencia, Spain
Paulo E. Cruvinel, Embrapa Instrumentation, Brazil
Almudena Rivadeneyra-Torres, University of Granada, Spain
Michael Niedermayer, Beuth University of Applied Sciences - Berlin, Germany
Sandrine Bernardini, Aix Marseille University, France
Matteo Tonezzer, CNR-IMEM, Trento, Italy

Printed from e-media with permission by:

Curran Associates, Inc.
57 Morehouse Lane
Red Hook, NY 12571

CURRAN ASSOCIATES INC.
proceedings
.com

Some format issues inherent in the e-media version may also appear in this print version.

International Academy, Research, and Industry Association (IARIA)
412 Derby Way
Wilmington, DE 19810

Phone: (408) 893-6407
Fax: (408) 527-6351

petre@iaria.org

Additional copies of this publication are available from:

Curran Associates, Inc.
57 Morehouse Lane
Red Hook, NY 12571 USA
Phone: 845-758-0400
Fax: 845-758-2633
Email: curran@proceedings.com
Web: www.proceedings.com

Table of Contents

ALLSENSORS 2020

Forward

The Fifth Conference on Advances in Sensors, Actuators, Metering and Sensing (ALLSENSORS 2020) covered related topics on theory practice and applications of sensor devices, techniques, data acquisition and processing, and on wired and wireless sensors and sensor networks.

Sensor networks and sensor-based systems support many applications today above ground. Underwater operations and applications are quite limited by comparison. Most applications refer to remotely controlled submersibles and wide-area data collection systems at a coarse granularity. Other remote sensing domains and applications are using special sensing devices and services. Transducers and actuators complement the monitoring and control and constitute an area of interest related to sensors. They make use of specific sensor-based measurements and convey appropriate control actions.

ALLSENSORS 2020 was intended to serve as a forum for researchers from the academia and the industry, professionals, standard developers, policy makers, investors and practitioners to present their recent results, to exchange ideas, and to establish new partnerships and collaborations.

The accepted papers covered a large spectrum of topics on techniques and applications, best practices, awareness and experiences as well as future trends and needs (both in research and practice) related to all aspects of sensor-based applications and services.

We take here the opportunity to warmly thank all the members of the ALLSENSORS 2020 technical program committee as well as the numerous reviewers. The creation of such a broad and high quality conference program would not have been possible without their involvement. We also kindly thank all the authors that dedicated much of their time and efforts to contribute to the ALLSENSORS 2020. We truly believe that thanks to all these efforts, the final conference program consists of top quality contributions.

This event could also not have been a reality without the support of many individuals, organizations and sponsors. In addition, we also gratefully thank the members of the ALLSENSORS 2020 organizing committee for their help in handling the logistics and for their work that is making this professional meeting a success.

We hope the ALLSENSORS 2020 was a successful international forum for the exchange of ideas and results between academia and industry and to promote further progress on the topics of sensors.

ALLSENSORS 2020 Chairs

ALLSENSORS 2020 General Chair
Jaime Lloret Mauri, Polytechnic University of Valencia, Spain

ALLSENSORS 2020 Steering Committee
Michael Niedermayer, Beuth University of Applied Sciences - Berlin, Germany
Paulo E. Cruvinel, Embrapa Instrumentation, Brazil
Sandrine Bernardini, Aix Marseille University, France
Matteo Tonezzer, Italian National Research Council - Institute of Materials for Electronics and Magnetism (CNR - IMEM), Italy

ALLSENSORS 2020 Publicity Chair
Daniel Andoni Basterrechea, Universitat Politecnica de Valencia, Spain

ALLSENSORS 2020 Advisory Committee
Manuel Vieira, CTS-ISEL, Portugal
Manuela Vieira, ISEL-ADEETC ; CTS-UNINOVA; DEE-FCT-UNL, Portugal

ALLSENSORS 2020
Committee

ALLSENSORS 2020 General Chair
Jaime Lloret Mauri, Polytechnic University of Valencia, Spain

ALLSENSORS 2020 Steering Committee
Michael Niedermayer, Beuth University of Applied Sciences – Berlin, Germany
Matteo Tonezzer CNR-IMEM, Trento, Italy
Paulo E. Cruvinel, Embrapa Instrumentation, Brazil
Sandrine Bernardini, Aix Marseille University, France

ALLSENSORS 2020 Publicity Chair
Daniel Andoni Basterrechea, Universitat Politecnica de Valencia, Spain

ALLSENSORS 2020 Advisory Committee
Manuel Vieira, CTS-ISEL, Portugal
Manuela Vieira, ISEL-ADEETC ; CTS-UNINOVA; DEE-FCT-UNL, Portugal

ALLSENSORS 2020 Technical Program Committee
Francesco Aggogeri, University of Brescia, Italy
Amin Al-Habaibeh, Nottingham Trent University, UK
Ammar Al-Jodah, Monash University, Australia
Kawiwat Amnatchotiphan, Rangsit University, Thailand
Darius Andriukaitis, Kaunas University of Technology, Lithuania
Roberto Beghi, Università degli Studi di Milano, Italy
Roc Berenguer Pérez, TECNUN - Technological Campus of the University of Navarra, Spain
Sandrine Bernardini, Aix Marseille University, France
Xavier Boddaert, Mines Saint Etienne | Centre Microélectronique de Provence (CMP), France
Ismail Butun, Mid Sweden University, Sweden / Abdullah Gul University, Kayseri, Turkey
Maria Candelaria Hernandez Goya, Universidad de La Laguna, Spain
Juan Vicente Capella Hernández, Universitat Politècnica de València, Spain
Vítor Carvalho, 2AI-EST-IPCA / Algoritmi Research Centre - UM, Portugal
Paula María Castro Castro, Universidade da Coruña, Spain
Debashish Chakravarty, IIT Khaargpur, India
Nan-Fu Chiu, National Taiwan Normal University,Taiwan
Paulo E. Cruvinel, Embrapa Instrumentation, Brazil
Emiliano Descrovi, Polytechnic University of Turin, Italy
Chérif Diallo, Université Gaston Berger (UGB), Senegal
Attilio Frangi, Politecnico di Milano, Italy
Orlando Frazão, INESC TEC, Porto, Portugal
Kelum Gamage, University of Glasgow, UK
Félix J. García Clemente, University of Murcia, Spain

Sergey Yurish, Excelera, S. L. | IFSA, Spain
Lan Zhang, AIST, Japan
Mohd Zamani Zulkifli, International Islamic Universiti, Malaysia

Copyright Information

UHF Printed Sensor for Force Detection

Almudena Rivadeneyra
Pervasive Electronics Advanced Research Laboratory (PEARL)
Department of Electronics and Computer Technology
University of Granada, 18071
Granada, Spain
email:arivadeneyra@ugr.es

Andreas Albrecht
Institute for Nanoelectronics
Technical University of Munich, 80333
Munich, Spain
email:andreas.albrecht@tum.de

Paolo Lugli
Faculty of Science
Free University of Bozen-Bolzano, 39100
Bozen-Bolzano, Italy
email: paolo.lugli@unibz.it

Markus Becherer
Institute for Nanoelectronics
Technical University of Munich, 80333
Munich, Spain
email: markus.becherer@tum.de

José F. Salmerón
Pervasive Electronics Advanced Research Laboratory (PEARL)
Department of Electronics and Computer Technology
University of Granada, 18071
Granada, Spain
email: jfsalmeron@ugr.es

Abstract— **In this contribution, we show the advances in the direction of designing Radiofrequency Identification (RFID) antennas with sensing capabilities. In this particular case, we have integrated a force/pressure sensor made of a silicon-based organic polymer in one of the arms of a dipole antenna made of silver paste. The sensor response to external forces modifies the resonance frequency of the dipole antenna that can be detected by an external RFID reader, building up a wireless force sensor system.**

Keywords— flexible; force sensor; pressure; printed electronics; Ultra-High Frequency band.

I. Introduction

In this paper, we focus on the Ultra-High Frequency (UHF) band (860 MHz) that is commonly used for Radiofrequency Identification (RFID) tags and communications. In particular, lots of effort has been made in the past decades to develop antennas operating in this frequency band with the so-called printed electronics [1]-[3]. The reasons behind this are the attractive features that such technology offers with respect to conventional ones, like the feasibility of creating electronics in virtually any substrate, its cost-effectiveness and large-scale manufacturing, among others [4]. There are many examples in the literature where printed UHF antennas are embedded in RFID tags with sensing capabilities [5]-[7]. However, these tags require the utilization of silicon chips to transmit the information, leading to hybrid electronics, which slows the fabrication process and makes more difficult their industrialisation [8]. An alternative that has arisen interest in the last years is the implementation of wireless chipless sensors. The characteristic of these sensor tags is the design of sensors whose information is associated with their electromagnetic properties, such as the resonance frequency or the threshold power magnitude [9].

What we describe in this paper is precisely an UHF chipless sensor for pressure detection. The sensor is fabricated by screen printing of silver and poly(dimethylsiloxane) (PDMS) and its working principle is the variation in the resonance frequency when a certain pressure is applied in the UHF antenna.

The rest of the paper is structured as follows. In Section 2, the fabrication of the sensor and its characterization are presented. The results of the sensor' characterization are shown in Section 3, together with the discussion. Finally, the main conclusions are drawn in Section 4.

II. Materials and Methods

The silver (Ag) screen printing paste employed in this work to print the antenna was LOCTITE ECI 1010 0.2KG E&C by Henkel (Germany) used without modifications. An array of pillar was made of polydimethylsiloxane (PDMS) formulated as in [10], but deposited with screen printing. All pastes were printed onto thermally pre-heated (100°C for 30 min) polyethylene terephthalate (PET) Melinex 506 of DuPont of a thickness of 100 µm. A manual screen printer (Nino from Coruna, Switzerland) was used to print with a screen with 120 threads/cm of mesh density. After printing, the pastes were dried at 100°C for 30 min in an Memmert oven before printing the next type of paste.

The E5061B ENA Vector Network Analyzer of Keyight was utilized for the S_{11} parameter measurements, as described in [11]. Similar capacitive pressure sensors were already studied in [12].

III. Results and Discussion

We investigated the use of our thin pressure sensors without a dielectric, as these are shorted at a certain pressure. Figure 1 shows the patterned area that acts as the sensor. The dielectric is structured in pillars and the contact area corresponds precisely to the areas between pillars when certain pressure is applied in the patterned area. At UHF frequency, the sensor device behaves as a capacitor in series with one of the antenna dipole arms. When pressure is applied, the sensor device behaves as a series resistor, ideally a short-circuit, leading to a change in both the resonance frequency and the magnitude, as shown in Figure 2.

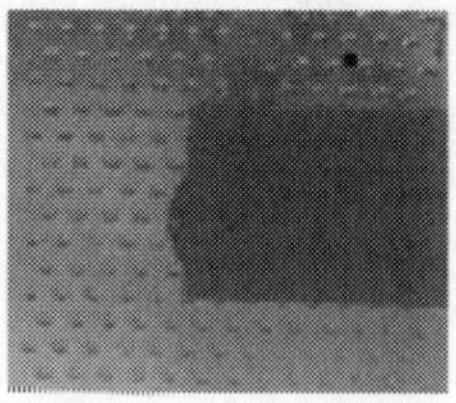

Figure 1. Pressure-sensing area.

We studied the frequency response, represented in Figure 2, by pressing and releasing several times with a plastic clamp (button area) over the sensor area.

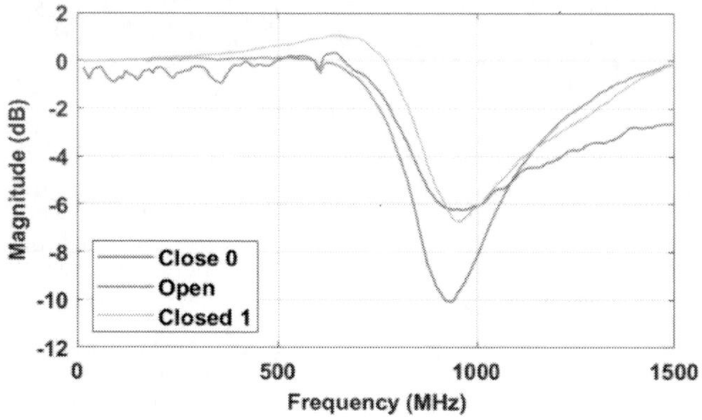

Figure 2. S_{11} magnitude for open and close states. Close 0 corresponds to the first attemp of closing the button, followed by Open when the button is released and finally Close 1 when the button is pressed again.

The dipole antenna that can be modelled as RLC series circuit was designed to resonate at 868 MHz when the sensor is pressed. When the sensor is released, a small series capacitance is added to the dipole series capacitance causing a shift of the resonance frequency upwards. This detuning of the resonance frequency is enough to be discriminated by an RFID reader, but it is not enough to inhibit the wireless link between the reader and the sensor tag.

IV. Conclusions

In this contribution, we present the possibility of designing a printed UHF sensor for force detection based on PDMS and silver on a flexible substrate. In particular, there is a shift in the resonance frequency as well as a change in its magnitude when the force is applied in the area where the structured PDMS has been deposited. When pressing the mentioned area, the resonance frequency is increased and its magnitude decreases. This solution paves the way for including sensor information in printed RFID antennas. In the future, we will study in depth the influence of the force applied on the resonance frequency together with the analysis of the area where the structured PDMS is located.

Acknowledgment

This work has been partially supported by the fellowship H2020-MSCA-IF-2017-794885-SELFSENS and the TUM Graduate School.

References

[1] A. Falco, J. F. Salmerón, F. C. Loghin, P. Lugli, and A. Rivadeneyra, "Fully printed flexible single-chip RFID tag with light detection capabilities", Sensors, 2017, vol. 17, no. 3, pp. 534.

[2] M. Akbari, M. W. A. Khan, M. Hasani, T. Bjorninen, L. Sydanheimo, and L. Ukkonen, "Fabrication and Characterization of Graphene Antenna for Low-Cost and Environmentally Friendly RFID tags", IEEE Antennas and Wireless Propagation Letters, 2015, vol. 15, pp. 1569-1572.

[3] S. Kim, T. Le, M. M. Tentzeris, A. Harrabi, A. Collado, and A. Georgiadis, "An RFID-enabled inkjet-printed soil moisture sensor on paper for "smart" agricultural applications", In "Book An RFID-enabled inkjet-printed soil moisture sensor on paper for "smart" agricultural applications" (IEEE, 2014, edn.), pp. 1507-1510.

[4] S. M. F. Cruz, L. A. Rocha, and J. C. Viana. "Printing technologies on flexible substrates for printed electronics": "Flexible Electronics" (IntechOpen, 2018).

[5] J. Virtanen, L. Ukkonen, T. Bjorninen, A. Z. Elsherbeni, and L. Sydanheimo, "Inkjet-printed humidity sensor for passive UHF RFID systems", IEEE Transactions on Instrumentation and Measurement, 2011, vol. 60, no 8, pp. 2768-2777.

[6] A. Martínez-Olmos, J. Fernández-Salmerón, N. Lopez-Ruiz, A. Rivadeneyra Torres, L. F. Capitan-Vallvey, and A. Palma, "Screen printed flexible radiofrequency identification tag for oxygen monitoring", Analytical chemistry, 2013, vol. 85, no 22, pp. 11098-11105.

[7] R. Nair et al., "A fully printed passive chipless RFID tag for low-cost mass production", The 8th European Conference on Antennas and Propagation (EuCAP 2014). IEEE, 2014. pp. 2950-2954.

[8] A. Rivadeneyra, F. C. Loghin, and A. Falco. "Technological Integration in Printed Electronics": "Flexible Electronics" (IntechOpen, 2018).

[9] R. Nopper, R. Has, and L. Reindl, "A wireless sensor readout system—Circuit concept, simulation, and accuracy", IEEE Transactions on Instrumentation and Measurement, 2011, vol. 60, no 8, pp. 2976-2983.

[10] S. El-Molla et al., "Integration of a Thin Film PDMS-Based Capacitive Sensor for Tactile Sensing in an Electronic Skin", Journal of Sensors, 2016, vol. 2016.

[11] R. Colella et al., "Comparison of fabrication techniques for flexible UHF RFID tag antennas [wireless corner]", IEEE Antennas and Propagation Magazine, 2017, vol. 59, no. 5, pp. 159-168.

[12] S. C. Mannsfeld et al., "Highly sensitive flexible pressure sensors with microstructured rubber dielectric layers", Nature materials, 2010, vol. 9, no. 10, pp. 859-864.

Screen Printable Electrochemical Capacitors on Flexible Substrates

Francisco J. Romero, Diego P. Morales, Almudena Rivadeneyra, Noel Rodriguez
Dept. Electronics and Computer Technology
University of Granada
Granada, Spain
e-mail: franromero@ugr.es, diegopm@ugr.es, arivadeneyra@ugr.es, noel@ugr.es

Markus Becherer
Institute for Nanoelectronics
Technische Universität München
Munich, Germany
e-mail: markus.becherer@tum.de

Abstract—**This work presents a novel approach for the fabrication of Electrochemical Capacitors (ECs) based on the screen-printing of a commercial carbon-based conductive ink on flexible substrates. This technique enables the fast and cost-effective production of ECs with high flexibility and outstanding performance over bending states and voltage cycling, as demonstrated by means of cyclic voltammetry and galvanometric charge-discharge measurements. Despite the fact that the specific areal capacitances achieved are lower than the ones obtained using other carbon-based materials (~22 μF/cm^2), the results show that, as soon as new screen-printable carbon-based pastes become available, this fabrication method will enable the mass production of ECs that can be attached to any surface as a conformal patch, as it is being required by a large number of the emerging technological applications.**

Keywords- Carbon; Conductive ink; Electrochemical Capacitor; Flexible Electronics; Screen-printing; Specific Capacitance.

I. INTRODUCTION

In recent years, flexible electronics has attracted the attention of many researches. This technology is expected to cause a disruption in the field of electronics devices, since it arises from the need to fulfill the demands required by novel technological applications, such as wearables or biomedical sensors, which cannot be addressed by means of the traditional silicon-based electronics [1]. Many of the advances in this context come with the emergence of new conductive and flexible materials. Examples of those are Carbon NanoTubes (CNTs) [2], graphene and its derivatives [3]-[5], or silver nanowires (AgNWs) and nanoparticles (AgNPs) [6][7]. Additionally, alternative fabrication processes enabling cost-effective processing on large flexible substrates are targeted. Those processes include printing technologies or laser treatment approaches, among others [8][9].

Thus, the combination of these two emerging lines of research has resulted in the development of many flexible electronics devices, including sensors [10][11], Radio Frequency Identification Tags (RFID) [12][13] and antennas [14][15]. Besides, apart from these latter, the flexible electronics progress is also requiring of flexible energy storage devices that, combined with energy harvesting technologies, contribute to the development of self-powered devices [16].

Numerous studies have been conducted to examine different materials as electrodes for the fabrication of flexible Electrochemical Capacitors (ECs). Among them, carbon-based materials are the preferred to play this role for several reasons: *i)* exceptionally high surface area, *ii)* relatively high electrical conductivity and *iii)* acceptable cost [17]. Examples of materials studied so far are Laser-Induced Graphene (LIG) [18][19], reduced Graphene Oxide (rGO) [20] and single walled CNTs [21]. Many researchers agree that carbon-based electrodes will play an important role in the supercapacitor technology and that is why a big effort is being devoted to further optimizing its properties through doping [22] or surface treatments [23]. Besides, the performance of the electrochemical capacitors does not only rely on the material of the electrodes, but also on the electrolyte used. Therefore, it is also important to achieve a proper interaction electrode-electrolyte. Then, different acid/base/salt-Poly(Vinyl Alcohol) (PVA) gel electrolytes have been widely studied for this purpose, being the PVA/phosphoric acid (PVA/H_3PO_4) and the PVA/sulfuric acid (PVA/H_2SO_4) the ones which report the best performance [24][25].

In this contribution, we present a novel approach for the fabrication of flexible ECs based on the screen-printing of a commercial carbon-based electrically conductive ink using PVA/H_3PO_4 as electrolyte. We have opted for a 2D architecture, which consists of several InterDigital Electrodes (IDEs) arranged on a flexible substrate, since this configuration offers some advantages over the conventional designs, such as lower thicknesses and smaller distances between electrodes [16]. This paper is organized as follows. Section II describes the materials and methods used. Section III presents the performance of the presented ECs and, finally, Section IV addresses the main conclusions.

II. MATERIALS AND METHODS

A. Materials

Transparent polyester films for water-based inks with a thickness of 160 μm (from ColorGATE Digital Output Solutions GmbH, Hannover, Germany) were used as a flexible substrate for the fabrication of the capacitors. The screen-printing carbon-based paste used in this work, product name: C-220, was provided by Applied Ink Solutions (Westborough, MA, USA). Both Poly(vinyl alcohol) (PVA, Mw 31,000-50,000, 98-99% hydrolyzed) and phosphoric acid (H_3PO_4, product name: 1005731000) were acquired from Sigma-Aldrich (St. Louis, MO, USA). Electrical access to the capacitive devices was achieved using a silver nanoparticles (AgNPs) screen printable ink (LOCTITE® ECI 1010 E&C from Henkel AG, Düsseldorf, Germany).

B. Devices Fabrication

Figure 1 shows the scheme for the fabrication of the carbon-based flexible electrochemical capacitors. First, the in-plane interdigital electrodes were printed on the flexible substrate using a 90 Nylon threads per centimeter (T/cm) mesh with a FLAT-DX200 screen printing machine (from Siebdruck-Versand, Magdeburg, Germany), as shown in Figure 1a and 1b. The capacitive structure considered has the following dimensions (number of fingers N: 20, width W: 1 mm, spacing S: 1 mm, interspacing *i*: 1 mm and length L: 1 cm), which results in an effective area of 4 cm^2, see Figure 1c. Following the manufacturer recommendations, the samples were dried at a temperature of 130 °C for 3 min to remove all residual solvent using a UF55 oven (from Memmert, Schwabach, Germany). Following the same screen-printing process, electrical contacts were printed using silver ink (Figure 1d), and the sample was dried afterwards again (this time at 120 °C for a duration of 15 min). Furthermore, the gel electrolyte was prepared by dissolving 1 g of PVA in 10 mL of de-ionized water (10 wt%) with stirring at 80 °C for 2 h using a VWR 12365-382 hot plate stirrer (from VWR International, Radnor, PA, USA). Once the PVA was completely dissolved, 1.2 g of H_3PO_4 was added to the solution and it was stirred for another hour [26]-[28]. The final homogeneous gel solution was drop casted (~1.5 mL) on the capacitive IDE structure covering all the effective surface area (Figure 1e). Finally, once the device is left standing overnight to remove the excess of water, the EC looks as shown in Figure 1f.

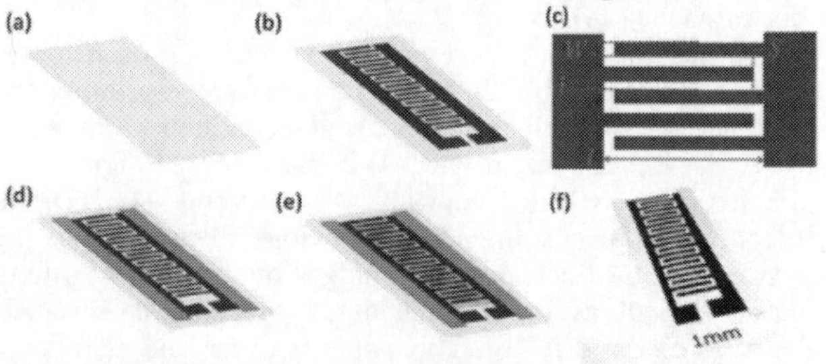

Figure 1. Schematic representation of the fabrication process of the flexible EC. (a) Flexible transparent substrate (thickness: 160 μm). (b) Capacitive IDE structure screen-printed on the substrate. (c) Dimmension of the interdigitally arranged electrodes (W: width, *i*: interspacing, L: length, S: spacing). (d) Silver electrical contacts screen-printed on each electrode. (e) PVA/H_3PO_4 electrolyte drop-casted on top of the IDE structure (blue shadow color has been selected to make the electrolyte visible). (d) Real view of the EC presented in this work.

C. Characterization

Microscope pictures were obtained with a ZEISS Axioscope 5 (from Carl Zeiss AG, Oberkochen, Germany). The sheet resistances were measured through the four-point method at a constant Direct Current (DC) of 100 μA using a probe head from Jandel connected to a B2901A Keysight (Keysight Technologies, Inc., CA, USA) Source Measuring Unit (SMU). Cyclic Voltammetry (CV) and charge-discharge measurements at Constant Current (CC) were performed using a 2602B Keithley SMU from Tektronix Inc. (Beaverton, OR, USA). The impedance of the samples was obtained using the impedance analyzer 4294A (from Keysight Technologies, Inc., CA, USA). The performance of the devices as a function of the temperature was studied using the climate chamber VCL4006 (from Vötsch Industrietechnik GmbH, Balingen, Germany). A custom bending setup was built to perform the bending tests using a PD4-N5918M420 stepper motor together with a GPLE60 precision planetary gear (from Nanotec Electronic GmbH & Co. KG, Feldkirchen, Germany). All the measurement setup was automated using the software LabView 2017 (from National Instruments Corporation, TX, USA).

III. Results and Discussion

Microscope images of the screen-printed electrodes are shown in Figure 2. On one hand, Figure 2a shows the printing resolution achieved. From the microscope images, it can be obtained that the average electrode width is W = 1.168 mm, while its interspacing and separation are found to be *i* = 0.892 mm and S = 0.902 mm, respectively, as a consequence of the paste spreading once it is deposited on the substrate. On the other hand, the porous nature of the carbon-based electrodes can be observed in Figure 2b. The sheet resistance of these conductive patterns is 503.6 ± 74.4 Ω/sq.

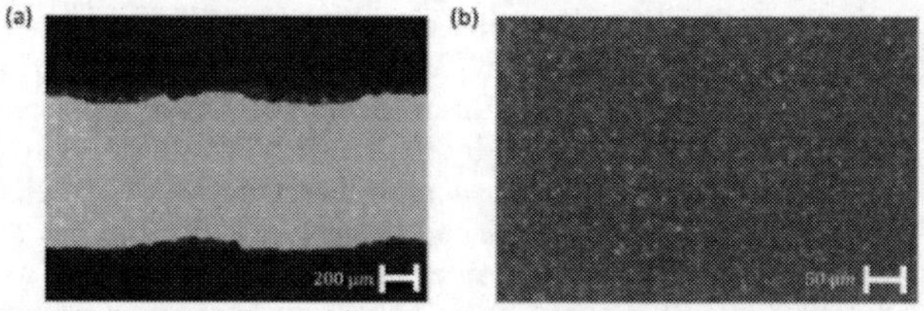

Figure 2. Microscope images of the screen-printed electrodes. (a) Interspacing between two consecutive electrodes (scale bar: 200 μm). (b) Electrode surface (scale bar: 50 μm).

First, the electrochemical performance of the ECs was investigated through Cyclic Voltammetry (CV). The experiments were conducted considering a potential window of ΔV = 1 V, from -0.5 V to +0.5 V, at different scanning rates (20 mV/s, 50 mV/s, 90 mV/s, 120 mV/s), as shown in Figure 1a. It can be noted that the CV curves maintain the quasi rectangular shape over the increasing scan rates, indicating a good reversible Electrostatic Double-Layer Capacitive (EDLC) behavior [29]. From these curves, the capacitance can be calculated as follows:

$$C_{cv} = \frac{1}{2\cdot\Delta V\cdot s}\cdot\left(\int_{-0.5}^{0.5} I(V)dV + \int_{0.5}^{-0.5} I(V)dV\right) \quad (1)$$

where ΔV is the potential window, s the scan rate and $I(V)$ the current response as a function of the voltage [20]. The results, depicted in Figure 3b, show an average capacitance of ~12.5 μF (~3.1 μF/cm^2). As seen, the capacitance does not suffer from a considerable decrease as the scan rate increases, which indicates a good interaction electrode-electrolyte [30].

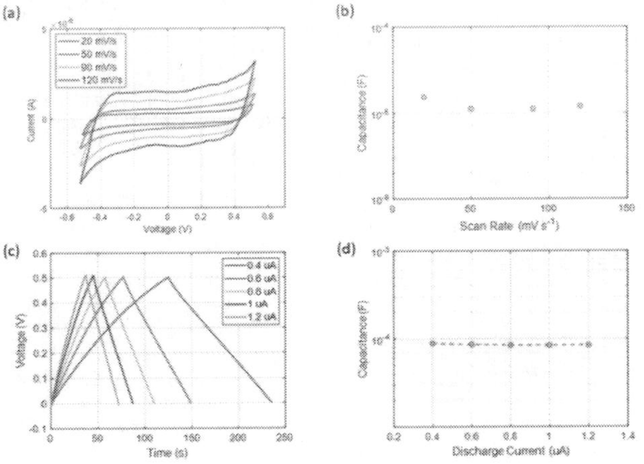

Figure 3. Evaluation of the specific capacitance of the ECs under different conditions. (a) Cyclic voltammetry curves at different scan rates. (b) Capacitance as a function of the scan rate extracted from the CV curves. (c) Galvanometric charge-discharge curves at different constant currents. (d) Capacitance as a function of the discharge current extracted from the CC curves.

Galvanostatic charge-discharge measurements are also commonly used for the characterization of ECs. The resulting curves associated with these measurements are displayed in Figure 3c. In this case, the quasi triangular symmetric shape demonstrates a good charge propagation across the carbon electrodes and negligible internal resistances [31]. In the same way, these results can also be used to calculate the specific capacitance by the following equation:

$$C_{cc} = \frac{I}{dV/dt} \quad (2)$$

where I is the discharge current and dV/dt the slope of galvanostatic discharge curve [22]. In this case, the specific capacitance obtained is around 86 μF (~22 μF/cm^2) with a slight decrease as the discharge current increases ($\Delta C/C_0$ = 4.7%), see Figure 3d. This specific areal capacitance is similar to that obtained with other non-treated carbon materials [32][33].

The outstanding performance of the ECs under different bending conditions (r = 1.25 cm, 0.75 cm and 0.5 cm) is demonstrated in Figure 4. It can be noted how the EC presents almost unchanged CC and CV curves for the different bending states, which would allow to use these ECs in conformal applications with no effect on their electrochemical performance.

The electrochemical cycling durability of the ECs has also been studied. The results, displayed in Figure 5, have shown that the capacitors are able to retain their capacitance even after 1000 bending cycles ($\Delta C/C_0$ < 1%). However, it can also be noticed how the rectangular shape of the CV curves is progressively deformed. This latter can be attributed to the appearance of reversible pseudocapacitive effects, indicating that an increasing number of continuous cycles boosts the electrosorption, redox and intercalation processes on the surface of the porous electrodes [20][34][35].

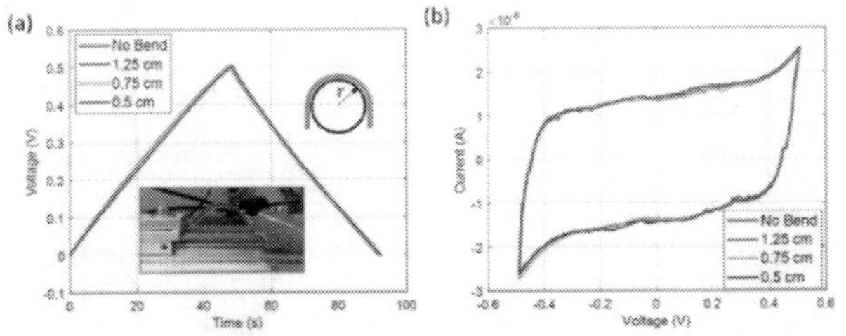

Figure 4. ECs performance under different bending conditions. (a) CC curves at the four different states (I = 1 μA). Inset shows a bent EC, while the diagram depicts the definition of bend radius. (b) CV curves for the four bending states considered (s = 100 mV/s).

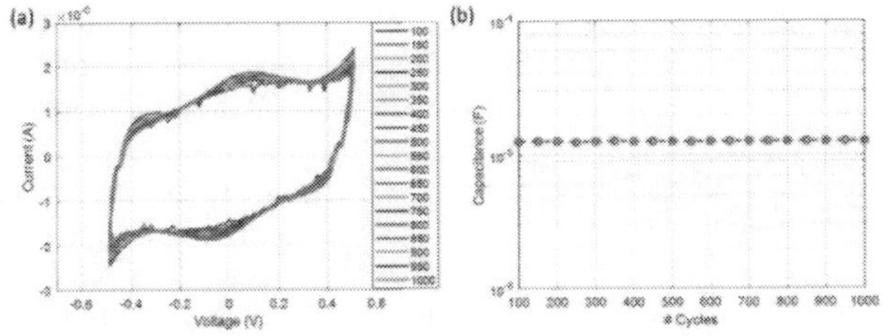

Figure 5. Cycle ability experiments. (a) CV curves obtained at the different cycles shown in legend. (b) Specific capacitance as a function of the number of cycles extracted from the CV curves.

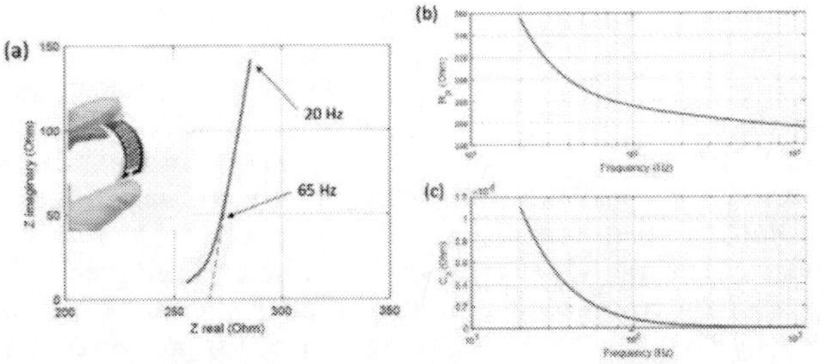

Figure 6. Electrochemical Impedance Spectroscopy (EIS) of the presented ECs. (a) Nyquist plot. (b) Equivalent resistance and (c) capacitance considering a simple model based on a R||C circuit.

The ECs have been further investigated using a Nyquist diagram (Figure 6), which shows the capacitive behaviour of the presented ECs as a function of the frequency. At low frequencies, the imaginary part of the impedances against the real one is almost linear (up to ~65 Hz), then a semicircle appears in the high frequency region indicating the transition between resistance and capacitance behaviours. It should also be noticed that, at this point, the curve faces the real axis at a ~45° angle, which is a common characteristic when a porous electrode is saturated with electrolyte [30][36][37]. Moreover, the interception with the real axis is associated with the Equivalent Series Resistance (ESR), which is estimated to be ~250 Ω. Lastly, Figure 6b and Figure 6c show the behaviour of the analyzed ECs if we simplify its model to a capacitance in parallel with a resistance.

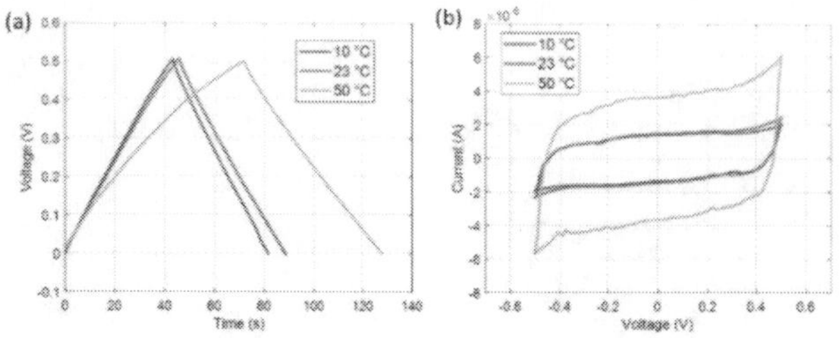

Figure 7. ECs performance under different bending conditions. (a) CC curves at the four different states. Inset shows a bent EC, while the diagram depictes the definition of bend radius. (b) CV curves for the four bending states.

Finally, the temperature effect on the performance of the ECs is represented in Figure 7. As demonstrated by both CC and CV experiments, the specific capacitance increases as the temperature incresases, as it has been demonstrated for several electrode/electrolyte systems, such as rGO-PVA/H_3PO_4 [37], CNT-PC/TEABF4 [38] and others [39]. This effect has been attributted to changes in the electrolyte, since an increase of the temperature possibly leads to the physisorbtion of the electrolyte ions [37][38].

IV. Conclusions

In summary, we report the fabrication of thin-film flexible electrochemical capacitors trough the screen-printing of a carbon-based conductive ink on a flexible substrate. Using PVA/H_3PO_4 as electrolyte, the devices present good performance as ECDL capacitors, which has been demonstrated trough cyclic voltammetry, charge-discharge experiments and electrochemical impedance spectroscopy. Although the specific capacitances obtained for this electrode material does not achieve those obtained with other carbon-based materials, further studies aim to treat the conductive ink in order to optimize its properties and increase the specific areal capacitance. It has been demonstrated that this method paves the way towards an alternative method for the large-scale and cost-effective fabrication of flexible electrochemical capacitors.

Acknowledgment

This work has been partially supported by the Spanish Ministry of Education, Culture and Sport (MECD) and the European Union through the pre-doctoral grant FPU16/01451, and its mobility program, the project TEC2017-89955-P and fellowship H2020-MSCA-IF-2017794885-SELFSENS.

References

[1] D. M. Sun, C. Liu, W. C. Ren, and H. M. Cheng, "A Review of Carbon Nanotube - and Graphene - Based Flexible Thin - Film Transistors," Small, vol. 9(8), 2013, pp. 1188-1205. DOI: 10.1002/smll.201203154.

[2] E. Castillo *et al.*, "An optimized measurement algorithm for gas sensors based on carbon nanotubes: optimizing sensor performance and hardware resources," IEEE Internet of Things Journal, vol. 6(5), 2019, pp. 9140-9146. DOI: 10.1109/JIOT.2019.2928231.

[3] H. Jang *et al.*, "Graphene - Based Flexible and Stretchable Electronics," Advanced Materials, vol. 28(22), 2016, pp. 4184-4202. DOI: 10.1002/adma.201504245.

[4] G. Eda, G. Fanchini, and M. Chhowalla, "Large-area ultrathin films of reduced graphene oxide as a transparent and flexible electronic material," Nature Nanotechnolgy, vol. 3, 2008, pp. 270–274. DOI: 10.1038/nnano.2008.83.

[5] F. J. Romero *et al.*, "In-Depth Study of Laser Diode Ablation of Kapton Polyimide for Flexible Conductive Substrates," Nanomaterials, vol. 8(7), 2018, 517. DOI: 10.3390/nano8070517.

[6] D. Langley *et al.*, " Flexible transparent conductive materials based on silver nanowire networks: a review," Nanotechnology, vol. 24, 2013, 452001. DOI: 10.1088/0957-4484/24/45/452001.

[7] W. Shen , X. Zhang , Q. Huang , Q. Xu, and W. Song, "Preparation of solid silver nanoparticles for inkjet printed flexible electronics with high conductivity," Nanoscale, vol. 6, 2014, pp. 1622-1628. DOI: 10.1039/C3NR05479A.

[8] S. Khan, L. Lorenzelli, and R. S. Dahiya, " Technologies for Printing Sensors and Electronics Over Large Flexible Substrates: A Review," IEEE Sensors Journal, vol. 15(6), 2015, pp. 3164-3185. DOI: 10.1109/JSEN.2014.2375203.

[9] H. Chang and H. Wu, "Graphene - Based Nanomaterials: Synthesis, Properties, and Optical and Optoelectronic Applications," Advanced Functional Materials, vol. 23(16), 2013, pp. 1984-1997. DOI: 10.1002/adfm.201202460.

[10] F. J. Romero *et al.*, "Design, fabrication and characterization of capacitive humidity sensors based on emerging flexible technologies," Sensors and Actuators B: Chemical, vol. 287, 2019, pp. 459-467. DOI: 10.1016/j.snb.2019.02.043.

[11] A. Salim and S. Lim, "Review of Recent Inkjet-Printed Capacitive Tactile Sensors," Sensors, vol. 17(11), 2017, 2593. DOI: 10.3390/s17112593.

[12] J. F. Salmeron *et al.*, "Properties and Printability of Inkjet and Screen-Printed Silver Patterns for RFID Antennas," Journal of Electronic Materials, vol. 43(2), 2014, pp. 604–617. DOI: 10.1007/s11664-013-2893-4.

[13] A. Albrecht, J. F. Salmeron, M. Becherer, P. Lugli, and A. Rivadeneyra, "Screen-Printed Chipless Wireless Temperature Sensor," IEEE Sensors Journal, 2019, 12011 - 12015. DOI: 10.1109/JSEN.2019.2940836.

[14] Y. Goliya *et al.*, "Next Generation Antennas Based on Screen - Printed and Transparent Silver Nanowire Films," Advanced Optical Materials, vol. 7(21), 2019, 1900995. DOI: 10.1002/adom.201900995.

[15] P. Lukacs, A. Pietrikova, J. Potencki, and G. Tomaszewski, "UWB Antenna Based on Nanoparticles of Silver on Polyimide Substrate," 38th International Spring Seminar on Electronics Technology (ISSE), May 2015, 15452268. DOI: 10.1109/ISSE.2015.7248031.

[16] M. Beidaghia and Y. Gogotsi, "Capacitive energy storage in micro-scale devices: recent advances in design and fabrication of micro-supercapacitors," Energy Environ. Sci., vol. 7, 2014, pp. 867-884. DOI: 10.1039/C3EE43526A.

[17] A. G. Pandolfo and A. F. Hollenkamp, "Carbon properties and their role in supercapacitors," Journal of Power Sources, vol. 157(1), 2006, pp. 11-27. DOI: 10.1016/j.jpowsour.2006.02.065.

[18] A. Lamberti, F. Clerici, M. Fontana, and L. Scaltrito, "A Highly Stretchable Supercapacitor Using Laser - Induced Graphene Electrodes onto Elastomeric Substrate," Advanced Energy Materials, vol. 6(10), 2016, 1600050. DOI: 10.1002/aenm.201600050.

[19] Z. Peng, J. Lin, R. Ye, E. L. G. Samuel, and J. M. Tour, "Flexible and Stackable Laser-Induced Graphene Supercapacitors," ACS Applied Materials and Interfaces, vol. 7, 2015, pp. 3414–3419. DOI: 10.1021/am509065d.

[20] Y. Chen, X. Zhang, D. Zhang, P. Yu, and Y. Ma, "High performance supercapacitors based on reduced graphene oxide in aqueous and ionic liquid electrolytes," Carbon, vol. 49, 2011, pp. 573 – 580. DOI: 10.1016/j.carbon.2010.09.060.

[21] M. Kaempge, C. K. Chan, J. Ma, Y. Cui, and G. Gruner, "Printable Thin Film Supercapacitors Using Single-Walled Carbon Nanotubes," Nano Lett., vol. 9(5), 2009, pp. 1872-1876. DOI: 10.1021/nl8038579.

[22] Z. Peng *et al.*, "Flexible Boron-Doped Laser-Induced Graphene Microsupercapacitors," ACS Nano, vol. 9(6), 2015, pp. 5868-5875. DOI: 10.1021/acsnano.5b00436.

[23] W. Wang *et al.*, "Tailoring the surface morphology and nanoparticle distribution of laser-induced graphene/Co3O4 for high-performance flexible microsupercapacitors," Applied Surface Science, In Press, 2019, 144487. DOI: 10.1016/j.apsusc.2019.144487.

[24] Q. Chen *et al.*, "Effect of Different Gel Electrolytes on Graphene Based Solid-State Supercapacitors," RSC Advances, vol. 4, 2014, pp. 36253-36256. DOI: 10.1039/C4RA05553E.

[25] W. Zhou *et al.*, "Flexible wire-like all-carbon supercapacitors based on porous core–shell carbon fibers," J. Mater. Chem. A, vol. 2, 2014, pp. 7250-7255.DOI: 10.1039/C3TA15280D.

[26] D. He *et al.*, "Fabrication of a Graphene-Based Paper-Like Electrode for Flexible Solid-State Supercapacitor Devices," Journal of Electrochemical Society, vol. 165(14), 2018, pp. A3481-A3486. DOI: 10.1149/2.1041814jes.

[27] J. Y.Shieh, S. H. Zhang, C. H. Wu, and H. H. Yu, "A facile method to prepare a high performance solid-state flexible paper-based supercapacitor," Applied Surface Science, vol. 313, 2014, pp. 704-710. DOI: 10.1016/j.apsusc.2014.06.059.

[28] R. Singh and C. C. Tripathi, "Electrochemical Exfoliation of Graphite into Graphene for Flexible Supercapacitor Application," Materials Today: Proceedings, vol. 5(1), 2018, pp. 1125-1130. DOI: 10.1016/j.matpr.2017.11.192.

[29] J. S. M. Lee, M. E. Briggs, C. C. Hu, and A. I. Cooper, "Controlling electric double-layer capacitance and pseudocapacitance inheteroatom-doped carbons derived from hypercrosslinked microporouspolymers," Nano Energy, vol. 46, 2018, pp. 277-289. DOI: 10.1016/j.nanoen.2018.01.042.

[30] G. A. M. Ali, L. L. Tan, R. Jose, M. M. Yusoff, and K. F. Chong, "Electrochemical performance studies of MnO2 nanoflowers recovered from spent battery," Materials Research Bulletin, vol. 60, 2014, pp. 5-9. DOI: 10.1016/j.materresbull.2014.08.008.

[31] J. Luo *et al.*, "Integration of micro-supercapacitors with triboelectric nanogenerators for a flexible self-charging power unit," Nano Research, vol. 8(12), 2015, pp. 3934–3943. DOI: 10.1007/s12274-015-0894-8.

[32] X. Zang *et al.*, "Evaluation of layer-by-layer graphene structures as supercapacitor electrode materials," Journal of Applied Physics, vol. 115, 2014, 024305. DOI: 10.1063/1.4861629.

[33] J. J. Yoo *et al.*, "Ultrathin Planar Graphene Supercapacitors," Nano Letters, vol. 11, 2011, pp. 1423–1427. DOI: 10.1021/nl200225j.

[34] J. Zhu *et al.*, "Multifunctional Architectures Constructing of PANI Nanoneedle Arrays on MoS 2 Thin Nanosheets for High-Energy Supercapacitors," Small, vol. 11(33), 2015, pp. 4123–4129. DOI: 10.1002/smll.201403744.

[35] D. J. You *et al.*, "Redox-active ionic liquid electrolyte with multi energy storage mechanism for high energy density supercapacitor," vol. 7(88), 2017, pp. 55702-55708. DOI: 10.1039/C7RA10772B.

[36] M. F. El-Kady, V. Strong, S. Dubin, and R. B. Kaner, " Laser Scribing of High-Performance and Flexible Graphene-Based Electrochemical Capacitors," Science, vol. 335(6074), 2012, pp. 1326-1330. 10.1126/science.1216744.

[37] M. Wang *et al.*, "All-Solid-State Reduced Graphene Oxide Supercapacitor with Large Volumetric Capacitance and Ultralong Stability Prepared by Electrophoretic Deposition Method," ACS Appl. Mater. Interfaces, vol. 7(2), 2015, pp. 1348-1354. DOI: 10.1021/am507656q.

[38] C. Masarapu, H. F. Zeng, K. H. Hung, and B. Wie, "Effect of Temperature on the Capacitance of Carbon Nanotube Supercapacitors," ACS Nano, vol. 3(8), 2009, pp. 2199–2206. DOI: 10.1021/nn900500n.

[39] H. Y. Jung, M. B. Karimi, M. G. Hahm, P. M. Ajayan, and Y. J. Jung, "Transparent, flexible supercapacitors from nano-engineered carbon films," Sci Rep., vol. 2, 2012, 773. DOI: 10.1038/srep00773.

Low-Cost Energy-Autonomous Sensor Nodes Through RF Energy Harvesting and Printed Technology

Fernando Moreno-Cruz

Infineon Technologies AG
Munich, Germany
Email: fernando.morenocruz@infineon.com

Francisco J. Romero, Noel Rodríguez,
Diego P. Morales and Almudena Rivadeneyra
University of Granada
Granada, Spain
Emails: franromero@ugr.es, noel@ugr.es,
diegopm@ugr.es, arivadeneyra@ugr.es

Abstract—**The irruption of Internet of Things and 5G in our society comes along with several technological challenges to overcome. From an overall perspective, the low-cost and environmental friendliness of these technologies need to be ensured for their universal deployment in different areas, starting with the sensors and finishing with the power sources. To address these challenges, the production and maintenance of a great number of sensor nodes incur costs, which include manufacturing and integration in mass of elements and sub-blocks, changing or recharging of batteries, as well as management of natural resources and waste. In this article, we demonstrate how Radio Frequency Energy Harvesting (RFEH) and printed flexible technology (a growing technology for sensors) can solve these concerns through cost-effective mass-production and utilization of energy harvesting for the development of energy-autonomous nodes, as part of a wireless sensor network. We present as illustration a sprayed flexible relative humidity sensor powered with RFEH under the store-and-use principle.**

Keywords–Radio frequency energy harvesting; printed flexible sensors; IoT; sprayed flexible technology; store-and-use principle.

I. INTRODUCTION

The concept of Internet of Things (IoT) is merging everyday objects, vehicles, buildings, etc., with electronics as part of a Wireless Sensor Network (WSN), giving new perspectives to a broad range of areas traditionally out of the innovation scope. In the following years, while it deploys, a lot of effort will focus on the expenses, security and energy sources of the WSN-nodes, as they occur to be the most critical issues. Under these circumstances, Energy Harvesting (EH) methods and low-cost hardware techniques such as *Radio Frequency Energy Harvesting (RFEH)* and *printed technology*, respectively, appear to be innovations to overcome successfully these matters and that aim at the same time at the series production and distribution.

Depending on the application, the energetic demands of the deployed nodes differ vastly. While the tendency in the low-power cases is the use of non-rechargeable chemical (lithium) batteries [1], in several situations is not an option due to:

- Longevity of a minimum time frame of months or years without compromising the quality of service.
- Large-scale deployment of nodes, materialized in impractical maintenance.
- Hard access to the devices (high structures, wild animals, etc.).
- Cost of the batteries during the whole product life.

Besides, the massive employment and disposal of batteries cost a big price to the environment in the shape of resources over-exploitation and wastes [2], [3].

On the other hand, EH takes advantage of the existing ambient energy such as thermal, solar, vibrational or electromagnetic waves among others; providing energy-autonomous systems that do not need batteries for their operation. Specifically, RFEH exploits the far field region of ambient radiation whose frequencies range between some kilohertzs and hundreds of gigahertzs [4].

Likewise, the usage of printed sensors solves a number of problems that often head towards an increase of the costs in manufacturing, integration and assembly. In contrast to traditional integrated sensors, printed ones can integrate at the same instance a broad combination of variables like environmental gas concentrations, temperature, human heartbeat, relative humidity or biopotentials, among others. Large-scale and multipurpose fabrication techniques allow as well their manufacture in a cost-effective way. Additionally, their flexible capabilities open the doors to use-cases as wearables whose manufacturing costs decrease, facilitating their broad utilization.

Having these two technologies together brings low costs in production (cheap printed materials and integration) and maintenance (no batteries), along with respect for the environment. Moreover, printed sensors present ultra-low power requirements, fitting perfectly with RFEH which stays in that energetic range in most of the scenarios.

This paper is organized as follows: Section II explains the general concepts of RFEH and flexible electronics technology, keeping a perspective under the common linker of IoT. Section III introduces and analyzes their integration and describes the proposed solutions in terms of hardware and working principle. Finally, Section IV presents the conclusions.

II. BACKGROUND

A. RF Energy Harvesting

An IoT energy harvester is a system that captures energy from ambient sources and converts it into electricity for further use. Normally, the goal will be powering wireless autonomous devices like nodes part of a WSN.

The selection of the source depends only on the ambient conditions around and on the application requirements, i.e., amount of energy needed, update period, part of the day of

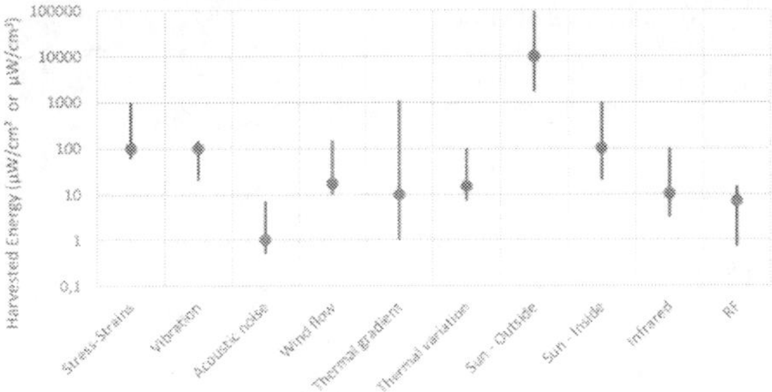

Figure 1. Comparison of different energy harvesting sources [4].

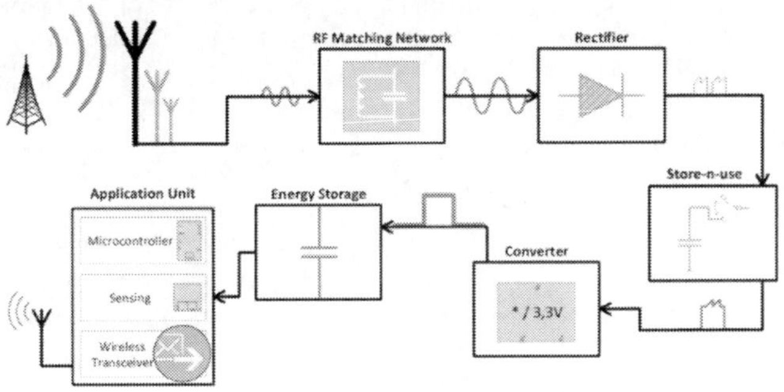

Figure 2. Block diagram of a basic RFEH complete system (with store-and-use principle).

operation, among others. Figure 1 compares the most common EH methods in terms of energy harvested.

RFEH grants clear advantages in contrast with the rest of techniques or wired options [2], [5]:

- Everywhere and every-time availability (unlike solar or thermal).
- Predictability and stability over time (unlike wind flow or vibrational).
- Wireless nature (unlike the common USB-powered option).
- Low-cost implementation (an antenna and a simple rectification circuit suffice).
- Small form-factor (within the interest frequency range).

However, as seen in the previous figure, the available power presents the mayor challenge, since extremely high efficiencies in the circuits are needed for its usage. Friis equation determines the inverse square relation with the distance to the signal source and with the efficiency of the rectifying and converting circuits [6]. Moreover, often the availability of the signal is permanent but not constant, e.g., Wi-Fi router duty-cycle or mobile phone random use [3], [7].

RFEH is usually categorized as "ultra-low power" (barely tens of microwatts), although it can be also employed as a wireless energy transfer technique. Using a dedicated signal emitter unlocks a broader range of applications more power consuming, reaching hundreds of microwatts. The advantage against the well-known inductive coupling (including resonant inductive) is the effective distance reached (it presents 20 dB attenuation per decade versus 60 dB [5]), although it has much lower source-to-load energy efficiency. That turns the maximum separation of a few centimeters into several kilometers.

The basic operation of a RFEH harvester (see Figure 2) starts with an antenna (or antennas) capturing the signal carrier of interest. A rectifier follows, which converts the microwave energy into dc, consisting of Schottky diodes or CMOS structures in diode configuration in nearly all the literature. For the best power transfer between these two stages, a matching network tuned at the target frequency is needed.

In order to obtain an appropriate and constant voltage level, a voltage regulation stage is essential, generally in form of a boost converter or a charge pump. Once at the desired level, the energy is stored in a capacitor, dimensioned according to the application needs.

Figure 3. Example of hybrid prototype between flexible electronics (flexible Kapton printed sensor) and rigid (microcontroller).

B. *Flexible Electronics Technology*

Together with the EH technology, flexible electronics has attracted significant attention in the field of WSNs. Recent advances show promising future prospects in diverse areas, such as wearables, electronic skin (e-skin) and even implantable devices [8], [9], which satisfy requirements that were not affordable with the current rigid silicon-based solutions.

In addition to its inherent properties (flexibility, lightness, transparency, etc.), the interest in flexible electronics relies on the possibility to reduce the manufacturing cost of large-area devices, since its associated fabrication processes are usually compatible with roll-to-roll techniques [10].

Over the years, diverse methods and materials have been presented for the manufacturing of flexible electronics, such as screen- and inkjet-printing of conductive pastes, or spray deposition and laser processing of nanomaterials [11]–[13]. However, the development of fully flexible IoT devices is still in early stages, and precisely because of that, most proof-of-concept designs are based on hybrid technologies in which the flexible part is limited to the sensors or antennas [14]–[16] and, more recently, to the energy storage devices [17], [18] (see Figure 3).

III. Energy-Autonomous and Low-Cost IoT Nodes

Within the IoT and WSN world exist several scenarios where the application requirements are not too demanding towards the update period or transmission range. With the inclusion of printed ultra-low power sensors and if the surrounding environment enhances its usage. RFEH appears as a singular method for powering the nodes, becoming an excellent composite for both technologies.

The complete IoT node consists of: i) printed sensor, a capacitive structure in this case for measuring the Relative Humidity (RH) of the air; ii) a microcontroller (μC) plus transceiver chip, the logic and communicator of the circuit (also able to be manufactured in bendable technology); iii) different antennas, for communication (868 MHz) and harvesting from Global System for Mobile communications (GSM) (949 MHz); iv) RFEH block, outputting directly regulated dc voltage to a v) storage capacitor.

In this manner, we achieve energy-autonomous and low-cost nodes, since we avoid the use of any sort of battery and the production, integration and maintenance phases are remarkably cheaper.

A. *Working Principle*

The working principle attends to the one described in Figure 4, commonly known as duty-cycled operation. In this manner, after a measurement and transmission cycle, the system will be most of its time in sleep mode (ultra-low power consumption or even disconnected), while the harvesting electronics charge the capacitors for a new measurement.

The wake-up process can be triggered in different ways:

- With a fixed period determined by the application, although within a certain time range where the capacitors are assured to be charged (Radio Frequency (RF) energy available is stable and predictable).
- With an extra wake-up radio that triggers the active mode [4].
- Or every time a certain voltage level is reached while charging.

In any case, the *minimum period* will depend only on the RF spectrum, i.e., how much energy is available around the node, and of course, on the application needs.

Once a measurement is carried out and sent, the gateway -or objective node depending on the communication topology- will forward the message to the cloud and answer the node in case of need. These points are assumed to not work with energy harvesting.

B. *Harvested Energy*

The power levels in city open-spaces nowadays go up to −30 dBm and even −20 dBm at bands of high usage such as GSM, tv broadcasting, license-free bands or wireless local networks [19]–[21]. Furthermore, with active emitting, the levels can reach in average more than −3 dBm [5].

The losses, from the source emission until the load, can be split in two parts. The first and largest are the propagation losses along the path, defined by the Friis transmission equation, and increased by presumable obstacles and misalignment of the antennas. The second part is related to the efficiency at the rectifier-converter-storage chain. Slight drops in this efficiency will stop the system from working, since the voltage levels are close to the thresholds of the actual silicon electronics.

The current state of the art in rectification and storage for the power levels mentioned satisfies the energy needs for several IoT use-cases, although the conversion stage gets harder to deal with due to the low levels of power and/or voltage. Most of the off-the-shelf converters are considered "low-power" (range of milliwatts) and are able to operate either with extremely low levels of voltage or power, but not with both together. This results in a harder employment of EH techniques, as the converter stage must be custom designed or, alternatively, this task is taken over by the rectifier, being then only valid under certain energy conditions.

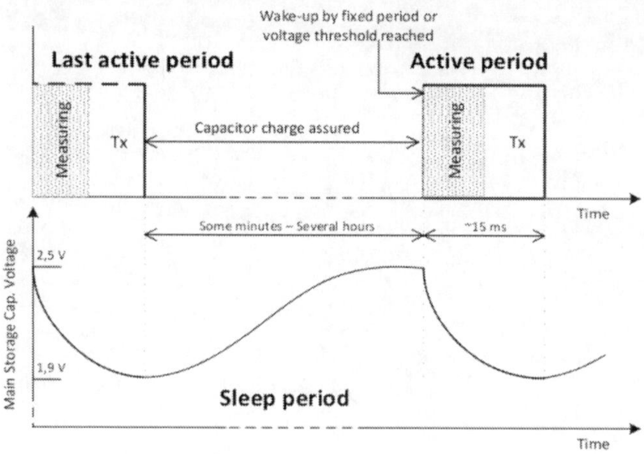

Figure 4. Working principle of an ultra-low power IoT node with duty-cycled operation and EH.

Nevertheless, making use of the store-and-use principle as an intermediate stage [22], more energetic bursts in periods can be output to the converter. In this way, and with a favorable environment as the mentioned before, the power harvested from some microwatts to hundreds of them, can be stored in the desired voltage level for its use by the application unit in a duty-cycled fashion.

In this direction, we have developed a battery-less harvesting block capable of capturing RF energy while using commercial low-power dc/dc converters (see Figure 5). Making use of an innovative autonomous switched capacitor design, we implemented the store-and-use principle, functioning not only as an energy adaption phase, but also as an impedance matching.

C. *Flexible Relative Humidity Sensor*

The developed IoT node integrates a flexible sensor intended for the monitoring of the ambient RH. The operation of this sensor, shown in Figure 6-a, is based on the outstanding sensitivity to humidity changes of the dielectric constant of Graphene Oxide (GO) [23], [24]. For that, a flexible PolyEthylene Terephthalate (PET) substrate was coated with a thin-layer of GO, which was prepared at a concentration of 0.4 wt% following a modified version of the Hummers and Offeman's method, as described in [25]. The spray-coating of the substrate ($38.5\,\mu L/cm^2$) was done using a manual airbrush similar to the presented in [26], [27]. Finally, once the GO layer was completely dried, a capacitive structure consisting of 16 InterDigitally arranged Electrodes (IDE) was screen-printed on its surface using a silver-based conductive ink (LOCTITE® ECI 1010 E&C from Henkel AG, Düsseldorf, Germany), as

Figure 5. Picture of developed RFEH block.

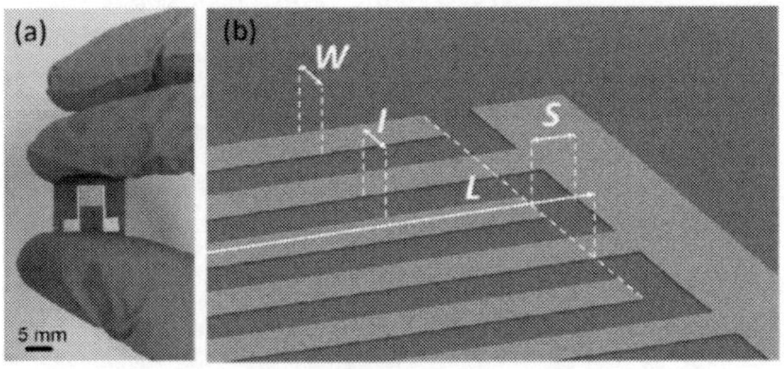

Figure 6. a) Flexible GO-based humidity sensor. b) Dimensions of the screen-printed pattern (W: width 150 µm, S: spacing, 225 µm, I: interspacing 225 µm, L: length 5 mm).

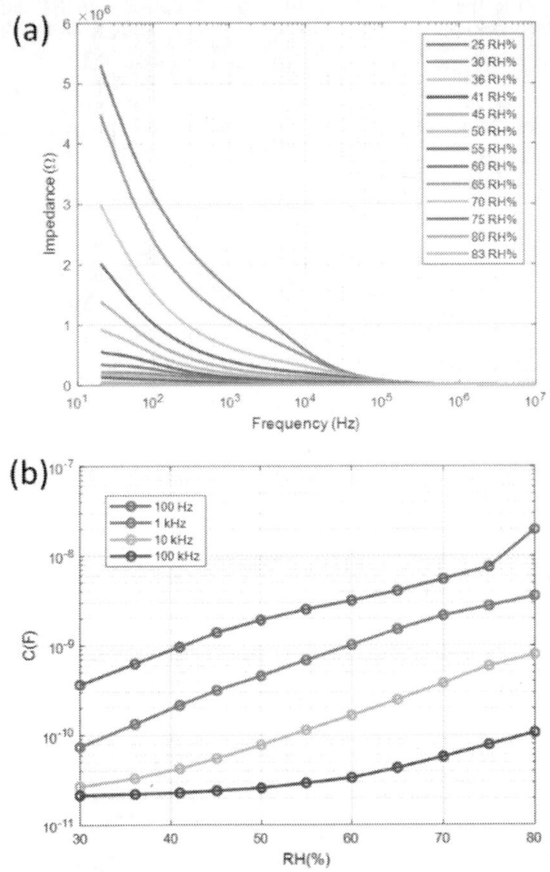

Figure 7. Impedance response of the sensor a) and extracted equivalent parallel capacitance b) as a function of the RH and frequency.

depicted in Figure 6-b. We opted for this configuration for two main reasons. Firstly, to have a more uniform layer on which the GO can be deposited with a better control of the thickness and, secondly, to minimize the impact of the substrate on the performance of the sensors. Electrical connections were glued to the electrodes using silver conductive paint (186-3600 RS Pro, RS Components, Corby, UK), following the manufacturer recommendations, which did not affect the thermal reduction of the GO.

The calibration curves obtained for this humidity sensor are shown in Figure 7. The experiments were performed using the climate chamber VCL4006 (from Vötsch Industrietechnik GmbH, Balingen, Germany) at a constant temperature of 40 °C to use the whole humidity range of the chamber. The results show that the impedance decreases with both increasing humidity and frequency values (see Figure 7-a). These impedance values were used to extract the equivalent parallel capacitance as a function of the RH at four different frequencies (100 Hz, 1 kHz, 10 kHz and 100 kHz) as shown in Figure 7-b. The sensitivity offered by this sensor depends on the frequency of the excitation signal, being 385.53 pF at 100 Hz, 70.07 pF at 1 kHz, 15.44 pF at 10 kHz and 1.72 pF at 100 kHz.

IV. Conclusion

In this article, we introduced a solution for the use of RFEH in conjunction with flexible printed sensors as a form of decreasing the costs of WSNs deployment. Besides the general cost reduction due to the omission of battery-recharge or substitution and wiring; the employment of innovative low-cost printed sensors provides an extra boost in manufacturing and integration savings.

The presented sprayed GO-based sensor is an example of how this technology can achieve satisfactory measurement results in an extremely cost-effective manner and with ultra-low power requirements. On the other end of the system, the store-and-use principle applied to RFEH provides lower levels from where the energy can be harvested, through energy accumulation and impedance matching between the rectifier and converter stages.

The future work encompasses the optimization of the energetic sub-blocks in order to reach lower levels, as well as the improvement of the sensor accuracy.

Acknowledgment

This work was partially supported by the ECSEL Joint Undertaking through the Electronic Component Systems for European Leadership Joint Undertaking under grant agreement

No 737434. This Joint Undertaking receives support from the German Federal Ministry of Education and Research and the European Union's Horizon 2020 research and innovation program and Slovakia, Netherlands, Spain, Italy.

In addition, the Spanish Ministry of Education, Culture and Sport (MECD) and the European Union supported it through the pre-doctoral grant FPU16/01451 and the fellowship H2020-MSCA-IF-2017794885-SELFSENS.

REFERENCES

[1] G. Zhou, L. Huang, W. Li, and Z. Zhu, "Harvesting ambient environmental energy for wireless sensor networks: a survey," Journal of Sensors, vol. 2014, 2014, pp. 1–20.

[2] P. Kamalinejad, C. Mahapatra, Z. Sheng, S. Mirabbasi, V. C. Leung, and Y. L. Guan, "Wireless energy harvesting for the internet of things," IEEE Communications Magazine, vol. 53, no. 6, 2015, pp. 102–108.

[3] H. Jayakumar, K. Lee, W. S. Lee, A. Raha, Y. Kim, and V. Raghunathan, "Powering the internet of things," in Proceedings of the 2014 international symposium on Low power electronics and design. ACM, 2014, pp. 375–380.

[4] F. Moreno-Cruz, A. Escobar-Molero, E. Castillo, M. Becherer, A. Rivadeneyra, and D. P. Morales, "Why use rf energy harvesting in smart grids," in 2018 IEEE 23rd International Workshop on Computer Aided Modeling and Design of Communication Links and Networks (CAMAD). IEEE, 2018, pp. 1–6.

[5] X. Lu, P. Wang, D. Niyato, D. I. Kim, and Z. Han, "Wireless networks with rf energy harvesting: A contemporary survey," IEEE Communications Surveys & Tutorials, vol. 17, no. 2, 2015, pp. 757–789.

[6] P. Nintanavongsa, "A survey on rf energy harvesting: circuits and protocols," Energy Procedia, vol. 56, 2014, pp. 414–422.

[7] X. Liu and E. Sánchez-Sinencio, "A highly efficient ultralow photovoltaic power harvesting system with mppt for internet of things smart nodes," IEEE transactions on very large scale integration (vlsi) systems, vol. 23, no. 12, 2015, pp. 3065–3075.

[8] C. Pang, C. Lee, and K.-Y. Suh, "Recent advances in flexible sensors for wearable and implantable devices," Journal of Applied Polymer Science, vol. 130, no. 3, 2013, pp. 1429–1441.

[9] A. Nag, S. C. Mukhopadhyay, and J. Kosel, "Wearable flexible sensors: A review," IEEE Sensors Journal, vol. 17, no. 13, 2017, pp. 3949–3960.

[10] I.-C. Cheng and S. Wagner, "Overview of flexible electronics technology," in Flexible Electronics. Springer, 2009, pp. 1–28.

[11] S. Khan, L. Lorenzelli, and R. S. Dahiya, "Technologies for printing sensors and electronics over large flexible substrates: a review," IEEE Sensors Journal, vol. 15, no. 6, 2015, pp. 3164–3185.

[12] V. Scardaci, R. Coull, P. E. Lyons, D. Rickard, and J. N. Coleman, "Spray deposition of highly transparent, low-resistance networks of silver nanowires over large areas," Small, vol. 7, no. 18, 2011, pp. 2621–2628.

[13] F. Wang et al., "Laser-induced graphene: preparation, functionalization and applications," Materials technology, vol. 33, no. 5, 2018, pp. 340–356.

[14] J. Bito, J. G. Hester, and M. M. Tentzeris, "Ambient rf energy harvesting from a two-way talk radio for flexible wearable wireless sensor devices utilizing inkjet printing technologies," IEEE Transactions on Microwave Theory and Techniques, vol. 63, no. 12, 2015, pp. 4533–4543.

[15] S.-E. Adami et al., "A flexible 2.45-ghz power harvesting wristband with net system output from- 24.3 dbm of rf power," IEEE Transactions on Microwave Theory and Techniques, vol. 66, no. 1, 2017, pp. 380–395.

[16] J. Fernández-Salmerón, A. Rivadeneyra, F. Martínez-Martí, L. Capitán-Vallvey, A. Palma, and M. Carvajal, "Passive uhf rfid tag with multiple sensing capabilities," Sensors, vol. 15, no. 10, 2015, pp. 26 769–26 782.

[17] S. Lehtimaki et al., "Performance of printable supercapacitors in an rf energy harvesting circuit," International Journal of Electrical Power & Energy Systems, vol. 58, 2014, pp. 42–46.

[18] J. Maeng, C. Meng, and P. P. Irazoqui, "Wafer-scale integrated micro-supercapacitors on an ultrathin and highly flexible biomedical platform," Biomedical microdevices, vol. 17, no. 1, 2015, p. 7.

[19] M. Russo, P. Šolić, and M. Stella, "Probabilistic modeling of harvested gsm energy and its application in extending uhf rfid tags reading range," Journal of Electromagnetic Waves and Applications, vol. 27, no. 4, 2013, pp. 473–484.

[20] A. Palaios, V. Miteva, J. Riihijärvi, and P. Mähönen, "When the whispers become noise: A contemporary look at radio noise levels," in Wireless Communications and Networking Conference (WCNC), 2016 IEEE. IEEE, 2016, pp. 1–7.

[21] M. Yılmaz, D. G. Kuntalp, and A. Fidan, "Determination of spectrum utilization profiles for 30 mhz–3 ghz frequency band," in Communications (COMM), 2016 International Conference on. IEEE, 2016, pp. 499–502.

[22] G. Singh, R. Ponnaganti, T. Prabhakar, and K. Vinoy, "A tuned rectifier for rf energy harvesting from ambient radiations," AEU-International Journal of Electronics and Communications, vol. 67, no. 7, 2013, pp. 564–569.

[23] S. Borini et al., "Ultrafast graphene oxide humidity sensors," ACS nano, vol. 7, no. 12, 2013, pp. 11 166–11 173.

[24] F. J. Romero et al., "Design, fabrication and characterization of capacitive humidity sensors based on emerging flexible technologies," Sensors and Actuators B: Chemical, vol. 287, 2019, pp. 459–467.

[25] ——, "Design guidelines of laser reduced graphene oxide conformal thermistor for iot applications," Sensors and Actuators A: Physical, vol. 274, 2018, pp. 148–154.

[26] Y. Zheng, R. Wu, W. Shi, Z. Guan, and J. Yu, "Effect of in situ annealing on the performance of spray coated polymer solar cells," Solar energy materials and solar cells, vol. 111, 2013, pp. 200–205.

[27] H.-W. Hsu and C.-L. Liu, "Spray-coating semiconducting conjugated polymers for organic thin film transistor applications," RSC advances, vol. 4, no. 57, 2014, pp. 30 145–30 149.

UV-assisted Chemiresistive Alcohol Sensor Based on Cobalt Doped Tin Dioxide

Mikayel Aleksanyan
Department of Physics of Semiconductors and Microelectronics
Yerevan State University
Yerevan, Republic of Armenia
e-mail: maleksanyan@ysu.am

Vladimir Aroutiounian
Department of Physics of Semiconductors and Microelectronics
Yerevan State University
Yerevan, Republic of Armenia
e-mail: kisahar@ysu.am

Artak Sayunts
Department of Physics of Semiconductors and Microelectronics
Yerevan State University
Yerevan, Republic of Armenia
e-mail: sayuntsartak@ysu.am

Valeri Arakelyan
Department of Physics of Semiconductors and Microelectronics
Yerevan State University
Yerevan, Republic of Armenia
e-mail: avaleri@ysu.am

Hayk Zakaryan
Department of Physics of Semiconductors and Microelectronics
Yerevan State University
Yerevan, Republic of Armenia
e-mail: hayk.zakaryan@ysu.am

Gohar Shahnazaryan
Department of Physics of Semiconductors and Microelectronics
Yerevan State University
Yerevan, Republic of Armenia
e-mail: sgohar@ysu.am

***Abstract*—In this paper, a sputtering ceramic target based on SnO_2 doped with 2 at.% Co was synthesized by solid-phase reaction method. A chemiresisive alcohol vapor sensor based on SnO_2<Co> was manufactured by the high-frequency magnetron sputtering method. The alcohol sensing properties of the SnO_2<Co> sensor under the ultraviolet (UV) illumination were examined at room temperature. The UV-assisted alcohol sensor showed a sufficient response to low concentrations of alcohol vapor at room temperature. The Co-doped SnO_2 sensor has also demonstrated a good response to alcohol vapors at elevated operating temperature (200 °C).**

Keywords* - *gas sensor; alcohol; UV radiation; room temperature; metal oxides.

I. INTRODUCTION

Today, alcohol vapor sensors have a great demand in various fields. Ethanol sensors are used in food industry, medicine and biotechnology. Ethanol sensors are also extremely important during the production of ethanol and alcoholic drinks to monitor the wine quality. They are used in processes such as: food–packages, clinical analysis, agronomic, vinicultural and veterinary analysis, also toxic waste and contamination analysis, fuel processing, Trends in Analytical Chemistry (TRAC) management and societal applications, as well as chemical processing in industry [1]-[5]. Several methods and strategies have been reported for the detection of ethanol, e.g., gas chromatography, liquid chromatography, refractometry and spectrophotometry, semiconductor gas sensors and so on [2][6][7].

The solid-state gas sensors based on Metal Oxide Semiconductors (MOSs) with different nanostructures have played an important role in environment monitoring, domestic and car safety, control in chemical processing due to their distinct advantages, such as simple implementation, low cost, high sensitivity, stability and reproducibility, low detection limit, easy production, nontoxicity, easy-achieved real-time response and compatibility with micro-fabrication processes [8]-[10]. Various MOSs materials, such as SnO_2, In_2O_3, WO_3, ZnO, TiO_2, Fe_2O_3, CuO, Ga_2O_3, CTO (CrTiO) with different nanostructures and dopant have been studied and showed promising results for detecting Volatile Organic Compounds (VOCs) [11]. Among these materials, the SnO_2 has good electrical and chemical properties. It is an n-type semiconductor with tetragonal rutile structure and it has a large energy band gap of 3.6 eV at 300 K. It has been widely exploited as an ultrasensitive gas sensor for the detection of carbon monoxide (CO), ammonia, ozone, carbon dioxide, hydrogen, hydrogen peroxide, nitrogen dioxide, ethanol and so on [12]-[14]. The wide range of possible applications has attracted many researchers to work on this material with different nanostructures, such as nanograins, nanorods, nanowires and nanofibers synthesized by various methods. It has a high sensitivity to reducing and oxidizing gases, fast response and recovery behavior and low sensitivity to humidity [15]-[17].

Although many conductometric gas sensors made of MOSs have been commercialized for the last decades, a lot of problems still need to be solved in order to improve the performance of gas sensing devices. The main issues are related to sensitivity, selectivity and stability but the lowering of sensor's operating temperature is still one of the main concerns. Resistive metal oxide based gas sensors normally operate at an elevated temperature (in a range of 200 °C to 400 °C). This results in higher power consumption, limits the use of the sensor in explosive environments, and causes difficulties for the sensor to be attached to electrical systems [18][19].

There are many studies aimed at applying new technologies and reducing operating temperatures. To ensure a low operating temperature, several techniques have been used, such as doping the metal oxides with additives, using catalytic particles, applying a high electric field across the sensor terminals and illuminating the sensors with UV radiation [20][21]. The irradiation of UV-assisted MOS sensors is an important alternative to activate chemical reactions on metal oxide surface and reduce the resistance of the thin sensing layer instead of the more common use of energy-demanding heating. Almost completely replacing the effect of thermal energy, UV irradiation greatly influences the adsorption and desorption processes of the gas on the semiconductor surface enhancing their reactivity with the analyte gas. Under the influence of UV illumination, as a result of the formation of electron–hole pairs, more neutral atoms and molecules of absorbed oxygen on the surface of the semiconductor become ions, which then interact with analyte gas. UV irradiation can also be used to clean the active surface of a gas sensing layer, but the more important function is to improve the sensitivity and selectivity of the gas sensor by reducing the operating temperature. If it is not possible to lower the operating temperature to room temperature by using UV irradiation, UV irradiation combined with heating can be used to stimulate the gas sensor [22]-[24].

In this paper, we focus on low temperature sensing of SnO_2 based thin film sensors under UV illumination. In Section 2, the fabrication steps of SnO_2<Co> sensor are presented. In Section 3, the studies of sensing properties of UV assisted ethanol sensor are presented. The conclusions are outlined in Section 4. The sensor exhibited good sensitivity to low concentration of ethanol vapors. Fabricated sensors have also sufficient selectivity and stability over time.

II. SENSOR FABRICATION

Sensitive layers based on SnO_2<Co> were deposited by RF magnetron sputtering technique. Firstly, appropriate quantities of the corresponding metal oxide powders (SnO_2+2 at.%Co_2O_3) were weighed and mixed thoroughly for 10 hours. Then, the mixture was subjected to pre-heat treatment at 800 ^{0}C for 5 hours (the initial annealing temperature was chosen based on the composition of the compound). The preheating of mixed powder eliminates the moisture of the metal oxide raw materials, which facilitates homogeneous mixing and milling of the powders (when the ceramic tablet is made of dry powders, it reduces the probability of formation of mechanical cracks during final annealing). Then, the mixed powder was milled for 20 hours until becoming fully homogeneous and pressed (with 2000 N/cm^2 pressure) in a form of a tablet (with 50 mm diameter). The sputtering ceramic target based on SnO_2 doped with 2 at.% Co (using the pressed tablet) was synthesized by solid-phase reaction method using thermal treatment in the atmosphere by the programmable furnace Nabertherm, HT O4/16 (with the controller of C 42). The final annealing was carried out at temperature range of 500 °C-1100 °C for 20 hours. The synthesized semiconductor solid solution was subjected to mechanical treatment in order to eliminate surface defects. So, a smooth and parallel target with a diameter of 40 mm and thickness of 2 mm was prepared as a magnetron sputtering target (see Figure 1).

The thin sensing layers were deposited on Multi-Sensor-Platforms by RF magnetron sputtering method using synthesized SnO_2<Co> target. The Multi-Sensor-Platforms were purchased by TESLA BLANTA (Czech Republic). The platform has a temperature sensor (Pt 1000) for controlling operating temperature. There are platinum heater and interdigitated electrodes on the ceramic substrate of the Multi-Sensor-Platform (see Figure 2). The heater and temperature sensor were covered with an insulating glass layer. Gas sensitive SnO_2<Co> layer was deposited onto the non-passivated electrode structure, so the Multi-Sensor-Platform was converted into gas sensor. Then, palladium catalytic particles are deposited on the surface of the magnetron sputtered sensing layer by ion-beam sputtering method for sensitization of active layer. The working conditions of the high-frequency magnetron sputtering and ion-beam sputtering are presented in Table I (the base pressure was 2×10^{4} Pa for both cases). The manufactured sensors were annealed in the air at 350 °C for 4 hours for homogenization of sensing films and stabilization their parameters. The fabrication steps of photo-assisted gas sensor are presented in Figure 1.

The thickness of the SnO_2<Co> thin film was measured by the Alpha-Step D-300 (KLA Tencor) profiler. The result of the study of the film-substrate transition profile is shown in Figure 3. The thickness of the SnO_2<Co> film was equal to 180 nm.

The electrical and gas sensing properties of the SnO_2<Co> thin layer was measured using a home-made computer-controlled gas testing system. The testing system has a test chamber, pressure sensor (Motorola-MPX5010DP) and a data acquisition system (PCLD-8115) [25]. For measurement of alcohol vapor concentration, the SnO_2<Co> based sensor (the Multi-Sensor-Platform) was attached in the test chamber connecting the six pins (two pins of temperature sensor, two pins of heater and two pines of resistance measurement electrodes, see Figure 2) with the corresponding inputs on sensor holder. The UV LED (λ=365 nm) was attached 0.5 cm away from the active layer with illumination of 2 mW/cm^2. The gas sensing properties of the SnO_2<Co> sensor were measured at room temperature in the dark and under UV illumination. The response of the sensor was measured also at 200 ^{0}C operating temperature in the dark. The working temperature of the sensor was adjusted by changing the voltage across the platinum heater. To have the necessary concentration of alcohol vapor in the chamber, the liquid ethanol was introduced into the chamber on the special hot plate designed for the quick conversion of the liquid ethanol to the gas phase. The response of the sensor is defined as $[(R_a-R_g)/R_a]\times100$ %, where R_a and R_g are the electrical resistances of active layer in air and target gas, respectively.

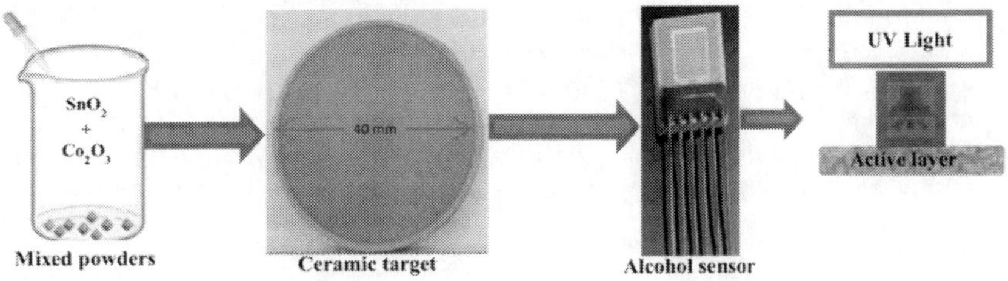

Figure 1. Schematic block diagram of the photo-assisted gas sensor fabrication.

TABLE I. THE WORKING CONDITIONS FOR DEPOSITION OF THIN LAYER AND CATALITIC PARTICLES.

Process	Sputtering duration	Working pressure	Power of generator	Substrate temperature	Cathode current	Anode voltage	Sputtering gas
Magnetron sputtering (RF)	20 m	2×10^{-1} Pa	60 w	200 ^{0}C	---	---	Ar
Ion-beam sputtering (DC)	3 s	5×10^{-1} Pa	---	100 ^{0}C	65 A	25 V	Ar

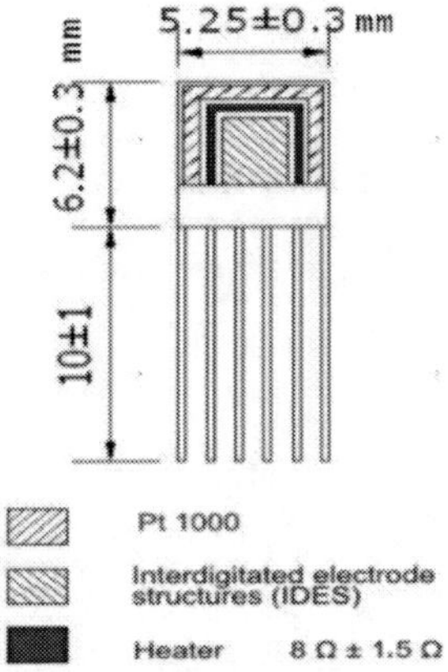

Figure 2. The schematic diagram of the Multi-Sensor-Platform.

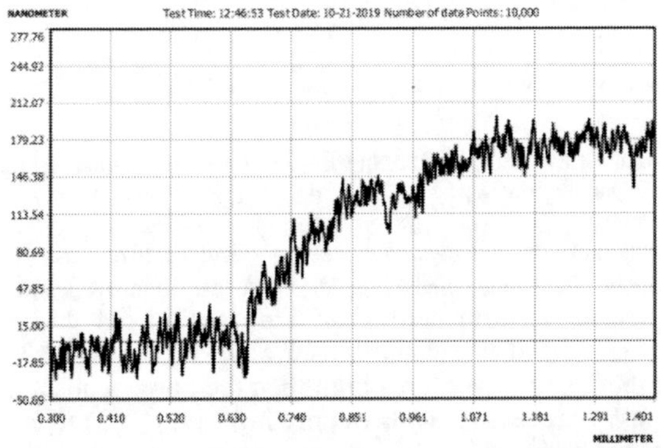

Figure 3. The thickness measurement result for the Co-doped SnO_2 film.

III. GAS SENSING PERFORMANCES

Initially, we tested the influence of the UV illumination on the baseline resistance of the SnO_2<Co> sensor at room temperature. It can be seen from Figure 4 that the value of R_0/R_{UV} (~350) ratio is larger than 1, indicating the decrease of the sensor baseline resistance under UV illumination. The response time of the Co-doped SnO_2 thin film under UV irradiation is a few minutes.

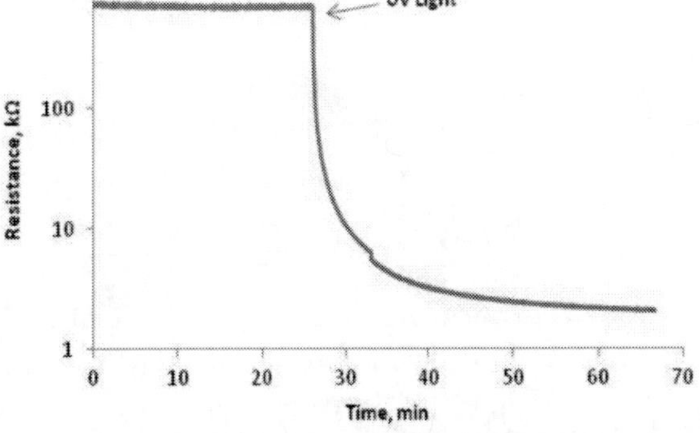

Figure 4. Resistance variation of the Co-doped SnO_2 sensing layer under the influence of UV irradiation at room temperature.

The manufactured sensor is resistive and its operation is grounded on changes of resistance of gas sensitive semiconductor layer under the influence of ethanol vapors caused by an exchange of charges between molecules of the semiconductor film and absorbed ethanol. The high operating temperature of these types of sensors is mainly due to the high activation energies of chemical reactions. For this reason, these types of sensors mainly do not sensitivity at room temperature. The UV light promotes the gas adsorption and desorption on the surface of the semiconductor participating to the sensing mechanisms [23].

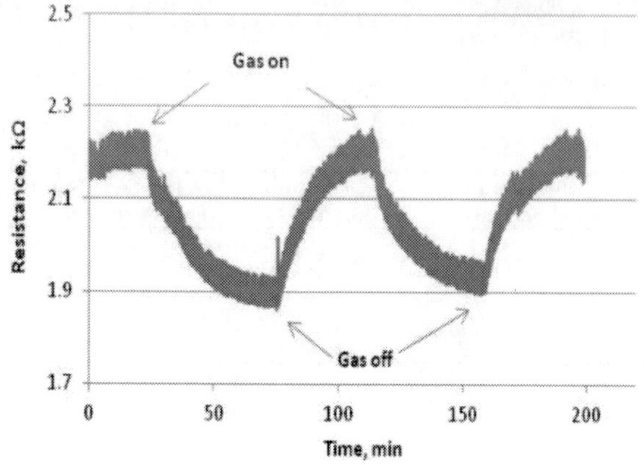

Figure 5. Resistance variation of the SnO_2<Co> sensor under the influence of UV irradiation at room temperature in the presence of 150 ppm ethanol vapors.

The thin film SnO_2<Co> based sensor did not show sensitivity to ethanol vapors at room temperature without UV irradiation. We measured the resistance variation (also the signal repeatability) of the SnO_2<Co> sensor in the presence of ethanol vapors under the influence of UV irradiation at room temperature. The resistance of the thin film changes by almost 400 Ω in the presence of 150 ppm ethanol vapors (see Figure 5).

Sensor response and recovery times are in minutes and it is clear that recovery times are faster because UV light more stimulate the desorption processes from the surface of the sensing layer.

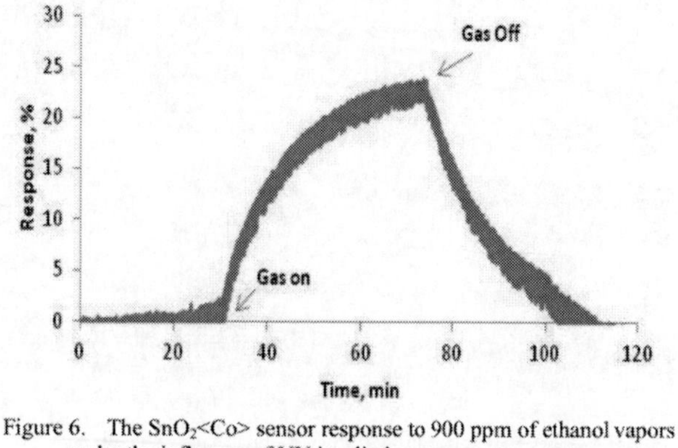

Figure 6. The SnO_2<Co> sensor response to 900 ppm of ethanol vapors under the influence of UV irradiation at room temperature.

Figure 6 shows the transient response of the SnO_2<Co> sensor in the presence of ethanol under UV light at room temperature. The response to 900 ppm ethanol vapors under UV illumination is sufficiently high (24 %).

We extracted the response vs. concentration curve for the Co-doped SnO_2 sensitive film. Figure 7 shows the dependence of response on the ethanol vapor concentration under the influence of UV irradiation at room temperature. The dependence has almost linear characteristic, which will allow not only to detect of ethanol vapors but also to accurately measure the low concentrations of this gas.

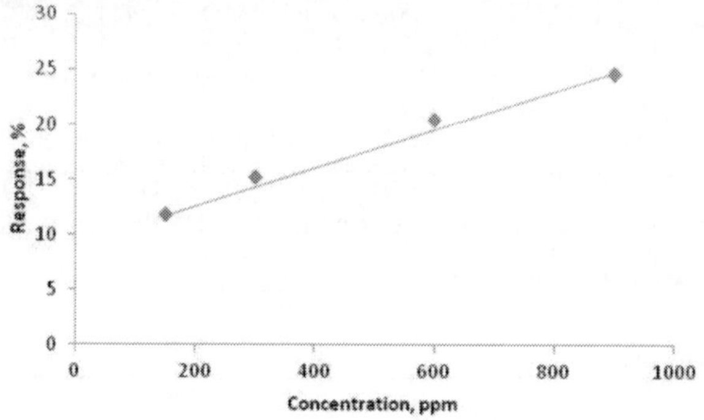

Figure 7. The dependence of response on the ethanol vapor concentration under the influence of UV irradiation at room temperature.

The resistance change of the Co-doped SnO_2 sensor under the influence of ethanol vapors at high operating temperature in dark conditions was also measured. The sensitive layer resistance decreases more than 25 times in the presence of 150 ppm ethanol vapors at 200 ^{0}C operating temperature (see Figure 8). The response and recovery times

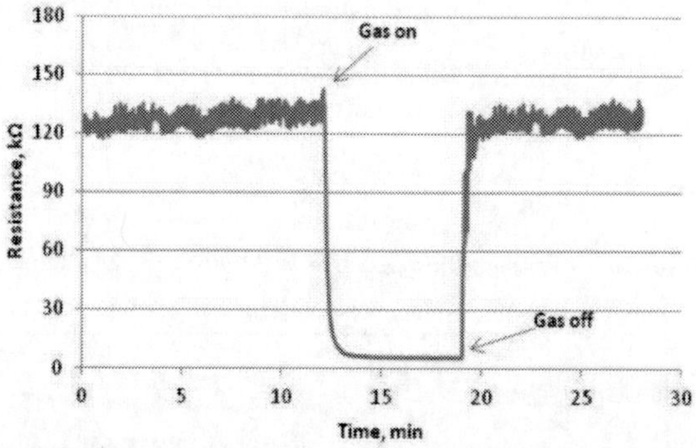

Figure 8. Resistance variation of the SnO_2<Co> sensor in the presence of 150 ppm ethanol vapors at 200 °C operating temperature in the dark.

of the sensor at high operating temperature are a few seconds. At high operating temperature in dark condition, the sensor performance is quite promising but the power consumption of fabricated sensor at 200 ^{0}C is about 2.5 W. It is more than two orders high then the power consumption (24 mW) needed the sensor operating with UV irradiation at room temperature.

IV. CONCLUSION

In summary, a simple technology has been used to manufacture semiconductor thin film sensor based on SnO_2 doped with 2 at.% Co. The fabricated SnO_2<Co> chemiresistive gas sensor showed a good sensitivity to different concentrations of ethanol vapor (from 150 to 900 ppm) at room temperature with the activation of low-powered UV LED (24 mW, 365 nm). The sensor displayed a good signal repeatability and long-term stability. These sensing characteristics made the present SnO_2<Co> based sensor a promising candidate for practically detecting ethanol vapors at room temperature.

ACKNOWLEDGMENT

This investigation was supported by 19YR-2K002 (Young Researchers 2019-2021) project of Ministry of Education, Science, Culture and Sport RA (Science Committee) .

REFERENCES

[1] M. A. Lakhanea, A. L. Choudharia, R. S. Khairnara, and M. P. Mahabolea, "Alcohol Sensor Based on Mg-STI zeolite Thick Films," Procedia Technology, vol. 24, pp. 595-602, 2016.

[2] A. Charishma, A. Jayarama, V. V. D. Shastrimath, and R. Pinto, "An Ethanol Sensor Review: Materials, Techniques and Performance," SAHYADRI International Journal of Research, vol. 1 3, pp. 37-46, June 2017.

[3] E. C. Ramaa et al., "Comparative study of different alcohol sensors based on Screen-Printed Carbon Electrodes," Analytica Chimica Acta, vol. 728, pp. 69-76, 2012, doi:10.1016/j.aca.2012.03.039.

[4] Y. Li et al., "In situ decoration of Zn_2SnO_4 nanoparticles on reduced graphene oxide for high performance ethanol sensor," Ceramics International, vol. 44, pp. 6836–6842, January 2018, doi:org/10.1016/j.ceramint.2018.01.107.

[5] Z. Qin et al., "Highly sensitive alcohol sensor based on a single Er-doped In_2O_3 nanoribbon," Chemical Physics Letters, vol. 646, pp. 12–17, 2016, doi:10.1016/j.cplett.2015.12.054.

[6] G. Feng, M. Zhang, S. Wang, C. Song, and J. Xiao, "Ultra-fast responding and recovering ethanol sensors based on CdS nanospheres doped with graphene," Applied Surface Science, vol. 453, pp. 513–519, May 2018, doi:10.1016/j.apsusc.2018.05.102.

[7] M. Shashikant, V. Lahade1, Mr. Pravin, and D. Pardhi, "Gas Sensing Technologies: Review, Scope and Challenges," International Journal of Recent Trends in Engineering & Research (IJRTER), vol. 04, pp. 108-115, February 2018, doi: 10.23883/IJRTER.2018.4073.M2XNS.

[8] Y. Shen et al., "Highly sensitive and selective room temperature alcohol gas sensors based on TeO_2 nanowires," Journal of Alloys and Compounds, vol. 664, pp. 229-234, 2016, doi: 10.1016/j.jallcom.2015.12.247.

[9] V. M. Aroutiounian et al., "Manufacturing and investigations of i-butane sensor made of SnO_2/multiwall-carbon-nanotube nanocomposite," Sensors and Actuators B, vol. 173, pp. 890-896, 2012, doi:10.1016/j.snb.2012.04.039.

[10] V. M. Arakelyan et al., "Gas sensors made of multiwall carbon nanotubes modified by tin dioxide," Journal of Contemporary Physics (Armenian Academy of Sciences), vol. 48, pp. 176-183, 2013, doi:10.3103/S1068337213040063.

[11] G. Korotcenkov and B. K. Cho, "Metal oxide composites in conductometric gas sensors: Achievements and challenges," Sensors and Actuators B, vol. 244, pp. 182-210, June 2017, doi:10.1016/j.snb.2016.12.117.

[12] V. Aroutiounian et al., "Thin-film SnO_2 and ZnO detectors of hydrogen peroxide vapors," Journal of Sensors and Sensor Systems, vol. 7, pp. 281-288, April 2018, doi: /10.5194/jsss-7-281-2018.

[13] H. S. Jeong, M. J. Park, S.H. Kwon, H. J. Joo, S. H. Song, and H. I. Kwon, "Low temperature NO_2 sensing properties of RF-sputtered SnO-SnO_2 heterojunction thin-film with p-type semiconducting behavior," Ceramics International, vol. 44, pp. 17283–17289, June 2018, doi:10.1016/j.ceramint.2018.06.189.

[14] V. Aroutiounian et al., "Nanostructured sensors for detection of hydrogen peroxide vapours," Sensors & Transducers, vol. 213, pp. 46-53, June 2017.

[15] G. Korotcenkov and V. Nehasil, "The role of Rh dispersion in gas sensing effects observed in SnO_2 thin films," Materials Chemistry and Physics, vol. 232, pp. 160-168, June 2019, doi:10.1016/j.matchemphys.2019.04.069.

[16] G. Korotcenkov and B. K. Cho, "Thin film SnO_2-based gas sensors: Film thickness influence," Sensors and Actuators B, vol. 142, pp. 321-330, October 2009, doi:10.1016/j.snb.2009.08.006.

[17] M. S. Aleksanyan, "Methane sensor based on $SnO_2/In_2O_3/TiO_2$ nanostructure," Journal of Contemporary Physics (Armenian Academy of Sciences), vol. 45, pp. 77-80, 2010, doi:10.3103/S1068337210020052.

[18] N. Li, Y. Fan, Y. Shi, Q. Xiang, X. Wang, and J. Xu, "A low temperature formaldehyde gas sensor based on hierarchical SnO/SnO_2 nano-flowers assembled from ultrathin nanosheets: Synthesis, sensing performance and mechanism," Sensors and Actuators B, vol. 294, pp. 106-115, September 2019, doi:10.1016/j.snb.2019.04.061.

[19] I. Kortidis, H. C. Swart, S. S. Ray, and D. E. Motaung, "Detailed understanding on the relation of various pH and synthesis reaction times towards a prominent low temperature H_2S gas sensor based on ZnO nanoplatelets," Result in Physics, vol. 12, pp. 2189-2201, March 2019, doi:10.1016/j.rinp.2019.01.089.

[20] E. Espid, A. S. Noce, and F. Taghipour, "The effect of radiation parameters on the performance of photo-activated gas sensors," Journal of Photochemistry & Photobiology A, vol. 374, pp. 95–105, January 2019, doi:10.1016/j.jphotochem.2019.01.038.

[21] J. Cui, L. Shi, T. Xiea, D. Wang, and Y. Lin, "UV-light illumination room temperature HCHO gas-sensing mechanism of ZnO with different nanostructures," Sensors and Actuators B, vol. 227, pp. 220–226, 2016, doi:10.1016/j.snb.2015.12.010.

[22] E. Espid and F. Taghipour, "Development of highly sensitive ZnO/In_2O_3 composite gas sensor activated by UV-LED," Sensors and Actuators B, vol. 241, pp. 828–839, 2017, doi:10.1016/j.snb.2016.10.129.

[23] B. Gong et al., "UV irradiation-assisted ethanol detection operated by the gas sensorbased on ZnO nanowires/optical fiber hybrid structure," Sensors and Actuators B, vol. 245, pp. 821–827, 2017, doi:10.1016/j.snb.2017.01.187.

[24] A. Ilina et al., "UV effect on NO_2 sensing properties of nanocrystalline In_2O_3," Sensors and Actuators B, vol. 231, pp. 491–496, 2016, doi:10.1016/j.snb.2016.03.051.

[25] Z. Adamyan et al., "Nanocomposite sensors of propylene glycol, dimethylformamide and formaldehyde vapors," J. Sens. Sens. Syst., vol. 7, pp. 31-41, 2018, doi:10.5194/jsss-7-31-2018.

Development of pH Sensor Module with Wireless Transmission Function

Lan Zhang, Jian Lu, Ryutaro Maeda
Research Center for Ubiquitous MEMS and Micro Engineering (UMEMSME)
National Institute of Advanced Industrial Science and Technology (AIST)
Tsukuba, Japan
e-mails: {chou-ran, jian-lu, maeda-ryutaro}@aist.go.jp

Abstract— **In our previous work, we developed a solid-state pH sensor for real time pH measurement. In this work, we discuss the use of this sensor for extension applications in the health monitoring field. The pH sensor system needs to be super compact in size and have a bio-friendly interface in order to provide a good user experience. In this paper, we introduce a smaller transistor and a new sensing material for realizing an optimized sensor structure and measurement system. The measured results show that the antimony-based pH sensor has a reasonable responsivity for pH real-time monitoring.**

Keywords - pH; field effect transistor; health condition; calibration; wireless transmission.

I. INTRODUCTION

Recently, Micro-Electro-Mechanical Systems (MEMS) technology has undergone many advances, such as super compact size, high sensitivity and high uniformity of working functions. Based on the MEMS technique, we developed a solid-state pH sensor that has already been used in some application fields, not only in chemical engineering, but also in industry and agricultural science [1] [2].

In this study, we would like extend the given sensor for applications in the health monitoring field. Figure 1 shows the schematic view of our proposed pH sensor measurement system. The typical electrodes were fabricated using the MEMS technique for realizing high dimensional and high performance homogeneity. The sensor system combines the measurement and transmission boards (see insert images). The electrodes connect the gate terminal of a Metal-Oxide-Semiconductor Field-Effect Transistor (MOSFET). The specific FET is loaded on the measurement board and used to measure the pH value of target solutions. The transmission board has a wireless or a Bluetooth module to transmit the tested date to the user terminal devices (smart phone or PC), respectively. Figure 1 also shows the potential application fields of the given pH sensor: (1) the compact sensing system unit could be set in a nappy or a diaper, for real-time monitoring the health condition of children or old people; (2) the compact sensor could be packaged with a bio-friendly surface; (3) the ultra-small low-power wireless sensor node may also be implanted into animal body to measure the urine condition of pets.

The rest of the paper is structured as follows. In Section 2, we are going to describe the fabrication method of sensor electrodes and system. In Section 3, some preliminary measurement results will be presented. In Section 4, we will present a discussion and conclusion on this work.

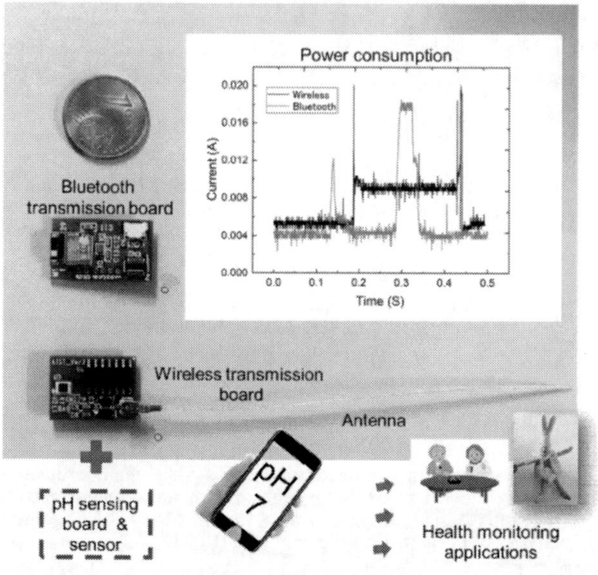

Figure 1. Smartphone based wireless pH sensor system and its potential applications.

II. SENSOR FABRICATION AND SPECIFICATION

In our previous works, we already comprehensively presented the fabrication processes of Indium Tin Oxide (ITO) -based pH sensor electrode [1]. Silicon wafers with 200-μm-thick SiO_2 for passivation layers were used to fabricate the MEMS devices in this work. After under-metal and sensing layers generation, photolithography and metal etching methods were used to generate the sensing electrode and the bottom electrode layers with high precision. Then, to pattern the sensing area and protect it with a long life time, a fluoropolymer thin film coating was fabricated on the sensor electrode. Finally, O_2 plasma was used to remove the photoresist and other residuals. On the other hand, in this work, the comparison sensor with the following specification of thick film antimony for the working electrode was used: the sensing area has a 4-mm diameter circular window.

III. PRELIMINARY MEASUREMENT RESULTS

A. *Metal-oxide-semiconductor field-effect transistor measurement*

To provide a good user experience, the pH sensor system components should also be improved, because a small sensor node can minimize the discomfort of the users. The components on boards should be optimized with the size as small as possible. After the measurement board can be shrunk to a very compact size, the sensor system will also have a tiny size. In the new sensor system, an n-channel MOS transistor (with very low price, lower than 20 Japanese yen) was used on the sensing board for testing the pH value of solutions.

The performance of the small MOS transistor was measured. The output current of the transistor has a range from 0.875 V to 0.890 V, correspondingly to the measured pH value from 7 to 4. The responsivity of the new sensor has a reasonable value of 5 mV/pH.

B. *Performance comparison of different sensing electrodes and different transmission systems*

We did a performance comparison of different sensing electrodes. Figure 2 shows the digital output of the pH sensor with different sensing materials versus the measured pH values. As the results show, the ITO- and antimony-based pH sensors have similar output/pH values (the relative error between the two sensors does not exceed 5% in average). Both sensors can keep a linear output proportional to the changes in the pH value. The very small different slope between the fitting curves showed that the antimony-based pH sensor has a relatively higher sensitivity (see Figure 2 fitting curves). However, the antimony-based pH sensor also suffers from a larger deviation error comparison with ITO-based pH sensor. On the other hand, some researchers prefer the antimony-based pH sensors to apply on bio-sensing technology, for a better biocompatibility [3]. We can understand the merits and demerits of sensing materials, reasonably. After correct calibration, the sensor node can be used in field measurements to prove its stability and reliability. We also tested the power consumption of wireless and Bluetooth transmission systems; we found that they have similar power consumption at the mW level, but Bluetooth has an inner antenna, which causes the Bluetooth-based pH sensor system to be very compact in size, with larger application potentials.

IV. DISCUSSION AND CONCLUSION

We developed a solid-state pH sensor for real time pH monitoring. In this work, we extend its applications into the health monitoring field. In order to realize the solid-state pH sensor with super compact size and bio-friendly interface to provide a good user experience, a small transistor and a new sensing material are introduced for fabricating the sensor structure and measurement system, respectively. As the results show, the antimony-based pH sensor has a reasonable responsivity for pH real-time monitoring. Super compact solid pH sensors can provide mass data of target solutions and water to help companies realize an Internet of Things management system.

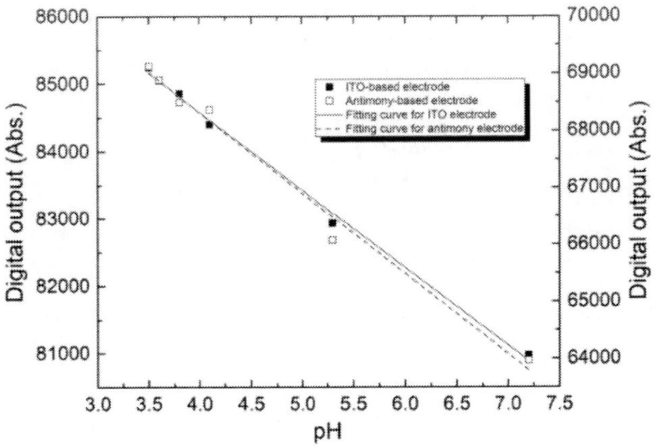

Figure 2. The output voltage of the pH sensor with different sensing electrodes against the measured pH values.

ACKNOWLEDGMENT

This study was support by Tsukuba Innovation Arena (Tsukuba, Ibaraki, Japan), collaborative research program of "Kakehashi".

REFERENCES

[1] L. Zhang, J. Lu, H. Okada, H. Nogami, T. Itoh, and S. Arai, "Low-Power Highly Sensitive pH sensor with μ-dots protective structures for monitoring rumen in cows in real-time," IEEE Sens. J. vol. 17, pp. 7281 - 7289, 2017.

[2] L. Zhang, J. Lu, H. Okada, H. Nogami, and T. Itoh, "Development of ITO- and FET-based cow rumen sensor for long-term pH value monitoring," Symposium on Design, Test, Integration and Packaging of MEMS/MOEMS (DTIP), vol. 2016, pp.92-96, May 2016.

[3] T. Kazuyoshi, A. Saad Mohammad, K. Daiki, K. Kagemasa, and K. Minoru, " Development of one electrode type pH sensor measuring in microscopic region," The International Journal of Applied Electromagnetics and Mechanic, vol. 52, pp.1417-1424, 2016.

Low Cost Measurement System for the Precise Monitoring of the Instantaneous Rotational Speed of an Internal Combustion Engine

Dimitrios N. Pagonis, Sofia Peppa
Naval Architecture Department
University of West Attica
Athens, Greece
emails: D.N.Pagonis@uniwa.gr, speppa@uniwa.gr

Grigoris Kaltsas
Electrical and Electronics Engineering Department
University of West Attica
Athens, Greece
email: gkaltsas@uniwa.gr

Abstract— **The work presented in this paper concerns the development of a novel low-cost measurement system for monitoring with high accuracy the instantaneous rotational speed of a low power industrial engine. The system has been successfully employed for monitoring the rotational speed of a typical four cylinder engine; a speed recording with a resolution of 0.04 degree of crank angle has been obtained, revealing its suitability for fault diagnosis and engine performance optimization applications. Key features of the proposed measurement configuration are very high monitoring accuracy, low-cost and ability to be installed on-site to an already operating engine with no major modifications; the above suggest numerous potential applications.**

Keywords-measurement system; encoder; instantaneous rotanional speed; 3D printing; fault diagnosis; internal combustion engine.

I. INTRODUCTION

Optimizing the performance of an engine has been the goal of numerous research efforts [1][2], since proper prediction of its main operation parameters (such as torque fluctuation during various loading, etc.) can significantly contribute to efficient fault diagnosis, fuel economy, gas emissions reduction and optimum engine performance in general. The value of the instantaneous rotational speed of the crankshaft is an important parameter employed widely in engine operation analysis and fault diagnosis [3]-[6], since it is relatively easily accessible employing low cost equipment. In general, there are two established methods for measuring the specific parameter: the timer/counter-based technique and the Analog-to-Digital Converter (ADC) based technique [7][8].

The vast majority of modern engine speed monitoring systems are based on the "magnetic pick-up" principle of operation, which is a timer/counter based method. In order to detect the engine's speed, a given number of dents of appropriate size and geometry are patterned on the surface of the metallic flywheel of the engine, which is attached to the rotating shaft; an inductive sensor is then employed to detect the presence of each dent as the engine is operating (Fig. 1). The rotational speed is deduced from the sensor's output pulse-train signal.

We should note that the maximum resolution of the above described system (i.e., maximum number of velocity measurements during a single rotation of the crankshaft) is mainly affected by the minimum resolution of the sensor, that is, the minimum size required for each dent in order to be magnetically detected.

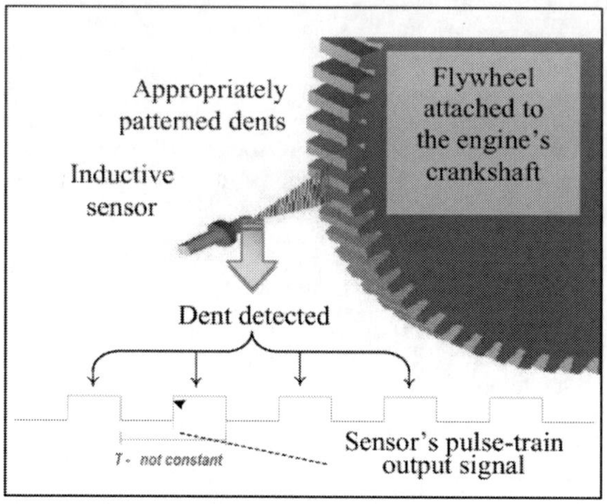

Figure 1. "Magnetic pick-up" principle of operation.

In a typical low power industrial engine [9], the above setup provides a maximum resolution of 120 measurements per cycle (i.e., the speed is measured every 3° of crankshaft rotation). In order to increase that figure, one should increment the number of dents available on the flywheel, resulting in an increase of its overall dimensions; thus, the maximum resolution of such a system is limited by the available space provided for the flywheel –a constrain that cannot be altered easily, especially in the typical case of low/medium power engine.

Although the measuring principle described above is widely adapted regarding engine rotational speed monitoring, other alternative methods have been reported in literature. In more detail, angular speed recording with high accuracy by employing an appropriate optical measurement system has been successfully performed in a low power four stroke, four cylinder industrial engine [10], while the development and installation of a speed monitoring system which is based on a rotary encoder (on a four stroke, six cylinder industrial engine) has also been described [11].

Both of the previously mentioned methods lead to substantial increase of the maximum resolution of speed monitoring (i.e. angular speed measurements with a resolution of less than 0.5° are reported) compared to the established "magnetic pick-up" principle of operation. We should note though that an important constraint for employing widely such monitoring systems and rendering them practically useful to typical industrial engines - already operating on-site, focuses on the need of altering the initial engine setup, in order for the measuring system to be installed. With our proposed method, this constraint is practically removed.

The rest of the paper is structured as follows. In Section II, we present the proposed measurement system, while in Section III, the obtained preliminary results after applying the system to a typical industrial engine are discussed. Finally, we conclude the work in Section IV.

II. Description of the Proposed Method

The proposed measurement system overcomes the restriction imposed by the size of the flywheel and the necessity of altering the initial engine setup in general. This is achieved by employing an incremental rotary encoder in order to measure the instantaneous rotational speed which is mounted directly on the engine's crankshaft through a custom-designed coupling, manufactured by a 3D printer.

Figure 2. Typical low power engine's flywheel attached to the crankshaft; the incremental encoder is mounted directly on the flywheel (region A) through an appropriate/custom-designed coupling.

In more detail, a low-cost commercially available sensor (IFM electronic, type RVP510) has been employed. The sensor was mounted on the engine's crankshaft (Fig. 2) through an appropriate coupling (Fig. 3) which is designed and then manufactured by a 3D printer, according to the specific engine's crankshaft design. Thus, in the proposed setup, the maximum resolution of the measurement system is not limited by the available space provided for the flywheel as in the case of a typical engine speed measuring

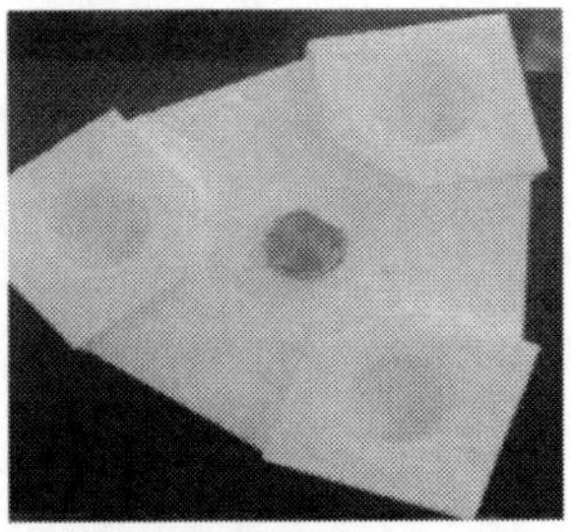

Figure 3. Appropriate coupling-manufactured by 3D printer; the encoder's shaft is visible at the center of the coupling.

system (i.e. the number of dents available to be magnetically detected) but only by the resolution of the employed encoder which is directly coupled to the crankshaft. Typical incremental rotary encoders can easily perform more than 2,000 measurements per revolution [12] while the specific industrial type encoder that was employed has a maximum resolution of 10,000 measurements per cycle.

Furthermore, the appropriate coupling –manufactured by 3D printer, can be custom-designed in order to fit to the crankshaft of basically any low/medium power already installed and working IC engine that needs to be monitored in a short time, eliminating the need for performing any alteration on the initial engine setup; the only addition necessary is the creation of a mechanical support for the encoder.

III. Results

Angular speed monitoring of 9,000 measurements per crankshaft rotation was successfully obtained employing the developed system on a typical low power four cylinder Diesel Engine, installed in the Department of Naval Architecture at the University of West Attica (Fig. 4). Note that all four cylinders firings are clearly noticeable at speed recording with an angular resolution of 0.04°.

We should point out that the speed profile presented in Fig. 4 is deduced directly from raw experimental data with no filtering applied for noise reduction purposes, making the specific method extremely immune to noise compared to similar results in literature [11], which are presented in Fig. 5. The above characteristic makes the system particularly suitable for fault diagnosis and engine performance optimization applications.

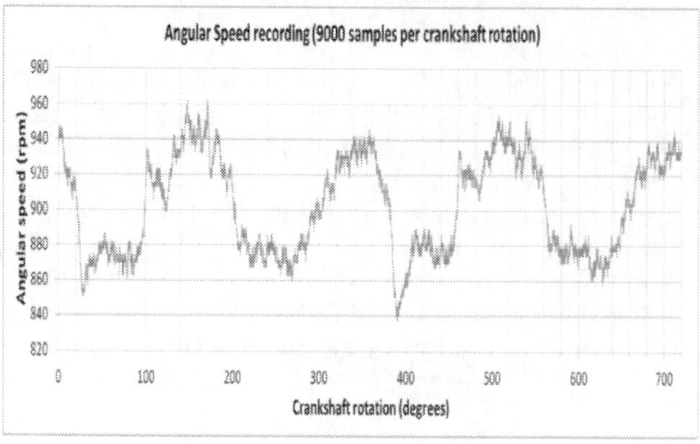

Figure 4. Angular speed monitoring of 9000 measurements per crankshaft rotation performed on a typical low power four cylinder Diesel Engine.

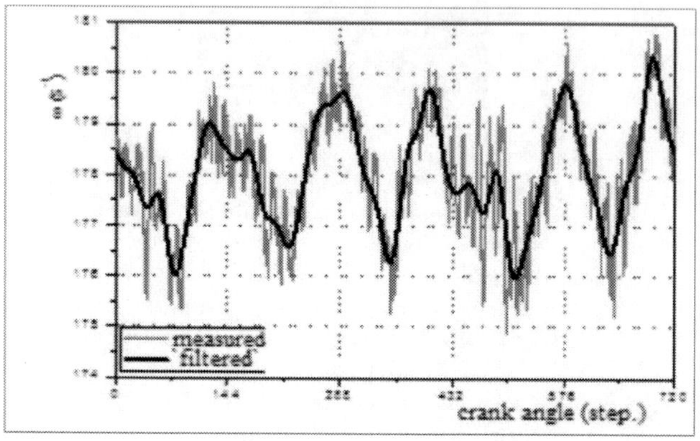

Figure 5. Angular speed monitoring before and after filtering at a four-stroke, six cylinder industrial engine [11].

An initial repeatability investigation has also been performed by recording rotational speed for a specific number of consecutive engine cycles. In more detail, the angular speed of the same engine was recorded for five consecutive engine cycles (i.e. 720° of crankshaft rotation) under the same operating conditions. The corresponding results are presented in Fig. 6; as we can clearly notice, there is a high concurrence between the different runs.

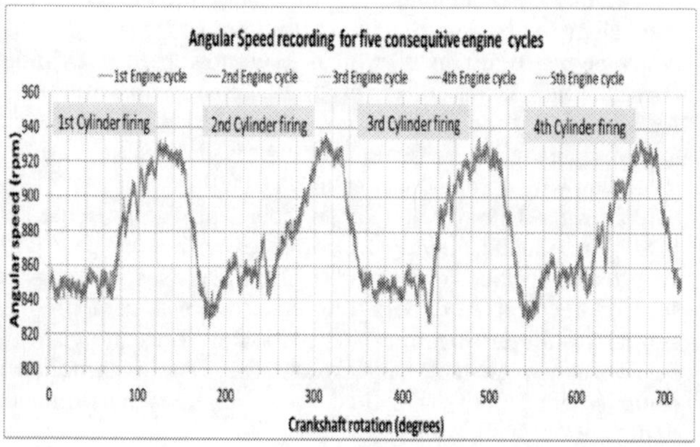

Figure 6. Rotational speed recording for five consecutive engine cycles (720 samples per crankshaft rotation).

IV. CONCLUSIONS

A novel low-cost measurement system for monitoring with high accuracy, the instantaneous rotational speed of an internal combustion engine has been developed. The system has been employed successfully for measuring the rotational speed of a typical industrial four cylinder engine with a resolution of 0.04 degree of crank angle, revealing its suitability for fault diagnosis and engine performance optimization applications.

The key features of the proposed measurement configuration are very high monitoring accuracy, low-cost and ability to be installed on-site, to an already operating engine with no major modifications, suggesting numerous potential applications.

Ongoing studies are focusing on fabricating a metallic coupling for long-term monitoring and also on determining how effectively the developed sensing arrangement can be employed in optimizing an engine's performance and in real-time fault diagnosis monitoring under different engine load conditions.

REFERENCES

[1] C. D. Rakopoulos, E. G. Giakoumis, and A. M. Dimaratos, "Evaluation of Various Dynamic Issues during Transient Operation of Turbocharged Diesel Engine with Special Reference to Friction Development", SAE Technical Paper 2007-01-0136, doi:10.4271/2007-01-0136, 2007.

[2] Z. S. Filipi and D. N. Assanis, "A nonlinear, transient single-cylinder diesel engine simulation for predictions of instantaneous engine speed and torque", Journal of Engineering for Gas Turbines and Power, vol. 123, pp. 951-959, 2001.

[3] M. Desbazeille, R. B. Randall, F. Guillet, M. El Badaoui, and C. Hoisnard, "Model-Based Diagnosis of Large Diesel engines Based on Angular Speed Variations of the Crankshaft", Mechanical Systems and Signal Processing, vol. 24, pp. 1529–1541, 2010.

[4] D. Taraza, "Estimation of the Mean Indicated Pressure from Measurements of the Crankshafts Angular Speed Variation" SAE Technical Paper 932413, doi:10.4271/932413, 1993.

[5] N. Cavina and F. Ponti, "Engine torque nonuniformity evaluation using instantaneous crankshaft speed signal", Journal of Engineering for Gas Turbines and Power, vol. 125, pp. 1050-1058, 2003.

[6] J. Yang, L. Pu, Z. Wang, Y. Zhou, and X. P. Yan, "Fault detection in a diesel engine by analyzing the instantaneous angular speed", Mechanical Systems and Signal Processing, vol. 15(3), pp. 549-564, doi:10.1006/ mssp.2000.1344, 2001.

[7] Y. Li, F. Gu, G. Harris, A. Ball, N. Bennett, and K. Travis, "The measurement of instantaneous angular speed", Mechanical Systems and Signal Processing, vol. 19, pp. 786–805, 2005.

[8] N. V. Kirianaki and S. Y. Yurish, "High Precision, Wide Speed Range Rotation Sensing with UFDC1", Sensors & Transducers, vol. 59, pp. 426-431, 2005.

[9] IVECO N45 MST technical manual, https://www.fptindustrial.com/global/en/engines/construction/n45, accessed 10/03/2020.

[10] D. N. Pagonis, G. Theotokatos, and G. Livanos, "Accurate instantaneous engine speed recording by employing an optical measurement system-Application to a typical low power industrial engine", SAE Technical Papers 2 2013-01-0304, doi:10.4271/2013-01-0304, 2013.

[11] S. Biocanin and M. Biocanin, "Measurement Crankshaft Angular Speed of an OM403 Engine", Serbian Journal of Electrical Engineering, vol.14 (2), pp. 257-275, 2017.

[12] N. Dumbravescu and S. Schiaua, "Possibilities to increase the resolution of photoelectric incremental rotary encoders", Materials Science in Semiconductor Processing, vol. 3, pp. 557-561, 2000.

Screen Printed $BaTiO_3$ for CO_2 Gas Sensor

Fabien Le Pennec, Sandrine Bernardini, Mohamad Hijazi, Carine Perrin-Pellegrino, Khalifa Aguir and Marc Bendahan
Aix Marseille Univ, Université de Toulon, CNRS, IM2NP, Marseille, France
e-mails: {fabien.lepennec, sandrine.bernardini, mohamad.hijazi, carine.perrin-pellegrino, khalifa.aguir, marc.bendahan}@im2np.fr

***Abstract*—In this work, we report on a new evaluation of metal oxide based on carbon dioxide sensors, using barium titanate nano-powder. The sensing principle is based on a change in conductance of semiconducting oxides when carbon dioxide is present. The sensitive layer was deposited on a SiO_2/Si substrate by screen printing technology. The sensor responses were studied between 100 and 5000 ppm of carbon dioxide in the air with 50% relative humidity. The sensor presents good sensitivity toward carbon dioxide, with a stable baseline, and fast response and recovery time. These results are promising for carbon dioxide sensing.**

Keywords-Gas Sensor; CO_2; $BaTiO_3$; Metal Oxide; Environment.

I. INTRODUCTION

Carbon dioxide (CO_2) is one of the main gases responsible for the greenhouse effect and, consequently, the global warming trends. Hence, its monitoring is subject of a major societal challenge. With an outdoors concentration up to 500 ppm in urban areas, the ventilation balance is affected and the development of reliable low-cost CO_2 sensors at multiple sites becomes an industrial strategy. Nowadays, the most commonly used method to detect CO_2 is based on optical sensors. Despite their efficiency in CO_2 detection, these technologies are expensive, have high electric consumption and are not fully miniaturized. Metal oxide gas sensors show potential features such as low-cost, mass production, miniaturization, fast response and recovery times.

In 1991, Ishihara et al. [1] first proposed a composite material based on p and n-type semiconductors, by mixing copper oxide (CuO) and barium titanate ($BaTiO_3$) powders. In 2001, Liao et al. [2] showed that pure CuO and pure $BaTiO_3$ gave no response to CO_2. Since then, these pure materials have been definitively abandoned and only composites have been studied. But, the sensors of Liao et al. [2] were in the very basic form of large discs of sintered powders with unknown granularity, connected by Ag paste electrodes. Thus, we propose herein a new evaluation of $BaTiO_3$ based CO_2 sensors.

The rest of the paper is structured as follows. In Section II, we describe our approach based on $BaTiO_3$ nano-powder deposition on platinum interdigitated electrodes by screen printing, a low cost, and an easily used technique. Then, in Section III, the sensing results are discussed based on a change in conductance of $BaTiO_3$ when CO_2 are introduced. Finally, a conclusion is given in Section IV.

II. DESCRIPTION OF APPROACH AND TECHNIQUES

This description is composed of two parts; one is the sensing film fabrication; the other is the measurement system set-up.

A. Gas sensors

Our gas sensor is made of Ti/Pt interdigitated electrodes (5 and 100 nm, respectively) deposited on Si/SiO_2 by magnetron sputtering. $BaTiO_3$ thick films were deposited by screen printing on these electrodes to produce a CO_2 sensitive layer. $BaTiO_3$ nano-powder (<100 nm, 4 g) was mixed with glycerol (1.5 g) and screen printed on Si/SiO_2 substrate with interdigitated platinum electrodes spaced by 50 µm (Figure 1).

Figure 1. Sample image of SiO_2/Si substrate (4 x 4 mm^2) with platinum electrodes (bottom) and the final sensor with the $BaTiO_3$ thick film (top).

The deposited film was annealed at 400°C on a hotplate, in ambient air. The film structure was determined by X-Ray Diffraction (XRD) with a Philip's X'Pert MPD equipment (λ = 1.54 Å).

B. Setup

0.1 V DC voltage was applied to the sample while the electrical resistance was monitored by a homemade LabVIEW program using a Keithley Model 2450 Source Measure Unit (SMU) Instrument (Keithley, U.S.A.). Dry air (no humidity) was used as both the reference and the carrier gas. A gas dilution and humidification system generates an output mixture at the target CO_2 concentrations (1 to 5000 ppm) with a variable humidity (0% to 90%). The sensing properties of $BaTiO_3$ sensors were tested by measuring the sensor resistance for 5 min under CO_2 diluted in dry air and in humid air with a standard Relative Humidity (RH) value of 50 %. The sensors were operated at several temperatures from 200°C to 300°C on a hotplate. A constant total flow was maintained at 500 Standard Cubic Centimeters per Minute (SCCM) via mass flow controllers.

III. Results and Discussions

The XRD diffractogram of $BaTiO_3$ thick film (Figure 2) shows the presence of $BaTiO_3$ nanocrystals in the tetragonal phase of $BaTiO_3$ [3].

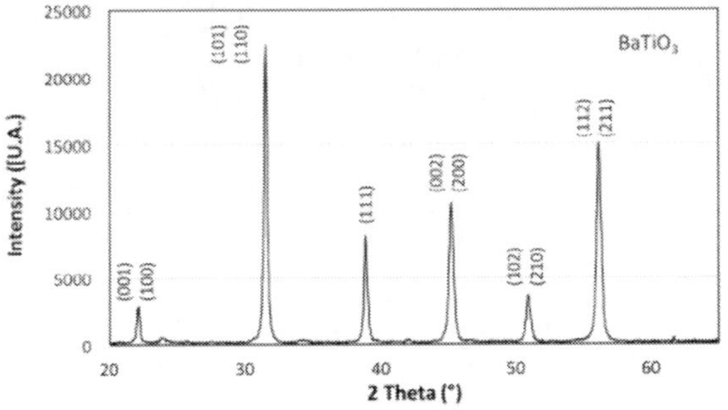

Figure 2. $BaTiO_3$ diffractogram using λ = 1.54Å (Philip's X'Pert MRD).

The $BaTiO_3$ sensors for different CO_2 concentrations provide a measurable response depending on the CO_2 concentrations in the 100 - 5 000 ppm range and 50% RH at various temperatures. The higher response amplitude variations were obtained at 280°C. Figures 3 and 4 show, respectively, the response and the sensitivity of the $BaTiO_3$ sensor under CO_2 in the air with 50% RH at 280 °C, the optimum working temperature. It gives reversible responses to CO_2 concentrations between 100 ppm and 5000 ppm.

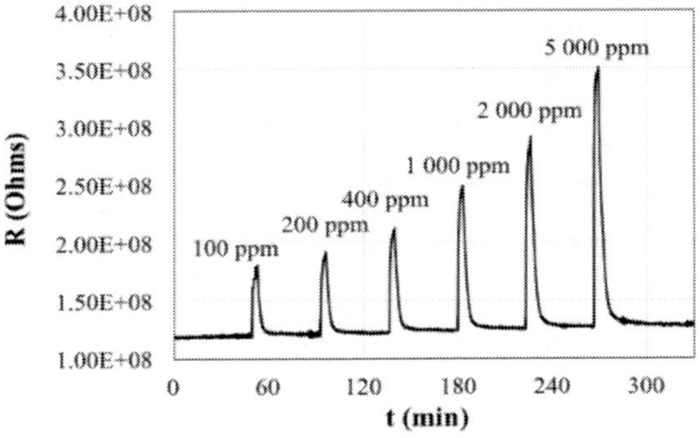

Figure 3. Resistive responses of $BaTiO_3$ to six CO_2 concentrations with 50% RH at 280°C.

The sensor response is defined in (1) as the ratio between the sensor resistance under CO_2 exposure and the sensor resistance in the air:

$$R = R_{gas} / R_{air} \quad (1)$$

where R_{air} is the sensor resistance through humid airflow and R_{gas} the sensor resistance in the presence of CO_2.

The response time was less than 2 minutes and the recovery time was about 5 minutes. The responses are proportional to the CO_2 concentrations, and they restored the original baseline in less than 5 minutes.

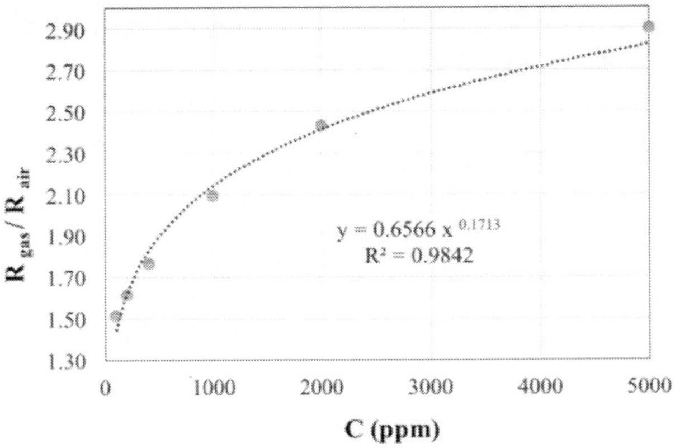

Figure 4. Sensitivity response of $BaTiO_3$ to different concentrations of CO_2 with 50% RH at 280°C.

These results are in agreement with the recent review on chemiresistive CO_2 gas sensors [4].

IV. Conclusions

This work reported preliminary results on a screen printing $BaTiO_3$ sensor working at an optimum temperature of 280°C and for 50% RH. Our experiments showed stable baseline responses with fast response/recovery times towards CO_2. These sensors seem promising for measuring indoor and outdoor air quality and for CO_2 detection. However, after a few weeks, using the same operational conditions, the sensor responses were weakened on the record. New experiments and analyses are in progress to understand this phenomenon.

Acknowledgment

The authors thank Mr. A. Combes and Dr. T. Fiorido for their technical support.

References

[1] T. Ishihara, K. Kometani, M. Hashida, and Y. Takita, "Application of Mixed Oxide Capacitor to the Selective Carbon Dioxide Sensor", J. Electrochem. Soc., 138, 1991, pp. 173-176, doi: 10.1149/1.2085530.

[2] B. Liao, Q. Wei, K. Wang, and Y. Liu, "Study on CuO–$BaTiO_3$ semiconductor CO_2", Sens. Actuators B:Chem., 80, 2001, pp. 208-214, doi: 10.1016/S0925-4005(01)00892-9.

[3] H. E. Swanson, R. K. Fuyat, and G. M. Ugrinic, "X-ray diffraction powder patterns" National Bureau of Standards, Circular 539, 3, 1954, pp. 44.

[4] Y. Lin and Z. Fan, "Compositing strategies to enhance the performance of chemiresistive CO_2 gas sensors", Materials Science in Semiconductor Processing, vol. 107, 2020, pp. 104820-104841, doi: 10.1016/j.mssp.2019.104820.

Data Analysis-Based Gas Identification with a Single Metal Oxide Sensor Operating in Dynamic Temperature Regime

Nicolas Morati, Thierry Contaret, Jean-Luc Seguin and Marc Bendahan
Aix-Marseille Univ, Univ Toulon, CNRS, IM2NP
Marseille, 13397, France
e-mails: nicolas.morati@im2np.fr; thierry.contaret@im2np.fr; jean-luc.seguin@im2np.fr; marc.bendahan@im2np.fr

Oussama Djedidi and Mohand Djeziri
Aix-Marseille Univ, Univ Toulon, CNRS, LIS
Marseille, 13397, France
e-mails: oussama.djedidi@lis-lab.fr; mohand.djeziri@lis-lab.fr

***Abstract*—This paper deals with a preliminary evaluation of a new data-driven approach aiming to discriminate several gases in a gas mixture, with a single Metal Oxide (MOX) sensor, under real conditions of use, i.e. in the permanent presence of a gas concentration. This method relies on a database obtained using temperature modulation of the sensor, for fixed gas concentrations. The database is increased by extracting the temporal attributes of the signal, and then reduced using principal component analysis to extract only useful information. Gas discrimination is achieved by the online projection of measurements in the principal space consisting of the two main components. Experimental results obtained on a test bench show the effectiveness of the proposed approach: carbon monoxide, ozone and nitrogen dioxide are clearly discriminated using one single MOX gas micro sensor.**

Keywords-MOX gas sensor; temperature modulation; temporal attributes; multivariate analysis; gas discrimination.

I. Introduction

The quality of outdoor and indoor air has become a very important health, societal and political issue. The health issue is recognized by institutions (World Health Organization in the leading position) and, for populations, air quality has become a major concern. The most harmful pollutant gases to health include carbon monoxide (CO), ozone (O_3), nitrogen dioxide (NO_2) and sulphur dioxide (SO_2). The variety of pollutants being large and the harmful concentrations for health being very low, it has become imperative to design detection systems that are both highly sensitive and highly selective. Today, only measurements by on-site sampling and laboratory analysis can meet these requirements, but remain expensive and incompatible with real-time monitoring. The development of highly sensitive, reliable, portable and low-cost detection systems is still limited because they are not sufficiently selective. Metal oxide (MOX) gas sensors are readily available and widely used in portable and low-cost gas monitoring devices because of their high sensitivity, stability and attractive lifetime. However, this type of gas sensor suffers from an inherent lack of selectivity, since the gas detection mechanism is rather nonspecific and more or less any type of reducing or oxidizing gas is detected. To overcome this low selectivity, MOX type gas sensors are most often assembled to form an electronic nose. The electronic nose is a complex system consisting of a set of multiple sensors, an information processing unit, software with digital pattern recognition algorithms, and databases with reference libraries [1][2]. The challenges of miniaturization and reduction of energy consumption involve minimizing the number of sensors. For this purpose, it is necessary to increase the amount of information provided by one sensor using advanced measurements, such as temperature modulation or fluctuation enhanced sensing [3]-[5].

The purpose of this study is to provide gases identification methods that can discriminate several gases with a single MOX sensor, under real conditions of use, i.e. in the permanent presence of a gas concentration. As a first step of the study, we report here on the evaluation of a new method based on temperature modulation of the sensor and data treatment using temporal attributes of the sensor response. The used methodology and the experimental set-up are described in Sections II and III, respectively. In Section IV, we present the results for three air quality gases (O_3, NO_2 and CO). Then, the capability of discriminating gases was evaluated using Principal Component Analysis (PCA). We conclude the work in Section V.

II. Methodology

The methodology is summarized in Figure 1. First, a database is created by measuring the sensor's resistance when modulating its operating temperature for fixed gas concentrations. Then, the database is increased by extracting the temporal attributes of the obtained signal, and then reduced using principal component analysis to extract only useful information. Gas discrimination is achieved by the online projection of measurements in the principal space consisting of the two main components. PCA is a robust and unsupervised model recognition approach commonly used for multivariate data analysis. It is a statistical procedure that converts a set of observations of possibly correlated variables into a new set of values called principal components. PCA has proven its effectiveness in many areas of application [6]-[8], including electronic noses [2].

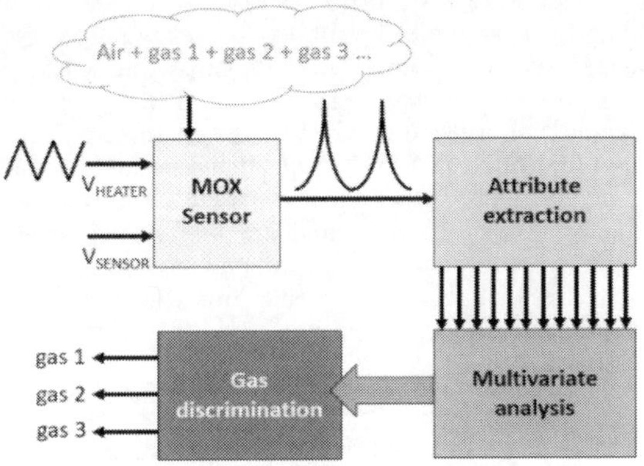

Figure 1. Summary of the used methodology.

III. EXPERIMENTS

In order to obtain a large amount of data, we have chosen to operate our microsensor in variable temperature mode: the heating voltage of the sensitive layer is varied triangularly between two extreme values with a very small voltage step. The maximum value of the triangular signal will correspond to the optimal detection temperature for the targeted gases. The sensor must have a transducer with a fast and efficient heating system. The sensor used in this study comes from a new technology developed by the IM2NP laboratory and the NANOZ-SAS company [9]. The sensor device has two distinct heaters and four detection zones offering several operating modes in single or multi-sensors. Figure 2 shows a picture of the sensor indicating the contact pads for the four sensors, the two heaters and the ground.

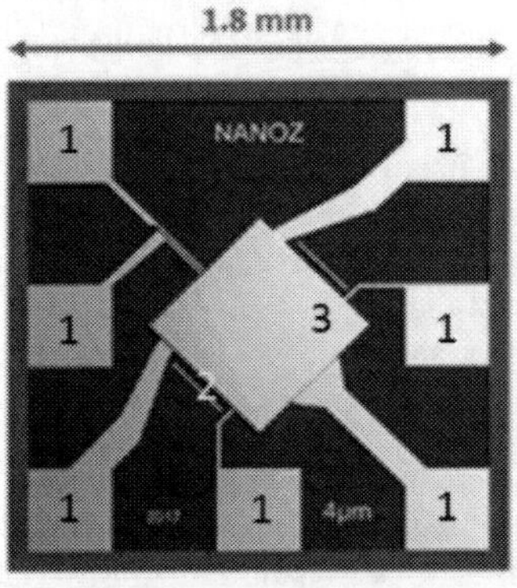

Figure 2. IM2NP - NANOZ sensor device [9]:1- Contact pads; 2- SiO2 membrane; 3- WO3 sensing layer covering the two heaters and the four detection zones. The transducer design showing the four sensitive zones and the two heaters is hidden for copyright reasons.

One of the innovations of our sensor is that the heating element is located on the same plane as the sensing element, on a SiO_2 membrane. The heaters and sensing electrodes were first realized in a sputtered platinum thin film using classical photolithography. Then, the WO_3 thin sensing layer was deposited by reactive magnetron radio-frequency sputtering and annealed at a temperature well above the operating temperature during two hours to improve its nano-crystallization and stability. As part of this study, we chose to operate in single sensor mode according to the diagram in Figure 3. We note R_{S1}, R_{S2}, R_{S3} and R_{S4} the sensor resistances of the four detection zones, and R_{H1} and R_{H2} the resistances of the two heaters.

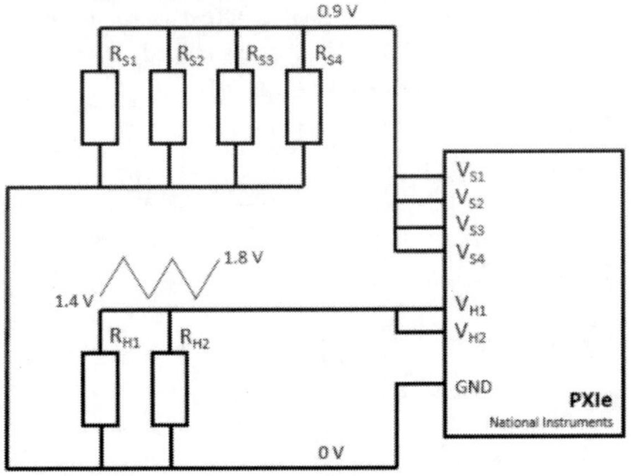

Figure 3. Electrical configuration of the sensor. V_{S1}, V_{S2}, V_{S3} and V_{S4} are the voltage across sensor resistances R_{S1}, R_{S2}, R_{S3} and R_{S4}, respectively. V_{H1} and V_{H2} are the voltage across heating resistances R_{H1} and R_{H2}, respectively.

The four sensors are biased at 0.9V using National Instrument PXIe 4140 source meter. The two integrated heaters are powered by a staircase waveform of amplitude 0.4V centered on 1.6V, as illustrated in Figure 4. The voltage value 1.8V allows to heat the sensitive layer at a temperature of 252 °C. This temperature corresponds to an optimal detection of the tested gases. The voltage of 1.4V corresponds to a temperature of 199 °C, which is the limit of detection. The staircase waveform is generated by programming the PXIe 4113 voltage source. The variation between each step is 10mV and the duration of each step is 1s. The configuration and control of the PXIe devices are performed with our developed LabVIEW application.

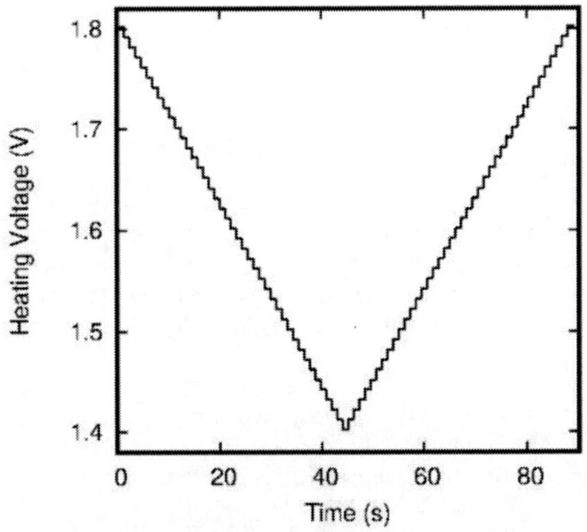

Figure 4. A period of the voltage applied to the heaters.

The sensor device is placed in a 3D-printed prototype test chamber developed in the IM2NP laboratory. This chamber enhances the gas flow hydrodynamics, in particular the gas concentration homogeneity and the reduction of flow recirculation and dead volumes [10]. To generate gas concentrations and measure sensor responses, we developed an experimental test bench shown in Figure 5. The dilution system provides a concentration range of 200 ppb to 16 ppm in order to test the limit thresholds of the tested pollutants. Mixed gases are admitted and evacuated from the test chamber via distribution valves.

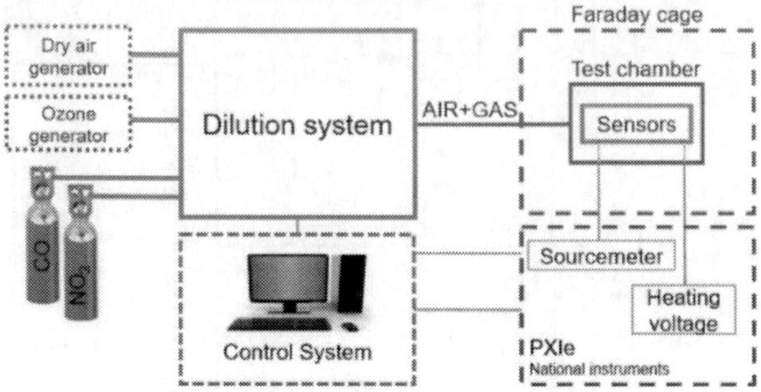

Figure 5. Experimental set up for micosensor characterization.

IV. RESULTS

This work is focused on the monitoring of air quality using metal oxide sensors. The microsensor has been exposed to three gases related to the air quality: ozone (O_3), nitrogen dioxide (NO_2) and carbon monoxide (CO). For each gas, we have chosen three concentrations close to the sanitary thresholds (see Table I). The WO_3 sensitive thin film deposited on our specific transducer enables to detect all these concentrations.

TABLE I. VARIOUS GASES CONCENTRATION USED IN EXPERIMENTAL SET UP.

Gases	Concentrations		
	C1	*C2*	*C3*
NO_2	200 ppb	400 ppb	800 ppb
O_3	80 ppb	110 ppb	160 ppb
CO	2 ppm	8 ppm	16 ppm

For each gas concentration, we proceeded with the following protocol:

- constant exposure of the sensor to a given gas concentration;
- biasing sensors at $V_S=V_{S1}=V_{S2}=V_{S3}=V_{S4} = 0.9V$.
- heating of the sensitive layer at the optimum detection temperature ($V_H = V_{H1} = V_{H2} = 1.8V$) during 5 minutes;
- heating of the sensitive layer using staircase waveform during four periods of the signal described in Figure 4;
- return to the optimal detection temperature.

In Figure 6, we present an example of the response of the sensor (bottom curve) to the staircase waveform in thermal modulation (top curve) for an ozone concentration. We have obtained similar responses for all gases, but all responses have different signal parameters. The proposed gas discrimination method is based on the characterization of the temporal attributes of the signal, including certain statistical parameters. Indeed, these mathematical moments enable to characterize a distribution and are interesting to take into account when studying transient phenomena. In our case, they can characterize mechanisms related to gases adsorption-desorption processes on the surface of the sensitive layer.

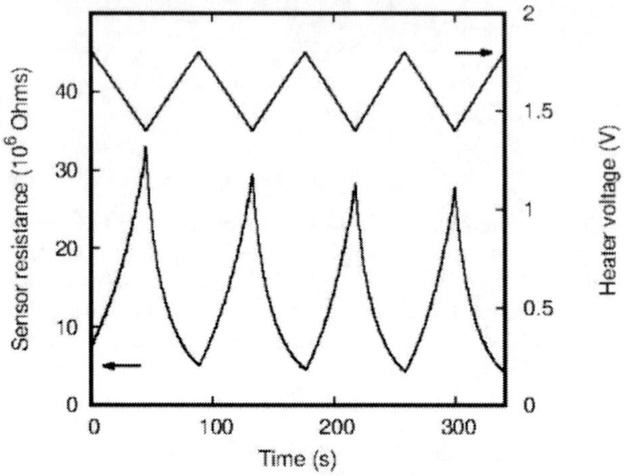

Figure 6. Example of sensor response (bottom curve) to triangular temperature variation (top curve) for 160 ppb of O_3.

To obtain a sufficient number of variables and to constitute a statistics database, we calculated the following temporal attributes for each gas response:

- peak to peak value.
- mean value.
- the root mean square value.
- the third standardized moment called skewness.
- the fourth standardized moment called kurtosis.
- the crest factor.
- the shape factor.
- the variance.

From the sets of calculated parameters of each gas concentration, we have evaluated the possibility of identifying the three studied gases using Principal Component Analysis. In PCA, the score diagrams show the relationships between the analyzed variables (different concentrations of the three gases in our studies). PCA has been performed using the Pearson matrix calculation. The PCA variables are the parameters of the temporal attributes. All PCA variables have a significant length in the PC1 / PC2 plane. The scores graph of the first two principal components (PC1 and PC2) is given in Figure 7. We clearly observe three groups of data. Each group corresponds to a gas. A first separation can be made according to the component PC1.

The corresponding CO data have a strongly positive PC1, while the NO_2 and O_3 have negative PC1 values.

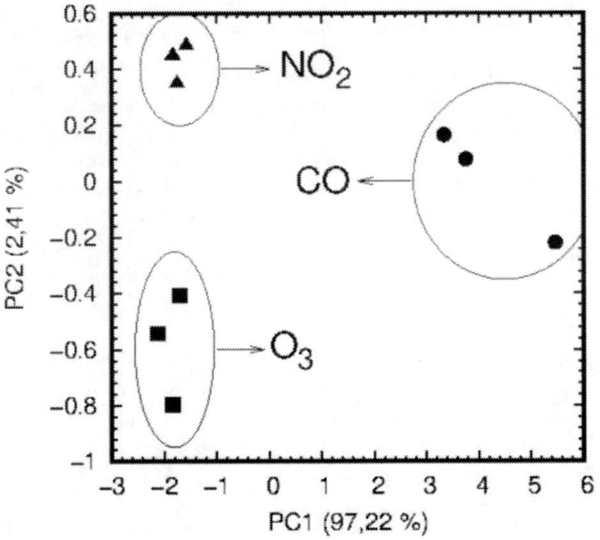

Figure 7. PCA scores plot.

The component PC2 makes it possible to separate these two gases. Indeed, the values of O_3 have a negative value of PC2. Conversely, the values for NO_2 have a positive value on PC2. The results of the PCA show that a clear distinction is possible between the three studied gases. Our results are consistent with other studies which have shown that the staircase waveform to modulate the temperature of sensing layer was the most effective to distinguish several gases with one single sensor [4].

V. Conclusion and Future Work

In this paper, we have presented a preliminary evaluation of a new gases identification method aiming to discriminate several gases with a single MOX sensor, under real conditions of use, i.e. in the permanent presence of a gas concentration. This method is based on temperature modulation of the sensing layer of the sensor, for a fixed gas concentration, followed by data treatment using temporal attributes of the sensor response. Finally, the PCA multivariable analysis method, applied to all data, has shown that it is possible to discriminate NO_2, O_3 and CO using one single MOX sensor.

After this preliminary step, more work is in progress in order to:

- study whether the number of temporal attributes can be reduced;
- increase the database by adding more gas concentrations and mixing the gases with each other and with humidity;
- apply and test classification algorithms such as Support Vector Machines, k Nearest Neighbors or Neural Networks.

Acknowledgment

Nicolas Morati would like to thank Région Sud of France and Nanoz SAS for financial support. We also thank Tomas Fiorido for his technical support throughout this work.

References

[1] J. Gutiérrez and M.C. Horrillo, "Advances in artificial olfaction: sensors and applications", Talanta, vol. 124, pp. 95–105, 2014.

[2] W. Hu et al., "Electronic Noses: From Advanced Materials to Sensors Aided with Data Processing". Advanced Materials Technologies, vol. 4, 2019, 1800488. https://doi.org/10.1002/admt.201800488.

[3] J. M. Smulko et al., "New approaches for improving selectivity and sensitivity of resistive gas sensors: a review." Sensor Review, vol. 35, pp. 340–347, 2015. https://doi.org/10.1108/SR-12-2014-0747

[4] S. M. Hosseini-Golgoo, F. Salimi, A. Saberkari, and S. Rahbarpour, "Comparison of information content of temporal response of chemoresistive gas sensor under three different temperature modulation regimes for gas detection of different feature reduction methods." J. Phys.: Conf. Ser. 939, 2017, 012005. https://doi.org/10.1088/1742-6596/939/1/012005

[5] S. Gomri et al., "A Noise Spectroscopy-Based Features Extraction Method to Detect Two Gases Using One Single MOX Sensor", IEEE Sensors Journal, Vol.19, No.20, pp. 9063-9070, 2019, DOI: 10.1109/JSEN.2019.2923699

[6] M. A. Djeziri, S. Benmoussa, and R. Sanshez. "Hybrid method for remaining useful life prediction in wind turbine systems. " Renewable Energy, vol. 116, pp. 173-187, 2018.

[7] L. Nguyen, M. A. Djeziri, B. Ananou, M. Ouladsine, and J. Pinaton. "Fault prognosis for batch production based on percentile measure and gamma process: Application to semiconductor manufacturing". in Journal of Process Control, Vol. 48. pp. 72-80, 2016.

[8] L. Nguyen, M. A. Djeziri, B. Ananou, M. Ouladsine, and J. Pinaton. "Health Indicator Extraction for Fault Prognosis in Discrate Manufacturing Processes", IEEE Transaction on Semiconductor Manufacturing, vol.28, no. 3, pp. 306-317, 2015.

[9] K. Aguir, M. Bendahan, and V. Laithier, "Heated sensitive layer gas sensor" patent N◦FR 13 59494, 2013, international extension in 2016, US20160238548

[10] F. E. Annanouch et al., "Hydrodynamic evaluation of gas testing chamber: Simulation, experiment", Sensors & Actuators: B. Chemical, vol. 290 pp. 598–606, 2019 DOI: 10.1016/j.snb.2019.04.023

Sensor and Electronic Circuits Development on Flexible Substrates through Additive Manufacturing Technologies for Textile Applications

Josue Ferri, Jorge Moreno, Ana Rodes, Elena Mira, Jose Maria Garcia
Smart Textiles and ICT Solution Research Group
Textile Research Institute (AITEX)
Alcoy, Spain
e-mail: josue.ferri@aitex.es, jmoreno@aitex.es, arodes@aitex.es, emira@aitex.es, jgarcia@aitex.es

Eduardo Garcia-Breijo, Raul Llinares
Instituto Interuniversitario de Investigación de Reconocimiento Molecular y Desarrollo Tecnológico (IDM), Universitat Politècnica de València
Departamento de Comunicaciones,
Universitat Politècnica de València,
Valencia, Spain
e-mail: egarciab@eln.upv.es, rllinares@dcom.upv.es

Abstract—**Printed electronics on flexible substrates have awakened special interest in the scientific community in recent years due to its potential applications. Some of these applications are directly connected to the use of textiles and fabrics as wearables. The present project has considered all the relevant topics that are needed to be taken into account in this type of development. The performance and constraints of both conductive inks and dielectric materials have been evaluated. The results achieved have been used to develop capacitive sensors that can bear the flexibility and stretchability conditions required by textile substrates, without undergoing any damage.**

Keywords - printed electronics; smart textiles; sensors; wearables; stretchable; flexible; screen- printing; textile; inkjet; flexography.

I. INTRODUCTION

Electronics that imitate the natural world by bending, flexing and stretching are becoming more and more significant as the technology is integrated into our lives, our environments and even our bodies. One of the most challenging applications is the combination of electronics with textiles or fabrics. This idea was defined as smart textiles [1] or smart fabrics [2]. The elements included in these solutions, such as conductive fibers, conductive filaments, conductive yarns, together with woven, knitted or non-woven structures, are able to interact with the environment of users [3]. Smart textiles are normally used as sensors and they are combined with external microprocessors units, in order to analyse the information and create some kind of action, such as an alert or activation. Smart textiles sensors can be mainly classified depending on their capability to measuring either resistivity or capacitance variations. On one hand, resistive sensors measure variations of resistance of a conductive structure that can be a wire or a conductive stretchable fabric [4]. On the other hand, capacitive sensors use more complex structures that allow to measure capacitance variations between two conductive materials that can be also conductive threads or conductive textiles. This idea has been successfully developed in order to measure parameters such as strain [5][6], pressure [7][8], respiration [9]-[11], humidity [12][13], gas [14] or temperature [15], among others. Moreover, sensors based on conductive surfaces such as electrocardiogram (ECG) [16][17], electromyography (EMG) [18] or electroencephalogram (EEG) [19] have also been implemented.

In addition to conductive threads or conductive fabrics, conductive particles or materials can also be printed on the surface of textiles [20]. Printed electronics [21] on flexible substrates [22][23] have drawn the attention of the scientific community during the last years, due to the great potential in terms of flexibility and possible final applications. Furthermore, these electronics have a lower cost than the current standard techniques, which is an added value [24], since they can be implemented with reel to reel industrial machines [25].

This paper is organized as follows. Section II presents the materials and manufacturing procedures used. Afterwards, Section III presents the experimental results and a discussion of them. Finally, section IV provides an overview of the conclusions.

II. MATERIALS AND METHODS

During the project, different prototypes have been developed using different technologies that can be used in smart fabrics. All of them were related to the design and development of fabrics with intelligent properties, investigating the scope and limitations of the technologies, in order to discover the potential of these applications.

Most common types of conductive inks are based on conductive nanoparticles or microparticles dispersed into a polymer matrix. These particles are based on carbon particles, metallic particles, such as silver and gold, as well as conductive oxides such as ITO or ZnO. These inks are usually dried or cured by heating; however, laser or UV curing is also possible. When the ink is cured by heat, the binder and solvent are removed, forming a conductive layer on the surface of the substrate. The required curing temperature depends on the type of ink, but the usual range covers from 100ºC to 250ºC for 5 to 30 minutes. Depending on the type of substrate, the curing procedure needs to be adjusted.

The use of printed electronics in textiles, despite it is in an early stage, is a very promising technology within the scope of the smart textiles field. Two critical parameters in the global design of the electronic system are the textile substrate in which the printing process is carried out, and the protection process of the printed ink. Each material or element has characteristics that will have an impact on the final application. Likewise, the typology of inks, their deposition and circuit design, with the added complexity of properties such as flexibility and elasticity, pose a challenge for their use. In addition, another aspect to consider is the interconnection between the flexible electronic and the rigid PCB electronic. Therefore, the selection of the connectors and the attachment systems are crucial.

The developed prototypes comply with the requirements of functionality and resistance. A careful selection of the appropriate materials to use was carried out, as well as the optimal conditions of application and manufacture. It should be noted that the knowledge acquired throughout the project, especially the one derived from the experimentation in the application of electronic inks on fabrics, will be very useful for future developments. Thus, the results achieved can be used in new and more complex applications, or in other environments, based on the previous knowledge acquired.

III. Results and Discussion

Initially, different ink characterization tests were carried out on different substrates, evaluating temperature and optimal curing time. These tests were developed taking into account the orientation of the tissues in relation to the printing direction, as well as other parameters, such as fabric roughness, fabric materials and possible surface finishes. These tests have been performed using different printing technologies depending on the substrate. It can be observed that in the case of the fabrics with higher thickness and higher diameter of thread, the samples did not show electrical conductivity and the values of resistance obtained were very high. The rougher a substrate is, the more quantity of ink is required during the printing process to reduce the negative effect of the substrate surface. In this type of substrates, screen-printing technology offers the best performance. On the other side, technologies such as flexography or inkjet enable a more precise control of the quantity of ink added and the line thickness.

Figure 1. Conductivity test on a stretchable substrate during a contract and relax process.

In addition, the behaviour of the inks printed on different elastic substrates, in terms of their adhesion and conductivity, has been evaluated. Stretching percentages have also been studied by assessing the variations in conductivity produced as a consequence of the undergone stretching. These variations in conductivity must be considered, in order to minimize the effect in the electronic performance. Figure 1 presents the test performed using strip lines of conductive material on stretchable substrate. Another aspect to consider is the negative effect of the contract-relax stretching repetitions, that can produce a considerable damage.

During the project, several prototypes based on capacitive sensors have been developed. This type of sensor offers the advantage of better supporting the conductive limitations than other types of resistive sensors. Initially, a study of the relative permittivity of the different materials used in this work was carried out. This assessment was applied to every non-conductive material, such as fabrics, dielectric inks, adhesives and films. The effect of these materials has been considered from the fabrication process point of view, but also from the sensor performance perspective.

IV. Conclusions

The tests carried out with conductive, dielectric and resistive inks, that can be stretched or flexed, enable to improve the durability of the circuits on flexible substrates, such as textiles. For this purpose, a specific selection of materials and a proper design of the fabrication process needs to be done. In addition, the design process of the electronic circuit must consider the existing constraints, in order to adjust or minimize the negative effect. On the other hand, it was observed that it is possible to reproduce electronic circuits on textiles, taking into account certain parameters of optimization of ink application and an adequate selection of tissues that facilitate the proper application and homogeneity.

Acknowledgment

This research was funded by the Conselleria d'Economia Sostenible, Sectors Productius i Treball, through IVACE (Instituto Valenciano de Competitividad Empresarial). Application No.: IMAMCI/2020/1.

References

[1] S. C. Das, D. Paul, M. Hasan, and E. H. Nizam, "Smart Textiles- New Possibilities in Textile Engineering," vol. 2013, no. November, pp. 1–3, 2013.

[2] A. Lymberis and R. Paradiso, "Smart fabrics and interactive textile enabling wearable personal applications: R&D state of the art and future challenges," *Proc. 30th Annu. Int. Conf. IEEE Eng. Med. Biol. Soc. EMBS'08 - "Personalized Healthc. through Technol.*, no. August, pp. 5270–5273, 2008.

[3] M. Stoppa and A. Chiolerio, "Wearable electronics and smart textiles: A critical review," *Sensors (Switzerland)*, vol. 14, no. 7, pp. 11957–11992, 2014.

[4] H. Jin, N. Matsuhisa, S. Lee, M. Abbas, T. Yokota, and T. Someya, "Enhancing the Performance of Stretchable

Conductors for E-Textiles by Controlled Ink Permeation," *Adv. Mater.*, vol. 29, no. 21, 2017.

[5] C. Mattmann, O. Amft, H. Harms, G. Tröster, and F. Clemens, "Recognizing upper body postures using textile strain sensors," in *Proceedings - International Symposium on Wearable Computers, ISWC*, 2007, pp. 29–36.

[6] T.-W. Shyr, J.-W. Shie, C.-H. Jiang, and J.-J. Li, "A Textile-Based Wearable Sensing Device Designed for Monitoring the Flexion Angle of Elbow and Knee Movements," *Sensors*, vol. 14, pp. 4050–4059, 2014.

[7] Y. Enokibori, A. Suzuki, H. Mizuno, Y. Shimakami, and K. Mase, "E-textile pressure sensor based on conductive fiber and its structure," *Proc. 2013 ACM Conf. Pervasive ubiquitous Comput. Adjun. Publ. - UbiComp '13 Adjun.*, pp. 207–210, 2013.

[8] M. Sergio, N. Manaresi, M. Tartagni, R. Guerrieri, and R. Canegallo, "5.4: A Textile Based Capacitive Pressure Sensor," *Sensors, 2002. Proc. IEEE*, pp. 1625–1630 vol. 2, 2002.

[9] C. R. Merritt, H. T. Nagle, and E. Grant, "Textile-based capacitive sensors for respiration monitoring," *IEEE Sens. J.*, vol. 9, no. 1, pp. 71–78, 2009.

[10] N. Molinaro *et al.*, "Wearable textile based on silver plated knitted sensor for respiratory rate monitoring," *Proc. Annu. Int. Conf. IEEE Eng. Med. Biol. Soc. EMBS*, vol. 2018-July, pp. 2865–2868, 2018.

[11] L. Guo, S. Ratnarathorn, L. Berglin, U. Wiklund, and L. Sandsjö, "‘ Disappearing Sensor ’ -Textile Based Sensor for Monitoring Breathing," *I nt.Conf.Control .Autom .Syst.Eng*, p. 1, 2011.

[12] C. Gonçalves, A. F. da Silva, J. Gomes, and R. Simoes, "Wearable e-textile technologies: A review on sensors, actuators and control elements," *Inventions*, vol. 3, no. 1, pp. 1–13, 2018.

[13] B. Li, G. Xiao, F. Liu, Y. Qiao, C. M. Li, and Z. Lu, "A flexible humidity sensor based on silk fabrics for human respiration monitoring," *J. Mater. Chem. C*, vol. 6, no. 16, pp. 4549–4554, 2018.

[14] Y. Ju Yun, W. G. Hong, N.-J. Choi, B. Hoon Kim, Y. Jun, and H.-K. Lee, "Ultrasensitive and Highly Selective Graphene-Based Single Yarn for Use in Wearable Gas Sensor," *Sci. Rep.*, vol. 5, no. 1, p. 10904, 2015.

[15] R. Polanský *et al.*, "A novel large-area embroidered temperature sensor based on an innovative hybrid resistive thread," *Sensors Actuators, A Phys.*, vol. 265, pp. 111–119, 2017.

[16] T. Pola and J. Vanhala, "Textile electrodes in ECG measurement," *Proc. 2007 Int. Conf. Intell. Sensors, Sens. Networks Inf. Process. ISSNIP*, pp. 635–639, 2007.

[17] X. Tao, V. Koncar, T. H. Huang, C. L. Shen, Y. C. Ko, and G. T. Jou, "How to make reliable, washable, and wearable textronic devices," *Sensors (Switzerland)*, vol. 17, no. 4, 2017.

[18] C. L. Ng and M. B. I. Reaz, "Evolution of a capacitive electromyography contactless biosensor: Design and modelling techniques," *Meas. J. Int. Meas. Confed.*, vol. 145, pp. 460–471, 2019.

[19] F. Seoane, M. Thordstein, and S. Academy, "Textile Electrodes for EEG Recording — A Pilot Study," pp. 16907–16919, 2012.

[20] J. Ferri, J. Lidón-Roger, J. Moreno, G. Martinez, and E. Garcia-Breijo, "A Wearable Textile 2D Touchpad Sensor Based on Screen-Printing Technology," *Materials (Basel).*, vol. 10, no. 12, p. 1450, Dec. 2017.

[21] S. Khan, L. Lorenzelli, and R. S. Dahiya, "Technologies for printing sensors and electronics over large flexible substrates: A review," *IEEE Sens. J.*, vol. 15, no. 6, pp. 3164–3185, 2015.

[22] J. Chang, X. Zhang, T. Ge, and J. Zhou, "Fully printed electronics on flexible substrates: High gain amplifiers and DAC," *Org. Electron.*, vol. 15, no. 3, pp. 701–710, 2014.

[23] Z. Li *et al.*, "Highly conductive, flexible, polyurethane-based adhesives for flexible and printed electronics," *Adv. Funct. Mater.*, vol. 23, no. 11, pp. 1459–1465, 2013.

[24] V. Subramanian *et al.*, "Printed electronics for low-cost electronic systems: Technology status and application development," *ESSCIRC 2008 - Proc. 34th Eur. Solid-State Circuits Conf.*, pp. 17–24, 2008.

[25] B. Salam, X. C. Shan, C. Zhanhong, and B. K. Lok, "Multilayer Roll-to-Roll Screen-Printing for Printed Electronics Applications," *2018 IEEE 20th Electron. Packag. Technol. Conf.*, pp. 359–362, 2019.

The Use of the Arduino Embedded System as a Prototype of a Mobile System Controlling a Person's Breathing Using a Sensor Printed on a T-shirt

Jarosław Wojciechowski
Faculty of Material Technologies and Textile Design
Institute of Material Science of Textiles and Polymer Composites
Lodz University of Technology
116 Zeromskiego Street, 90-924
Lodz, Poland
e-mail: jaroslaw.wojciechowski@p.lodz.pl

Ewa Skrzetuska
Faculty of Material Technologies and Textile Design
Institute of Material Science of Textiles and Polymer Composites
Lodz University of Technology
116 Zeromskiego Street, 90-924
Lodz, Poland
e-mail: ewa.skrzetuska@p.lodz.pl

Abstract— **The aim of this idea is to show an early stage draft for measuring the electrical resistance in a designed/elaborated textile printed sensor with a mobile Arduino microcontroller. The textile sensor was developed by the screen printing technique based on a water dispersion of carbon nanotubes printing composition. By stretching and squeezing the T-shirt during breathing, we change the electrical resistances of the printed sensor. The measured resistance corresponds to the number of breaths of a person wearing it. The microcontroller can calculate the number of breaths as a number of electrical resistance peaks which can lead to monitoring human live parameters.**

Keywords - textile actuator; t-shirt; textronic; monitor; microcontroller; Arduino; human body; carbon nanotubes; screen printing; printing composition; textiles.

I. Introduction

Manufacturing textronic systems is not an easy task. In order for the garment to meet certain properties, it is necessary to pay attention to a number of factors. When creating a design of clothes, one cannot forget about the requirements that accompany electronic products (including accuracy, measuring range), the behavior of the selected textile products (including low weight, flexibility), as well as the applicable principles of materials science and automation. The proper selection of textiles and electronic systems as well as their mutual integration is a big challenge for scientists. With the increase in technology development, the quality of manufactured systems has improved. Textronic products are created mainly using everyday clothes by combining them with a miniaturized electronic system, sensors, and a power supply system.

The creation of textronic systems is possible due to the use of sensors. The characteristic properties of some raw materials from which textile products are made include piezoelectric and electrostatic properties, as well as shape memory. Materials using these features are called intelligent and they combine the functions of both the sensor and the activator.

The most common sensors are sensors that provide information in one of the electrical quantities, such as voltage, current, and electrical resistance. This is due to the fact that electric current is a signal that is easily amplified, transmitted over long distances, further processed using digital techniques and computers, and saved. Their properties change under the influence of an external stimulus, which may be e.g. a mechanical stimulus or an electrical impulse.

Several research works [4]-[8] conducted at the Institute of Material Science of Textiles and Polymer Composites in Lodz, Poland, showed a real possibility of creating flat fiber products with sensory properties containing carbon nanotubes. The aim of the presented work is an early stage draft for measuring the electrical resistance of the designed/elaborated printed textile sensor on the chest part of a garment [6][8], using a mobile Arduino microcontroller. The measured electrical resistance corresponds to the number of breaths of a person wearing it. The Arduino microcontroller can calculate the number of breaths as a number of electrical resistance peaks.

The rest of the paper is structured as follows. In Section II, we present the state of the art in the topic of sensors controlling human live parameters. In Section III, we present the practical measurement and aim of calculations we may follow. Finally, we conclude the work in Section IV.

II. State of the Art

The idea of using Arduino is not new [1]. [1] describes the LilyPad Arduino, a fabric based construction kit that enables novices to design and build their own soft wearables and other textile artifacts. An assortment of sensors and actuators elements can be sewn to cloth substrates and each other with conductive thread to build e-textiles. In [2], the authors investigate aspects regarding the use of wearable electronic sensors, embedded in clothing for monitoring the health using simple electronics such as Arduino board to perform signal analysis processes. In [3], there is a breathing rhythm and an electrocardiography (ECG) measured using flexible substrates on a T-shirt with bi-axial accelerometers involved. The work in [3] is a slightly similar to ours, but ours is much easier to do and simpler to use in everyday life.

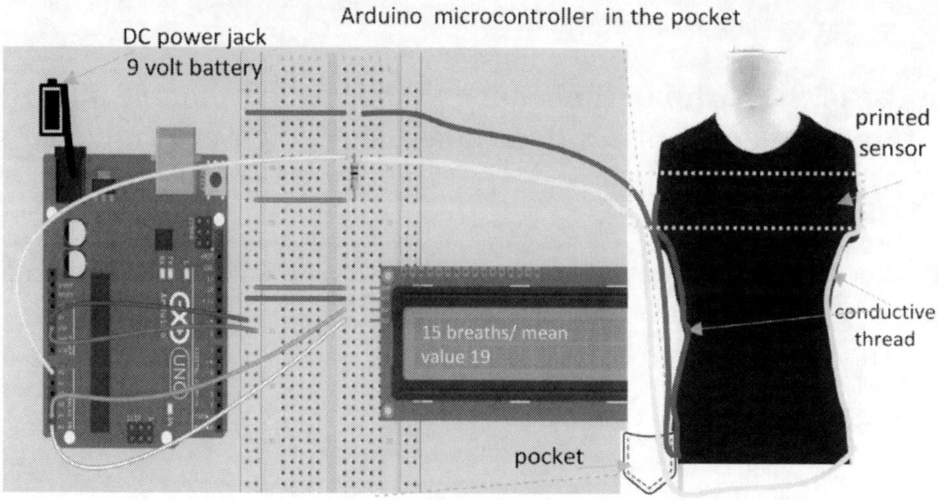

Figure 1. The microcontroller and textile sensor connection diagram – (own study, Arduino graphics taken from [10])

III. Practical Measurement

A. Research apparatus

- Arduino or Genuino Board connected to measuring electrodes,
- T-shirt with print containing sensors receiving and transmitting information about the tested subject [4].

B. Idea of research

The aim of the research is to measure the electrical resistance with the Arduino microcontroller [9][10] of an elaborated textile sensor for changes of electrical resistance during normal activity of a human who is wearing a T-shirt. The number of breaths may be calculated by the logic inside Arduino by counting the picks of resistance within 60 seconds. An exemplary architecture diagram is showed in Figure 1. We will use two resistors: the first resistor is 10k Ω and the second is represented by the textile sensor. From the point of view of Ohm's law, it is important that the resistors are connected in series. The resistor with a known resistance of 10k Ohm is between the ground and the cable connected to the A0 pin, while the tested textile sensor resistor is between the cable connected to the A0 pin and 5V from Arduino.

According to Ohm's law, the current flowing in the system is the quotient of voltage and resistance of a given system.

$$I = U / R \tag{1}$$

where I is the current, U is the voltage, and R isthe resistance.

Our system consists of two resistors connected in series with values that we will denote by R1 and R2. R1 will be our known resistor, while R2 will be a textile sensor. Current I flows through the system. Such current flows through both R1 and R2. The voltage drop is in the whole system and in each of the resistors the voltage changes proportionally to its value. The voltage that falls on the whole system is the voltage taken from Arduino, i.e., 5V - we will denote it as U. Having the above in mind, we can determine the following formula:

$$U / (R1 + R2) = U1 / R1 \tag{2}$$

$$R2 = ((R1 * U) / U1) - R1 \tag{3}$$

where R1 is the known resistor 10k Ohm and R2 is the resistance of the textile sensor.

Formula (3) may be calculated inside the microcontroller. The values can be stored in the Arduino memory for 60 seconds interval. An average value of peaks, corresponding to the number of human breaths, may be calculated and displayed on the LCD. By normal breathing, we perform the change of the textile sensor electrical resistance, we change the value of resistance which is connected to the center pin of the resistor series. This changes the voltage at the center pin. This voltage is the analog voltage that we will read as an input by the *Analog-to-Digital Converter (ADC)*. In case of difficulties with the calculation of the number of peaks, we may add a derivative element between the textile sensor at A0 pin and 5V power pin. The potential use of internal timer may make the calculations easier. It all depends on how the measurements proceed.

IV. Conclusions

Works currently carried out by the authors allow to state that it is possible to measure breaths of humans by using a T-shirt textile sensor. The authors are aware of the challenges of changing human body size, ambient humidity, temperature, pH of sweat, and the related need to calibrate the sensor in various atmospheric conditions.

As future work, first, we will work on miniaturization, even by removing the LCD and the big battery, and adding a Bluetooth module. Secondly, we will build a mobile Android app to present the data on the smartphone.

REFERENCES

[1] L. Buechley, M. Eisenberg, J. Catchen, and A. Crockett "The LilyPad Arduino: Using computational textiles to investigate engagement, aesthetics, and diversity in computer science education" Conference on Human Factors in Computing Systems – Proceedings, pp. 423-432, 2008.

[2] R. M. Aileni, A. C. Valderrama, and R. Strungaru „Wearable Electronics for Elderly Health Monitoring and Active Living (Book Chapter)" Ambient Assisted Living and Enhanced Living Environments: Principles, Technologies and Control, pp. 247-269, 2017.

[3] P. Jourand, H. De Clercq, R. Corthout, and R. Puers "Textile Integrated Breathing and ECG Monitoring System" Katholieke Universiteit Leuven, ESAT-MICAS, Kasteelpark Arenberg 10, B-3001 Leuven, Belgium, Procedia Chemistry 1 pp. 722–725, 2009.

[4] W. Urbaniak-Domagała, E. Skrzetuska, M. Komorowska, and I.Krucińska "Development Trends in Electronics Printed: Intelligent Textiles Produced with the Use of Printing Techniqueson Textile Substrates" Published: September 28th 2016 Printed Electronics - Current Trends and Applications. Edited by Ilgu Yun, ISBN 978-953-51-2527-3, Print ISBN 978-953-51-2301-9, 146 pages, Publisher: InTech, Chapter 7, http://dx.doi.org/10.5772/62962

[5] I. Krucińska, E. Skrzetuska, and W. Urbaniak-Domagała "Printed Textiles with Chemical Sensor Properties" Printed Textiles with Chemical Sensor Properties.FIBRES & TEXTILES in Eastern Europe 2014; 22, 4(106), pp. 68-72.

[6] N. T. Furtak, E. Skrzetuska, and I. Krucińska "Development of Screen-printed Breathing Rate Sensors" FIBRES & TEXTILES in Eastern Europe 2013, 21, 6(102), pp. 84-88.

[7] E. Skrzetuska, M. Puchalski, and I. Krucińska "Chemically driven printed textilesensors based on graphene and carbon nanotubes." Sensors, 2014, Vol. 14, pp. 16816-16828,ISSN: 1424 - 8220.

[8] Nanocyl, Safety Data Sheet for AQUACYL ™ carbon nanotubes from the NC7000 line, https://www.nanocyl.com/wp-content/uploads/2016/07/DM-TI-02-TDS-NC7000-V08.pdf, date of download 07.11.2019r.

[9] https://starter-kit.nettigo.pl/2018/10/budujemy-prosty-omomierz-na-arduino/, last accessed date: 8.12.2019

[10] https://www.arduino.cc/en/Tutorial/AnalogReadSerial, last accessed date: 8.12.2019.

Sensors-Based Virtual Reality Environment for Volumetric CT Analyses of Agricultural Soils Samples

Leonardo C. Botega[1,2,3], Paulo E. Cruvinel[1,2]
[1]Embrapa Instrumentation, São Carlos, SP, Brazil
[2]Post-Graduation Program in Computer Science - Federal University of São Carlos, SP, Brazil
[3]UNIVEM - University Centre Euripides of Marilia, Marilia, SP, Brazil
Email: botega@univem.edu.br, paulo.cruvinel@embrapa.br

Abstract—**Virtual Reality (VR) is based on the use of sensors, and the customization of its use for agricultural analysis is still a challenge. This study presents a solution for the analysis of agricultural soils based on sensor devices, signal conditioning, X-ray tomographic images, and a VR interface. In such a context, tomographic images from soil samples can be submitted though a user interface to a process of manipulation and volumetric visualization based on graphic-computational resources which add functionalities like immersion for the user's interaction with the samples. Validation was based on a case study involving the analysis of the porosity of agricultural soils samples in which preferential paths for water flow were reconstructed and manipulated by VR interaction techniques. In fact, by using 59.6 keV of energy and a time window of 10 seconds for sampling of each tomographic projection, it was possible to reconstruct digital tomographic images from agricultural soils to be analyzed using such a system. Results indicated both a new and non-invasive way for the evaluation of the spatial organization and physical properties of agricultural soils and its potential use for food production.**

Keywords-X-ray Sensors; Virtual Reality Sensors; Digital Image Processing; X-ray Tomography; Agricultural Soil Porosity; Decision-making Process.

I. Introduction

Evaluating the current evolution in the soil sciences, one can observe an increasing interest in the scientific community in the development and application of non-invasive techniques for the study of physical characteristics of agricultural soils. Since the 1980s, one of the noninvasive methods used for the evaluation of water movement into soil due to morphology as well as aggregates distribution has been the application of sensors and Computed Tomography (CT) for agricultural soil imaging [1]–[8]. From that time, it has been observed an expressive decreasing in the use of the invasive gravimetric and neutron probes techniques for water content measurements in agricultural soils [9][10]. Additionally, combined with the development of CT, new methods of three-dimensional (3-D) reconstruction have been developed, mainly motivated by the lack of information from two-dimensional models for a precise diagnosis in studies that require volumetric information [11]. Other challenges regarding such aspects were associated with the image reconstruction process, as well as with reconstruction algorithms, computational capacity, and handling large amounts of data [12]. Therefore, since then, it has been understood tomographic reconstruction must consider large amounts of data and the need to have a large processing capacity [13][14].

Moreover, owing to the advent of precision agriculture, it has become imperative to have adequate models for management based on data analyses not only related to spatial variability, but also due to the temporal variability in the areas used for agriculture. In this sense, the standardization of data storage and the architecture of distributed information systems that allow integration of different types of data in a simple and transparent way have become quite important for the development of new methods for non-invasive analyses in agricultural industry [15]-[20]. For example, digital agricultural soil images are obtained by tomography and take into account several projections. Moreover, because one soil sample is scanned at different angles, a large amount of data needs to be computationally processed. Nowadays, the use of tomography not only allows us to obtain information about soil density and moisture at the pixel level, but also allows quantification of the pore volume and its representation in three dimensions. The soil pores vary in size and shape and can be interconnected.

In 1982, Bouma highlighted the importance of determining the continuity of the pore network for the flow of water in soil [21]. Therefore, not only pore diameter, but also pore continuity, interferes with the process of redistribution of soil water. In such a context, it is important to assess the porosity of the soil, because, depending on the soil management strategy adopted for planting, restriction of soil water flow may occur, thus compromising plant growth. To determine the soil porosity, volumetric measurements are conventionally used [22][23]. For this, it is necessary to collect undisturbed soil samples for quantitative evaluation of its porosity based on the use of tomographic scanners.

Methods based on volumetric reconstruction have been developed for such a purpose, mainly due to the inadequacy of information provided by two-dimensional models for accurate diagnosis in studies that need volumetric information. Thus, such methods suggest the composition of surfaces and volume of the samples under analyses and contribute to the increase of precision in the process of information extraction. However, it is still a challenge gathering all the information from agricultural soils, i.e., the continuity, size, and shapes of the pores in a soil sample, among others.

CT is one methodology that allows observing the structural components of the soil, allowing better visualization of the behavior of the structure and soil porous space. However, the interconnection for preferential flow requires additional methods which can be beyond what CT can provide. Sensors-based VR techniques can be combined with CT to assist noninvasive research through immersive and interactive processes.

VR was born in the eighties to help differentiate traditional computational simulations of the synthetic worlds, and researchers like Bolt [24] and Lanier [25] played a key role in its development. VR transports a person into a fully immersive and interactive experience with a degree of realism. Academics, software developers, and researchers are still trying to define a VR based on their own experiences. However, it is possible to observe in specialized literature that all of them technically consider the term related to a immersive and interactive experience, i.e., based on images generated by computers, rendering, or not in real time [26]-[29]. In fact, the concept of sensors-based VR is related to the use of sensors in external devices, i.e., digital gloves, video-helmets, digital caves, digital tables, among others. In 1994, Machover stated that the quality of a VR system is a significant consideration, because it stimulates the user to the maximum in a creative and productive way, providing feedback coherently regarding the user's movements [30].

Presently, only some units of research have developed projects using sensors-based VR applications in the area of scientific visualization, such as tomographic reconstruction, due to the high cost and technical difficulties involved in such processes. However, some proposals have appeared to minimize the difficulties of development and maintenance of the systems and necessary programs.

Additionally, a better organization of human resources has now been observed to integrate areas of the knowledge leading to the application of such advanced methods based on the connection and use of those technologies. Thereby, the main objective of this work is to present the development of a VR system to support the analysis of 3D reconstructed soil samples using innovative immersive visualization and interaction techniques by integrating sophisticated external sensors-based devices.

Specifically, this paper presents the organization and implementation of a synthetic environment that makes possible the visualization, analysis, and manipulation of soil samples produced by an algorithm of volumetric reconstruction of X-ray tomographic images through graphic computational tools and non-conventional sensors-based VR devices, aiming immersion and user interaction at the scene entities, making possible the non-destructive analysis of agricultural soil samples, as shown by a case study in Soil Science.

The materials and methods used in this work are described in Section 2. In Section 3, the obtained results are discussed, and the conclusions are presented in Section 4.

II. MATERIALS AND METHODS

The conceptual and methodological structuring applied to the development of the sensors-based VR system dedicated to the inspection of digital tomographic images from agricultural soils uses data obtained by means of a volumetric reconstruction algorithm. Figure 1 shows a general view of the sensors-based VR system dedicated to the tomographic inspection of agricultural soil samples, as well as the dataflow. From this tomographic image data, soil samples can be reconstructed, imported, and treated by several VR processes, focusing on the analysis related to the soil science area.

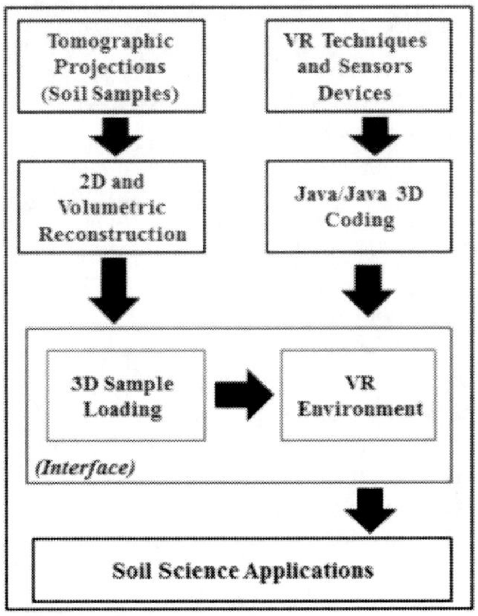

Figure 1. General view of the sensors-based VR system customized for the inspection of tomographic samples of agricultural soils, as well as a view of the dataflow from the acquisition process to the visualization process.

The software system was organized based on the concept of classes. In object-oriented programming, a class is an extensible program code template used for creating objects, providing initial values for states (member variables), and implementations of behavior (member functions or methods). In this work, the following classes have been considered: *Reconstruction*, *Loader*, *Transformations*, *Polygonal Attributes Extraction*, *Filter*, *Transparency*, *Illumination*, *Coloring*, *Conventional Collision*, *Non-conventional Collision*, *Conventional Model Manipulation*, *Non-conventional Model Manipulation*, *Conventional Scene Manipulation*, *Non-conventional Scene Manipulation*, *Quaternion*, *Visualization*, and *VR Environment*.

All classes were implemented using the Java programming language and the *Java3D* API [31].

A CT scanner from Embrapa Instrumentation was used to obtain the tomographic image data. All of the tomographic projections allowed image reconstruction, i.e., turning possible generation of mass attenuation coefficient maps given in cm^2/g with spatial resolution equal to or larger than 1 mm. All of the soil samples were submitted to the acquisition process using an amount of energy of 59.6 keV and a time window equal to 10 seconds for sampling of the points for the tomographic projection.

For two-dimensional reconstruction, an algorithm of *Filtered Back-Projection* (FBP) was used, with a filtering based on the use of the *Hamming's* window, implemented under 1-D *Fast Fourier Transform* (FFT), using the C++ language [32]. After that, a suitable filtering technique was also used with the 2-D reconstructed images. The filtering technique was based on the use of the *Wavelet Daubechies Transform* (WDT), which allowed filtering of only certain image areas preserving borders and details, i.e., through using a window with 76 coefficients [33].

An interpolation-based overlapping algorithm of reconstructed two-dimensional slices was adopted for volumetric reconstruction. Such a technique consists of setting up the plans generated by the function f(x, y, z_i) for i = 0... (n-1), where n is the number of reconstructed plans. Consequently, specific two-dimensional slices were interpolated to reconstitute the spaces left among these overlapped plans.

Figure 2 shows the overlapping original plans and the interpolated plans. This method was used to reduce the computational costs and the radiation time, with the use of interpolation in between the spaces of the reconstructed slices based on the use of *B-splines* [34]. Thus, with only a few slices, the algorithm was prepared to estimate and complete the entire information.

The sensors-based VR system for the inspection of agricultural soils samples was organized based on the CT images and a set of non-conventional sensors to support the VR environment. In addition, for the evaluation of the preferential paths for the water movement in soil, sensors were used to detect motion based on the use of gloves and the space based on 3-D visualization (using a CCD head-mounted display) as well as microelectromechanical actuators based on piezo-electrical devices [35][36]. Such sensors were necessary to translate movement and to help the users understand the relation of the workspace with the agricultural soil samples.

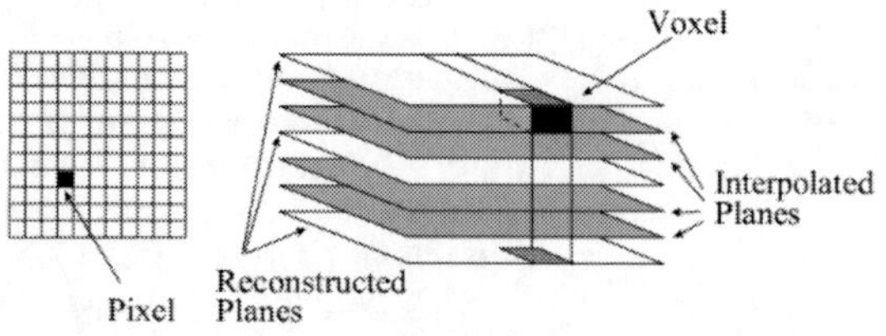

Figure 2. Volumetric reconstruction based on a set of reconstructed slices and the use of B-spline interpolator.

At the end of the process, the volumetric model is converted into the *Wavefront File Format* (.obj) using the *vtkOBJExporter* class from the *vtkOBJExporter.h* package of the visualization toolkit. This format has been chosen for its high performance and flexibility when importing such models to a virtual environment, where all their attributes can be customized for graphic APIs.

The *Attributes Extraction* class obtains the voxels data from a volumetric image, using those above-mentioned input non-conventional devices, i.e., supplying the users' information on a specific point of the volumetric representation. Initially, the objects of the classes *PickCanvas* and *PickResult* are instantiated, and these objects are responsible for activating the data extraction of a *Canvas3D* object and storing such data in vectors of event results. Based on user interest, a region can be selected and attributes extracted using a coordinate z, since it can be stabilized on the selected region in the display, allowing selection through a two-dimensional viewport in an intuitive way.

Thus, the available data for picking operations under instances of Shape3D and their respective methods are: the borders, with *getBounds*; the scene graphs, with *getLocale* and *numBranchGraph*; the geometries, with *getGeometry*; *ColoringAttributes*, with *get.ColoringAttributes*; the material under the Hue, Saturation, Lightness (HSL) and Red, Green, Blue (RGB) formats, with *getMaterial*; the *transparency,getTransparency*; and the polygons, with the *getAppearance.getPolygonAttributes.getPolygonMod* class.

In addition, an object is instantiated, belonging to the *PickIntersection* class, also of the *com.sun.j3d.utils.picking* package, responsible for sheltering the collision point between an entity/node and the two-dimensional cursor. Thus, this instance stores in its content the intersection product among an entity of *PickResult* with the chosen Canvas3D point, which is passed to the *getClosestIntersection* method as the parameter. The *PickIntersection* class can offer through its events: the distance between the point and the observer with the *getDistance* method; the coordinates of the point with the *getCoordinates* method; the coordinates of the closest vertex with the *getClosestVertexCoordinates* method; the normal straight line of the point with the *getNormal* method; and the transformation head offices with the *getMatrix* method.

The classes *PickIntersection* and *PickResult*, as well as the *Attributes Extraction* class, can allow the reading of each mass attenuation coefficient value, present in the tomographic volume. In this context, these values can be obtained through the gray level tones, which are represented by luminance, index "L" from the HSL pattern, obtained by using the class *getMaterial* method.

The *Non-conventional Scene Manipulation* class is one of the most important for user interactivity and immersion in the *VR environment*, since it allows user browsing in all directions through the synthetic scene, approximating and going into the reconstructed structures using data gloves *P5Glove* [37]. For the accomplishment of such events, the manipulation classes and the model of the scene are both based on another auxiliary class called *FPSGlove*, which is available in the *com.essentialreality* package offered by the device manufacturer. The *FPSGlove* classes is responsible for including all the parameters regarding non-conventional devices, and include the positioning, orientation, and finger bending, i.e., making it possible to detect the proximity and inclination, and thus launch a series of customized events.

On the other hand, in relation to the constructor method of classes, additional parameters of the same importance can be activated, such as: (1) *P5_Init*; (2) *P5_setForward*; (3) *P5_setMouseState*; (4) *P5_setFilterAmount*; and (5) *P5_setRequiredAccuracy*. These classes are responsible for initializing, determining the positive direction, and turning off the mouse, filtering the sign and determining the precision movements, respectively. Soon afterwards, the methods responsible for detecting the position of the glove in the real environment are declared. The methods are the *getXPosition*, *getYPosition* and *getZPosition*, which map the triggers mentioned before to launch an event type; it means, they monitor the values received by the glove through instances of the class *P5State*, a class responsible for determining the current state of the glove. Thus, through the *filterPos* method of *P5State*, the exact position of the device is obtained and then assigned to the methods to check if the limits were or were not outdated.

In a manner similar to the positioning detection methods still in the *FPSGlove* class, the methods *getYaw*, *getPitch*, and *getRoll* are described, as a solution for detecting the inclination of the device in the Y, X, and Z axes, to determine if the established limits for the flags were reached.

After having implemented the monitors and triggers of events with the auxiliary class, the *Non-conventional Scene Manipulation* class is also used with the ViewingPlatform class. In such a way, two other specific parameters are included, each of them related to the translation and rotation steps respectively. Such an arrangement is responsible for defining when the virtual models will be moved or leans in each movement of the device in the real world and recognized by the *FPSGlove* class.

Once such a process is concluded, the instance of the *Non-conventional Scene Manipulation* class should be harnessed to the object of the *ViewingPlatform* class of the current *Canvas3D* object, so that all of the movements can be related on the scene and not the volumetric model, i.e., through the *setViewingPlatform* method. The *Non-conventional Model Manipulation* is a class responsible for accomplishing the three-dimensional representation movement through real movements of the data glove *P5Glove*, where the user can change the positioning and orientation of models in real time in all directions and angles, contributing to the VR environment interactivity in six degrees of freedom. To operate such a process, it is important to consider the *Non-conventional Scene Manipulation* class, in which the current implementation uses the support *FPSGlove* class.

Thus, the *Non-conventional Model Manipulation* class is an extension of the *Behavior* class, a class that describes behaviors, customized for reactions to the movements of the device. Furthermore, after assigning the methods *getXPosition*, *getYPosition*, and *getZPosition* to obtain the positioning, and the methods *getYaw*, *getPitch*, and *getRoll* to obtain the orientation under instances of the *FPSGlove* class, the method *rotateQuaternion* is called. Such a method, responsible for converting rotations is accomplished based on the Euler angles in Quaternion coordinates and is useful to establish rotations with complex numbers and imaginary axis, in order to contribute to the movement's precision.

The *rotateQuaternion* method assigns to its class the axis and angles parameters in Euler coordinates and returns a quaternion description; a set used in the same *Quat4f* constructor, constructing a quaternion of float, and after a *setRotation* executes a rotation with instances of *Transform3D*.

At the end of the process, the product of *Non-conventional Model Manipulation* class is encapsulated in a *BranchGroup* object and assigned to the transformation group, *TransformGroup*, which conducts the three-dimensional representation movements in a distinct way from the previous class. In such a way, not only all of the movements' detection but also the effective positioning change and the entities orientation produce effects under the current models in the *Canvas3D* object.

The *Non-conventional Collision* class treats the implementation of a collision detection algorithm added to the *Non-conventional Scene Manipulation* class and is restricted to events that use non-conventional input data devices, specifically those provided by the data glove *P5Glove*. In that way, through the algorithm, the users are also prevented from crossing the faces of a three-dimensional representation during the browsing process in synthetic scenes, allowing only the cameras transpositions inside the empty spaces among such faces, simulating real physical processes.

Thus, each spatial position of the glove is tested as the current instance of itself; each direction of movement is limited to a specific moment, where the possible alternatives are: left, right, up, down, forward, and back. After identifying the positioning of the glove in the moment of a supposed collision, the *Non-conventional Collision* class can block the device movement. Thus, the last movement of the glove when a collision has been stopped is recorded, although the glove can freely be moved in the real environment. This is caused by a new instantiation of the current position of the glove, assigning empty vectors to them, in other words, initialized in the origin, i.e., causing the immediate stop of the device movement.

Additionally, at the same time, when accomplishing any other move that does not take them to a continuation of the blocking, the class interprets them and allows continuing the valid movements series through a new instantiation of the mapped positions of the glove, using as parameters the position where the collision began and the linear step was adopted by the class. At the end of this process, a *Shape3D* is added to *PhysicalBody* to detect the browsing of the scene being used by a user, allowing interaction and selection of each three-dimensional face. The algorithm of such a class allows both preventing the browsing to continue (or not) in a scene, as well as providing information of the direction of the glove movement since it became active.

The *Quaternion* class implements a conversion algorithm so that the system stops using just rotations on the x, y and z axes, and starts to accomplish orientations on some intermediate axis, defined by a vector that goes through the origin and reaches a point in space. Such a type of an axis can be represented by a specific coordinate of the real device, e.g., the Cartesian coordinates (x, y, z) of one of the eight LEDs present in the controller tower which is used with the glove [38].

To accomplish this operation, it uses imaginary bases and complex numbers, providing an alternative parameter for the *setRotation*, method of the *Transform3D* class, which allows using a quaternion as an argument. Thus, calling an instance of *Quaternion* to accomplish a rotation with the non-conventional device *P5Glove*, the orientation of the glove is interpreted by the *FPSGlove* class and translated by *Non-conventional Scene Manipulation* or *Model*, is converted from the Euler system to the *Quaternion* base, returned for the system new orientation coordinates, to then be executed by the *Quat4f* method of *Transform3D*, which encapsulates the entire functioning of the quaternion as previously described.

For the implementation of the *Visualization* class, the system interface prepares a volumetric tomographic image to be visualized. This way, the volumetric tomographic image is prepared to be adjusted to the 3-D model, i.e., to occupy the whole extension of the *Canvas3D* object, so that all of the spaces are taken advantage of, contributing to the visualization quality.

III. RESULTS AND DISCUSSIONS

Based on the use of the tomographic projections and the two-dimensional reconstruction FPB algorithm, it was possible to get volumetric images by means of use of the *B-spline* algorithm.

Figure 3 presents examples of the volumetric tomographic images obtained for stratified agricultural soil, degraded soil, and a clay soil sample, respectively. Based on the *Attributes Extraction* class, intrinsic characteristics of the scene and of agricultural samples could be obtained through the use of either the mouse or the *P5Glove*, with a data origin in the three-dimensional representations in the VR environment. The data set was divided into two categories: one concerning the scene, and the other concerning the CT measurements.

In relation to the first category, the synthetic scene data are related to: borders, which have represented the geometry limits or the geometry limits that involved it; the scene graph, that has represented the node hierarchy in the tree; the current geometry in the model and its composition, the distance of a certain voxel in relation to the coordinates chosen in the scene, the closest vertex to the chosen point in the scene, the three-dimensional coordinates, and the normal straight line in the closest face, which involved the chosen coordinates.

Secondly, concerning the tomographic data, the obtained data were: color attributes, which represented the individual color of each voxel, independent of illumination intensity; the mass attenuation coefficients values of the agricultural soils, which are represented by the colors of each analyzed voxel, and are related to the light intensity in each position; transparency attributes; and polygons attributes, and finally the saturation and matrix of the HSL coefficients.

An experiment for validation of the result was prepared considering a digital and volumetric tomographic image obtained from a latosol soil. For such a volumetric image, the value of an arbitrary voxel was taken as presented in Figure 4.

Based on the developed method, the attributes can be obtained from the latosol soil tomographic image at the sensors-based VR environment, i.e., under the two mentioned aspects, through the choice of any voxel coordinates, assuring the reliable recovery of the sample data.

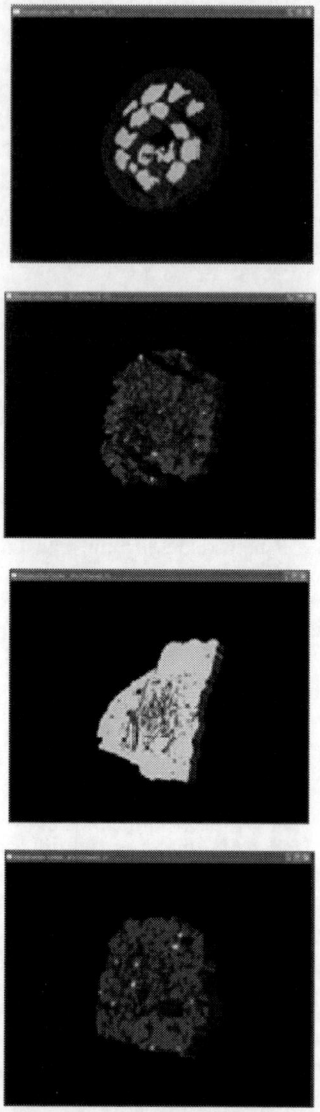

Figure 3. Volumetric images reconstructed by FBP and the B-Spline algorithm.

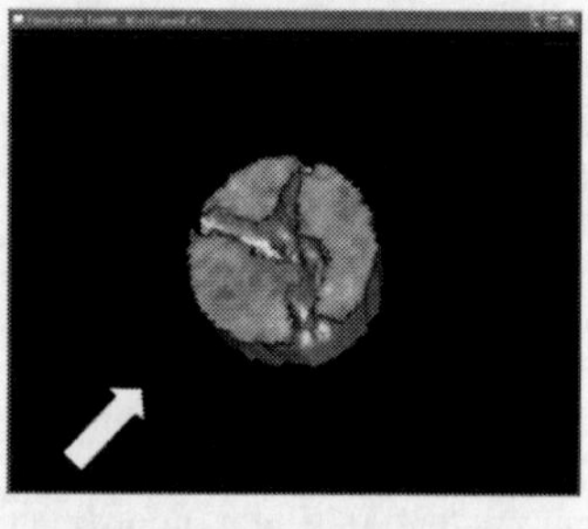

Figure 4. Resulting data obtained from a latosol soil sample where an arbitrary point is chosen using a conventional device (mouse) or a non-conventional one (glove). The coordinates of the voxel are directly selected and the respective information can be exhibited for the users.

As an example of such a result, attributes can be obtained and presented as below:

Colors:

Color=(0.03, 0.07, 0.04) | ShadeModel=SHADE_GOURAUD

Materials:

AmbientColor=(0.4, 0.4, 0.4)

EmissiveColor=(0.0, 0.0, 0.0)

DiffuseColor=(0.71, 0.70, 0.65)

SpecularColor=(0.3, 0.3, 0.3)

Shininess=128.0

LightingEnable=true

ColorTarget=2

Transparency Level: 0.3

Polygons: Planes

Gray Level: 156.82

Saturation: 22.86

Mass Attenuation Coefficient (cm²/g): 0.6521

Virtual borders:

Lower=-0.87 -1.0 -0.15

Upper=0.875 1.0 0.15

BranchGraphs: 3

Geometry: Triangles

Point Distance: 10.28

Closest Vertex: (0.92, -0.25, -10.24)

Point Coordinates: (0.75, -0.25, -10.26)

Point Normal Axis: (1.0, 0.0, 0.0)

In relation to the *Non-conventional Scene Manipulation*, the feedback produced by the class implementation has indicated absolute control of user browsing on the scene using the *P5Glove*. In this context, according to device positioning, the users can browse through the scene where the displacement of their hand is faithfully translated in scene movements, including moving the environment cameras in real time. Analogously, such movements are also translated in the three-dimensional displacements.

Practically, such movement with a glove should commence with closed hands, where the sensors are activated by bending fingers, thus starting the action. The *Non-conventional Model Manipulation* class simulates the manual support of 3-D samples, as well as its total movement inside the scene, with 6 degrees of freedom.

Also, the *Quaternion* class, when evaluated, presented an adequate conversion from Euler's coordinates to Quaternion's coordinates. In addition, the results of application of the *Transform3D* class produced smooth orientation changes. Table I presents an example of results for the 180° rotation, considering the initial position of the LED = (-1.0, 1.0, 0.0), and the origin of the three axes that is at coordinates (0.0, 0.0, 0.0).

Figure 5 presents the visual results of the applied transform. Such a result has demonstrated that the three rotations were composed by commutation of four other rotations of smaller angles. Also, the transposition of an orientation for another happened in a soft way, without leaps or arbitrary paths, leading to an intuitive result.

The three-dimensional samples were examined immersively by the Head Mounted Display through the *Visualization* class. First, *Canvas3D*, responsible for the rendering of three-dimensional images, was maximized to omit the parts related to the main interface in the device to focus only on the region where the sample was shown. Thus, each display of HMD forms an image which is shown and interpreted by the user's brain with a larger depth effect.

Secondly, such an effect also has allowed performing the analyses of the preferential paths of the water flow into the agricultural soil samples, called fingering effects, as well as the verification of the percentage of pores in the samples.

TABLE I - EXAMPLE OF RESULTS FOR THE ROTATION USING QUATERNIONS

Initial Position (sample point)	Quaternion	Final Position (sample point)
(0.0,0.0,0.0)	vector: (0.0,0.0,0.0) scale:0.9238	(0.7071,0,7071,0.0)
(0.7071,0.7071,0.0)	vector: (0.2705,0.2705,0.0) scale: 0.9238	(0.9999,0.9999,0.0)
(0.9999, 0.9999,0.0)	vector: (0.3826,0.3826,0.0) scale: 0.9238	(1.2928,1.2928,0.0)
1.2928,1.2928,0.0)	vector: (0.4947,0.4947,0.0) scale: 0,9238	(1.6862,1.6862,0.0)

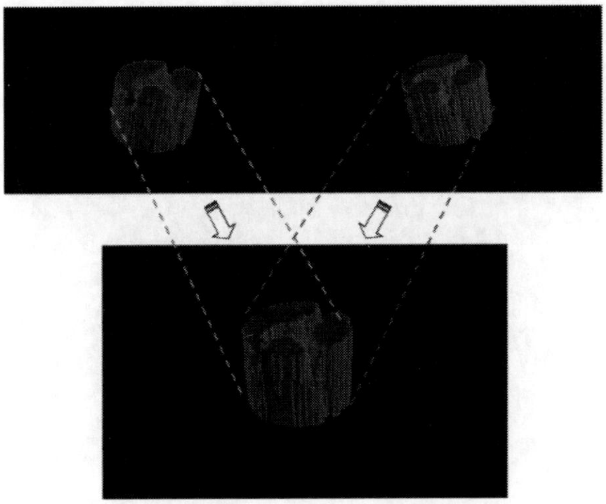

Figure 5. Representation of the rotation described around the stippled axis defined by the coordinate of LED = (1.0, 1.0, 0.0), and passing through the origin of the axis.

As described in the *Non-conventional Scene Manipulation* class, as the cameras are moved with the navigation processes, activated by keyboard interaction, or data glove *P5Glove*, the traveled paths can be demarcated; leaving the itinerary registered under visual and mathematical form. Furthermore, for each device movement identified, a new position for the camera is established, i.e., given by new coordinates (x, y, z).

Such positions are unique and occupied only one at a time. Thus, activated by the demarcation process, forming any point, the traveled path can be simulated for a certain water flow, i.e, when working with an agricultural sample. When accomplishing a certain movement, the current point occupied by the camera receives a *Shape3D* under the form of a blue sphere, which simulates the presence of a fluid drop occupying the previous position of the camera, leaving a bluish trace through where the camera passed. Similar to the simple scene manipulation, such demarcation obeys the laws imposed by the *Non-conventional Collision* class, i.e., the traveled path is prevented from passing over the non-porous faces of the agricultural sample, leading the flow of fluids to pass through the related pores, which are the preferential paths.

The process can be repeated several times in ways similar to real situations. It is also possible to make border calculation where the limits of three-dimensional samples are identified in space, as in the case of *Attributes Extraction* class through the use of *getBounds* on *Shape3D* instances combined with a three-dimensional borders detection algorithm called *Polytope*, available in the Bounds package of *Java3D* API.

Besides, by using such an algorithm has become possible drawing plans around of the surfaces of the soil samples images, i.e., to delimit their borders exactly. Thus, it allows the nonporous parts of the samples, including the internal ones, to be identified, allowing the verification of its volume in cm^3.

Figure 6 presents the results of the case study based on a tomographic image from degraded agricultural soil, where the sample is in gray tones and the water flow is represented with a blue color, demarcating the traveled paths.

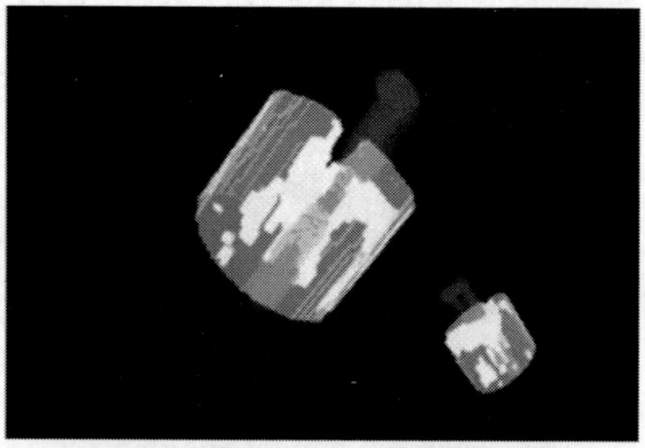

Figure 6. Result of the case study using a degraded soil sample, i.e., with representations of the non-porous soil portion (gray), emptiness (yellow), and water flow (blue) in between the soil pores.

In fact, once the non-porous part has been identified, the remaining portions were recognized based on the emptiness of the sample, which present the color that corresponds to those voxels in which there was an absence of the photons attenuation. The porous voxel was filled out with a semi-transparent yellow color, seeking a larger prominence close to the sample. With such available data, it is possible to calculate the total volume of the sample (sum of the non-porous parts with its complement) in cm^3. Thus, starting from the total volume and the individual volume of the non-porous part, it is possible to calculate exactly the volume represented by the emptiness of the three-dimensional sample.

IV. CONCLUSIONS

This work presented the development of a new method which considered the integration of a sensors-based VR environment with a CT for the dedicated inspection of agricultural soils. Results have shown both the possibility of accessing CT digital images of the agricultural soils and the opportunity of handling three-dimensional manipulation and graphic visualization processes through computational devices. Such a developed method allowed the addition of immersion and the user's interaction with soil samples. These resources involved rendering control, illumination, coloring, attributes extraction, and physical transformation, as well as the integration of non-conventional data input and output devices, such as a Head-Mounted Display (video-helmet), and digital gloves.

In addition, it was also observed that the *Java3D* API provided, in its group of classes, essential methods for HMD programming. Such development has encapsulated practically all of stereoscopy programming. Furthermore, the case study demonstrated the applicability of the method in visualization processes and agricultural soil sample analysis, considering the progress and facilities when accomplishing non-invasive inspections.

Finally, the integration of CT and sensors-based VR made possible the measuring of volumes of emptiness of the samples, i.e., the pores, and simulation of the water flow path for the formation of preferential fingering. Future work will consider embedded systems based on the use of the *Field Programmable Gate Array* (FPGA), as well as use of the augmented reality concepts.

ACKNOWLEDGMENT

This research was partially supported by the São Paulo Research Foundation (FAPESP, Process No. 17/19350-2), and the Brazilian Corporation for Agricultural Research (Embrapa, Process No. 11.14.09.001.05.06). We thank the institutional support received from the Computer Science Department of the Federal University of São Carlos (UFSCar), and the University Centre Euripides of Marilia (UNIVEM).

REFERENCES

[1] A. Petrovic, J. Siebert, and P. Rieke, "Soil bulk density analysis in three dimensions by computed tomographic scanning", Soil Science Society of America Journal, vol. 46, n. 3, pp. 445–450, 1982.

[2] J. M. Hainsworth and L.A.G. Aylmore, "The use of computer-assisted tomography to determine spatial distribution of soil water content", Australian Journal of Soil Research, n. 21, pp. 435–440, 1983.

[3] S. Crestana, S. Mascarenhas, and R. Pozzi-Mucelli, "Static and dynamic threedimensional studies of water in soil using computed tomographic scanning", Soil Science, vol. 140, n. 5, pp. 326–332, 1985.

[4] P. E. Cruvinel, R. Cesareo, S. Crestana, and S. Mascarenhas, "X-and gamma-rays computerized minitomograph scanner for soil science", IEEE Transactions on Instrumentation and Measurement, vol. 39, n. 5, pp. 745–750, 1990.

[5] Á. Macedo et al., "Wood density determination by X and gamma ray tomography", International Journal of the

Biology, Chemistry, Physics and Technology of Wood, vol. 56, pp. 535–540, 2002.

[6] A. Pedrotti et al., "Computed tomography applied to studies of a planosoil" (Original in Portuguese: Tomografia computadorizada aplicada a estudos de um planossolo). Brazilian Agricultural Research Journal, vol. 38, n. 7, pp. 819–826, Brazil, 2003.

[7] P.E. Cruvinel, M. L. F. Pereira, J. H. Saito, and L.F. Costa, "Performance optimization of tomographic image reconstruction based on DSP processors", IEEE Transactions on Instrumentation and Measurement , vol. 58, pp. 3295-3304, 2009.

[8] J. M. Beraldo, F. A. Scanavinno Junior, and P. E. Cruvinel, "Application of X-ray computed tomography in the evaluation of soil porosity in soil management systems", Engenharia Agrícola, vol. 34, n. 6, pp. 1162–1174, 2014.

[9] E. S. B. Ferraz and R. S. Mansell, "Determining water content and bulk density of soil by gamma-ray attenuation methods", Technical Bulletin, No. 807, IFAS, Florida, pp. 1-51, 1979.

[10] C. F. A. Teixeira, S. O. Moraes, and M. A. Simonete, "Tensiometer, TDR and neutron probe performance in the determination of soil moisture and hydraulic conductivity", (Original in Portuguese: Desempenho do tensiômetro, TDR e sonda de nêutrons na determinação da umidade e condutividade hidráulica do solo), Brazilian Journal of Soil Science, vol. 29, pp. 161–168, 2005.

[11] M. F. L. Pereira and P. E. Cruvinel, "A model for soil computed tomography based on volumetric reconstruction, Wiener filtering and parallel processing", Computers and Electronics In Agriculture, vol. 111, pp. 151-163, 2015.

[12] K. Slavakis, G. B. Giannakis, and G. Mateos, "Modeling and Optimization for Big Data Analytics", IEEE Signal Processing Magazine, pp. 18–31, 2014.

[13] V. Bolón-Canedo, N. Sánchez-Maroño, A. Alonso-Betanzos, "Recent advances and emerging challenges of feature selection in the context of big data", Knowledge-Based Systems, Elsevier, vol. 86, n.9, pp. 33–45, 2015.

[14] A. Ali, G. A. Shah, M. O. Farooq, and U. Ghani, "Technologies and challenges in developing machine-to-machine applications: A survey", Journal of Network and Computer Applications, vol. 83, pp. 124–139, 2017.

[15] S. S. Andrews, D. L. Karlen, and C. A. Cambardella, "The Soil Management Assessment Framework: A Quantitative Soil Quality Evaluation Method", Soil Science Society of America Journal, vol. 68, pp. 1945– 1962, 2004.

[16] A. Kaloxylos et al., "Farm management systems and the future internet era", Computers and Electronics in Agriculture, vol. 89, pp. 130– 144, 2012.

[17] U. Zimmermann et al, "A non-invasive plant-based probe for continuous monitoring of water stress in real time: a new tool for irrigation scheduling and deeper insight into drought and salinity stress physiology", Theoretical and Experimental Plant Physiology, vol. 25, n. 1, pp. 2-11, 2013.

[18] J. S. Selker, L. Graff, and T. Steenhuis, "Noninvasive time domain reflectometry moisture measurement probe", Soil Science Society of America Journal, vol. 57, n. 4, pp. 934-936, 1993.

[19] F. Palacios, M. P. Diago, and J. Tardaguila, "A non-invasive method based on computer vision for grapevine cluster compactness assessment using a mobile sensing platform under field conditions", Sensors, vol. 19, n. 17, pp. 3799-3818, 2019.

[20] H. Liu, R. Jia, X. Zhou, and L. Fu, "Virtual assembly of man-machine interactive mechanical seed-metering device based on matter-element identification", Transactions of the Chinese Society of Agricultural Engineering, vol. 32, n. 1, pp. 38-45, 2016.

[21] J. Bouma, "Measuring the conductivity of soil horizons with continuous macropores", Soil Science Society of America Journal, Madison, vol.46, pp. 438-441, 1982.

[22] Mualem, Y, "A new model for predicting the hydraulic conductivity of unsaturated porous media", Water Resources Research, vol.12, pp. 2184-2193, 1976.

[23] M. Kutilek and D. R. Nielsen, Soil Hydrology, Cremlingen-Destedt: Catena Verlag, 1994.

[24] R. A. Bolt, "Put-that-there: Voice and gesture at the graphics interface", in 7th International Conference on Computer Graphics and Interactive Techniques, Washington, USA, pp. 262–270, 1980.

[25] J. Lanier, Visual programming languages, Scientific American, 1984.

[26] L. C. Botega and P. E. Cruvinel, "Development of a Virtual Reality Environment for Agricultural Soil Analysis" (Original in Portuguese: Desenvolvimento de Ambiente de Realidade Virtual para Análise de Solos Agrícolas), in Proceedings of the Workshop of Virtual and Augmented Reality, Itumbiara, Brazil, 2007.

[27] K. Pimentel and K. Teixeira, Virtual reality through the new looking glass, McGraw-Hill, New York, 2nd edition, 1995.

[28] O. Gonzalez et al, "Development and assessment of a tractor driving simulator with immersive virtual reality for training to avoid occupational hazards", Computers and Electronics in Agriculture, vol. 143, pp. 111-118, 2017.

[29] L. Jacobson, Garage Virtual Reality, SAMS Publication, Indianapolis, 1994.

[30] C. Machover and S. Tice, "Virtual Reality", IEEE Computer Graphics and Application, vol. 14, n.1, pp. 15-16, 1994.

[31] Sun Microsystems. Java3D Documentation. [Online]. Available from: http://java.sun.com/javase/technologies/desktop/java3d.

[32] C. Kak and M Slaney, "Principles of computerized tomographic imaging," New york: The Institute of Electrical and Electronics Engineers, Inc., IEEE Press, 1988.

[33] I. Daubechies, "Ten lectures on wavelets", CBMS-NFS Regional Conference Series in Applied Mathematics, Philadelphia, PA: Society for Insdustrial and Apllied Mathematics (SIAM), vol. 61, 1992.

[34] T. N. E. Greville, "Spline functions, interpolation and numerical quadrature", Mathematical Methods for Digital Computers, Vol.2, A. Ralston and H.S. Wilf, eds., Wiley, New York, Ch. 8, pp. 156-168, 1967.

[35] S. Chen, L. Xu, and H. Li, "Research on 3D modeling in scene simulation based on Creator and 3dsmax," in IEEE International Conference, vol. 4, pp. 1736–1740, Mechatronics and Automation, 2005.

[36] E. F. S. Montero and D. J. Zanchet, "Virtual reality and medicine" (Original in Portuguese: Realidade virtual e a medicina), Brazilian Surgical Act, vol. 18, n. 8, pp. 489-490, 2003.

[37] C. Kenner. Essential reality p5glove sumary: Dual mode driver programming: [Online]. Available from: http://www.geocities.com/carl_a_kenner/p5.html.

[38] S. C. Biasi and M. Gattass. Use of quaternions to represent 3-D rotations. (Original in Portuguese: Utilização de quatérnios para representação de rotações em 3-D), Catholic University of Rio de Janeiro, February of 2002. [Online]. Available from: http://www.tecgraf.puc-rio.br/~mgattass.

Designing a Livestock Monitoring System and Evaluating the Performance of LoRa for a Farm

— Reforming agriculture by information and communications technology in Society 5.0 —

Atsushi Ito, Jinshan Luo
Department of Information Science
Utsunomiya University
Utsunomiya, Tochigi, Japan
at.ito@is.utsunomiya-u.ac.jp
kingsamlawsan@gmail.com

Yoshikazu Nagao
Department of Agriculture
Utsunomiya University
Moka, Tochigi, Japan
ynagao@cc.utsunomiya-u.ac.jp

Yuko Hiramatsu, Fumihiro Sato
Faculty of Economics
Chuo University
Hachioji, Tokyo, Japan
{susana_y, fsato}@tamacc.chuo-u.ac.jp

Takeo Watanabe
Tochigi Prefecture Dairy Co-operative
Utsunomiya, Japan
t-watanabe@tochiraku.or.jp

Abstract—**In this paper, we present an outline of our livestock monitoring system using long range (LoRa) in a low-power wide-area network and evaluate the performance of our LoRa device for use as a livestock monitoring system. We herein present the purpose of the project, an evaluation of LoRa transmission distance on a farm, and the application of our results. On the basis of our evaluation of LoRa, we confirm that it is a feasible technology for monitoring the behavior of livestock, particularly cows, on large farms.**

Keywords- grazing; high quality milk; behaviour tracking; ph of stomac; LoRa; AI.

I. INTRODUCTION

Several changes recently occurred in the methods of farm management in Japan. Farm size has become more extensive and efficient, promoting the American large-scale herd-management method. As a result, Japanese-style breeding management, which is based on a relationship of trust with livestock, has been lost. Breeding selection has dramatically improved the lactation ability of cows, but it led to a decline in body condition and weakening of reproductive behavior, primarily because of the lack of energy. Accordingly, artificial insemination at the correct time presents difficulties; it was reported in U.S. that the rate of successful pregnancies of cattle has been reduced to roughly 30% in the late 1990s (which was previously 60% in the late 1970s) [1], and in Japan to roughly 46% in 2009 (which was previously 60% in 1989) [2]. As a result, the number of cows and the production of raw milk have decreased.

Fine-grained, low-stress feeding management can reduce morbidity, increase reproductive efficiency, and improve the quality of raw milk. Breeding management that involves taking care of each animal and maximizing its individuality and ability can lead to the production of high-value-added milk. In this context, grazing is currently attracting attention for its ability to manage cows in a less stressful and more natural environment. The relationship between the production of high-value-added milk through pasturing and observing the feeding behavior of cows while grazing and the overall health status is not entirely clear.

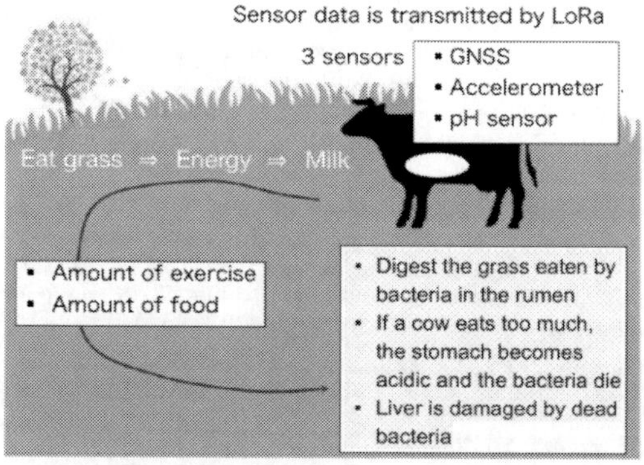

Figure 1. Cow's health condition

The aim of this paper is to clarify the relationship between grazing and the quality of raw milk and to subsequently develop a milk-quality-estimating system using sensors, information and communications technology, and Artificial Intelligence (AI).

This paper is organized as follows. In Section II, we explain the design of our proposed system. Section III introduces related research. In Section IV, we discuss the long-range (LoRa) [3] technology (included in ARIB STD-T108 in Japan [4]). In Section V, we explain an experiment for measuring the communication distance of LoRa in a different environment in detail. Finally, Section VI presents our research results and Section VII concludes the paper.

II. SYSTEM DESIGN

Generally, cow health must be maintained to ensure the production of high-quality raw milk. Fig. 1 shows the relationship between a cow's health and its behavior. An outline of this study is presented in Fig. 2.

To measure the effect of grazing, we set three technical targets as follows:

- Target 1: Real-time tracking of cow-feeding behavior
- Target 2: Real-time measurement of cow rumen pH levels
- Target 3: Application of a machine-learning model to estimate the quality of raw milk

The outline of each target is explained in the following subsections.

A. Real-Time Tracking of Cow-Feeding Behavior

Purpose: To understand the behavior of cows while grazing and investigate the relationship between this behavior and milk quality.

Tasks:

Develop a sensor box that can detect location (Global Navigation Satellite System, GNSS) and accelerometer data. Send the data to a server via LoRa.

- The number of steps and the number of chewing cycles are estimated from accelerometer data.
- Activity is estimated from the walking distance calculated using location data.

B. Real-Time Measurement of Cow Rumen pH Levels

Purpose: To understand the health situation of cows and clarify the relationship between the pH level and the quality of raw milk.

Tasks:

- Develop a pH sensor that can be used on rumen and that can send data external to the cow's body.
- Develop a communication system to send a pH sensor outside the rumen.

C. Machine-Learning Model for Estimating the Quality of Raw Milk

Purpose: To estimate the quality of raw milk from the behavior and pH level of cow rumen.

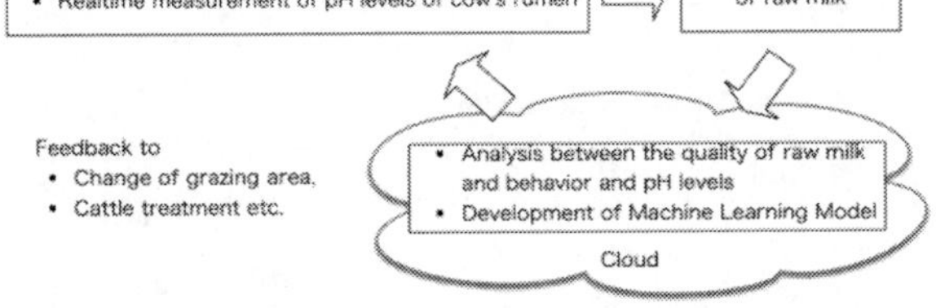

Figure 2. The outline of this study.

Task:

- Develop a machine-learning model to estimate the quality of raw milk from the behavior and pH level of cow rumen.

In the following two sections, related work and a technical outline of LoRa will be described.

III. RELATED WORK

Many studies have measured the behavior of livestock. In [5], a method was introduced to track the movement of cows using a black-and-white pattern of the surface of a cow house. In [6], a location-detection technique in a cow house using ultrawideband and tags was presented. In [7], a technique for observing the cow-feeding behavior using an accelerometer in a cow house was addressed. All of these technologies focus on the use of a cow house.

In [8], a technique for monitoring locomotion and posture activity was presented, but no function for transmitting data to the server in real time was provided. The work in [9] explains system aspects such as nodes, gateways, and servers and is based on a LoRa wide-area network (LoRaWAN). However, in that study, no real field tests were conducted. In [10], the performance of LoRa and custom protocols for monitoring livestock was discussed; however, hypothetical situations are always slightly different from the conditions on a real farm.

IV. LORA

Low-Power Wide rea (LPWA) [11] is a type of network that is becoming popular for LoRa license-free wireless communication technologies. This type of network can provide news services for long-distance communication (from several hundreds of meters up to several kilometers) in rural areas. Additionally, LPWA operates at the subgigahertz (sub-GHz) band, which has excellent penetration. It is expected that LPWA will be able to provide several useful features for Internet of Things (IoT) applications, such as low cost, low-power consumption, long-distance communication, connection of a significant number of IoT devices, and small-scale data transmission (ranging from 100 bps to 1 Mbps).

It is highly expected that LPWA will be used for communication technologies in IoT systems. This technology has the following features:

- Low cost
- Low-power consumption, except for Bluetooth Low Energy and ordinary near-field communication technologies, which require a generous power supply
- Long-distance coverage (from several hundreds of meters up to several kilometers)
- Connectivity to multiple devices
- Transfer of small amounts of data at speeds ranging from 100 bps to 1 Mbps

The most popular LPWA standard is LoRa [3]. The LoRa Alliance particularly defines LoRaWAN [12]. LoRa defines the modulation technology of the physical layer of a chip, and LoRaWAN also includes a media access control layer. Furthermore, LoRaWAN specifies the interoperability of

TABLE I. EFFECT OF SF AND BW ON TIME-ON-AIR (MS) (FROM THE ES920LR DATA SHEET IN [11])

(A) PAYLOAD IS 10 BYTES

Combination of BW x SF good for the long range communication (62.5KHz, SF=12)

		Spreading Factor (SF)					
		7	8	9	10	11	12
Band Width (BW) (KHz)	62.5	144	247	453	823	1483	2966
	125	72	123	226	412	741	1483
	250	36	62	113	206	371	741
	500	18	31	57	103	185	371

(ms)

Combination of BW x SF good to send large data (500KHz, SF=7)

(B) PAYLOAD IS 50 BYTES

		Spreading Factor (SF)					
		7	8	9	10	11	12
Band Width (BW) (KHz)	62.5	308	534	903	1642	2957	5587
	125	154	267	452	821	1479	2793
	250	77	133	226	411	739	1397
	500	38	67	113	205	370	698

(ms)

TABLE II. TEST PATTERNS.

	Category	*Features*	*Location*
Case 1	Forest	Trees and mountain	Oku-Nikko
Case 2	Farm for livestock (flat area)	Covered by grass	Utsunomiya Univ. farm
Case 3	Farm for livestock (mountain area)	Covered by grass	Ozasa Farm in Nikko
Case 4	City	Buildings	Eng. Department of Utsunomiya Univ.

LoRa devices. LoRa employs chirp spectrum spread, thereby allowing long-distance communication.

When using LoRa, two parameters must be included: bandwidth (BW) and spreading factor (SF). A smaller BW allows for communication across a longer distance, whereas a larger SF allows for communication over a longer distance. However, if we wish to achieve communication over even longer distances, we need to select appropriate parameters. The relationship between the BW and the SF of the ES920LR LoRa chip that we used in 2019 is described in Table I.

V. EXPERIMENT

We performed several trials to check the communication distance of LoRa.

A. Locations

In order to check the communication distance, we used four locations as follows:

(1) Oku-Nikko: flat, wide forest and marsh in the Nikko National Park (400 ha, roughly 4 × 4 km).
(2) Utsunomiya University Farm: flat farmland with some trees (50 ha, roughly 1 × 0.5 km).
(3) Near the Engineering Department: city area with buildings and factories surrounding the campus area.
(4) Ozasa Farm: one of the largest livestock farms in Japan (362 ha, roughly 4 × 4 km).

B. Devices and GNSS Data

We developed a LoRa device using the following parameters.

(Oku-Nikko)	(Farms and Utsunomiya Univ.)
– BW: 125KHz	– BW: 62.5KHz
– SF: 10	– SF: 12
– Tx power: 13dbm	– Tx power: 13dbm
– LoRa chip: RAK811	– LoRa chip: ES920LR
– Antenna gain: 0dbi	– Antenna gain: 0dbi

In these experiments, the transmitted data, including the GNSS location data, were 35 bytes. According to Table I, we estimated that one data could be transmitted within 5 s. Fig. 3 shows the receiver and transmitter that we used in the experiment conducted at Ozasa Farm, both of which used the same LoRa chip (ES920LR [13]). The transmitter had a GNSS receiver and sent location data to the receiver.

Receiver Transmitter

Figure 3. Receiver and Transmitter

C. Okumura-Hata Model

The Okumura–Hata model [14][15] is an approximate curve used for estimating the radio-wave propagation characteristics of wireless devices at the development stage of mobile communication systems in different environments in open areas; suburbs; and small, medium, and large cities. The equations shown in Fig. 4 were used for loss calculation. In the experiment, we measured not only the communication distance but also the fitting of the Okumura–Hata model. If

$$Loss(dB) = A + Blog(d) - \alpha + C$$

where

$A = 69.55 + 26.16\log[f(MHz)] - 13.82\log[h_b(m)]$

$B = 44.9 - 6.55\log[h_b(m)]$

f(MHz): frequency

d(km): distance

h_b(m): base station height

α and C depend on the location

For example, if the location is an open space, α and C are defined as follows:

$\alpha = \{1.1\log[f(MHz)] - 0.7\}hm(m) - \{1.56\log[f(MHz)] - 0.8\}$

$C = -4.78\{\log[f(MHz)]\}2 + 18.33\log[f(MHz)] - 40.94$

h_m(m): mobile station height

Figure 4. The Okumura–Hata model.

the results showed a good fit with the Okumura–Hata model, we would be able to use that model to estimate the reach of LoRa.

D. Experiments

We started performing LoRa tests in 2018 (see [16][17]) under different situations (e.g., in city, forest, and farm areas), as described in Table II. In [16][17], we reported the LoRa test results for three different cases (Cases 1, 2, and 4 in Table II) and confirmed that the communication distance closely fit the Okumura–Hata model.

We herein explain a recent experiment (December 3, 2019) conducted on a farmland in a mountainous area (Case 3 in Table II).

As previously noted, Ozasa Farm is one of the largest livestock farms in Japan (362 ha). Fig. 5 shows a panoramic view of the farm. We set a LoRa receiver at the center of the farm on a tripod (at a height of roughly 2 m) and then traversed the farm on foot holding two LoRa transmitters. As noted in Section 5-B, data including the GNSS location were transmitted every 5 s. We used a BW of 62 and an SF of 12 to achieve the highest possible sensitivity. Fig. 6(a) shows the trace of the transmitted location, and Fig. 6(b) shows the trace of the received data with location. The log shows that LoRa was able to cover almost all areas. Table III shows the message-receiving rate, which was on average greater than 80%. We believe that this result indicates that LoRa is a feasible measure for monitoring livestock. Fig. 7 shows fitting

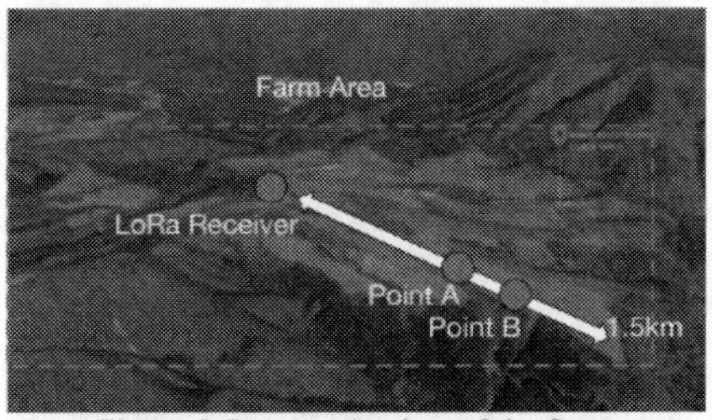

Figure 5. Panoramic view of the farm

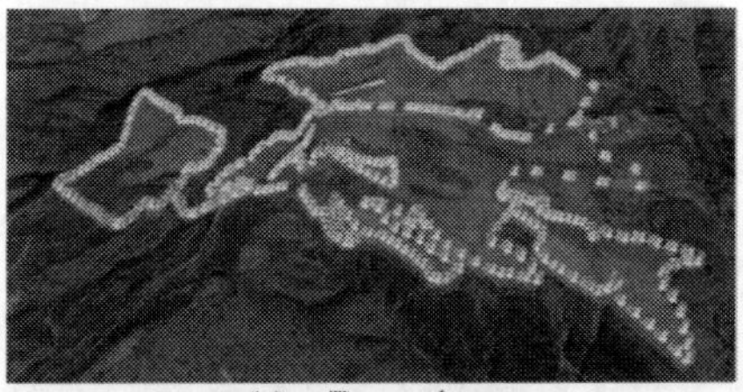
(a) Transmitter trace

(a) Received data

Figure 6. Results of the LoRa test.

TABLE III. MESSAGE-RECEIVING RATE.

	Device 1	*Device 2*	*Total*
Number of transmitted messages	2,884	2,507	5,391
Number of received messages	2,272	2,113	4,385
Message receiving rate	78.78%	84.28%	81.34%

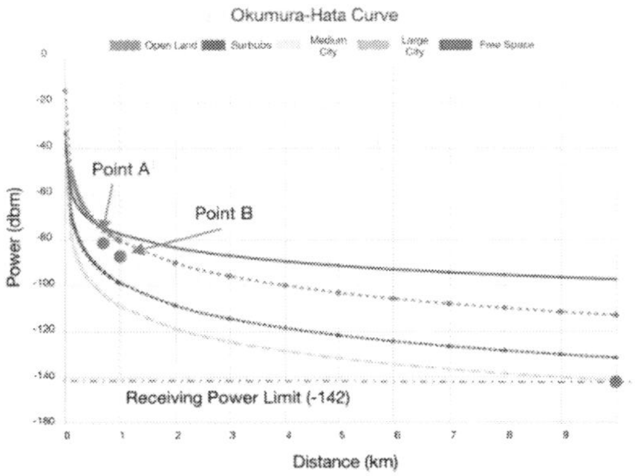

Figure 7. Fitting of the Okumura–Hata model.

of the Okumura–Hata model with these results. The results show that a loss occurred between open land and suburbs but that the results nonetheless met the requirements for Ozasa Farm. The Okumura–Hata model can, therefore, be used to estimate the potential of LoRa in a farm environment.

In the next step of our research, we will design sensor devices and a matching receiver for cows. If the transmitter sends data every 5 min and each data transmission requires 5 s, we will be able to obtain data from 60 cows using the same band. Each transmitter will have a GNSS device, allowing the scheduling of the transmission time for each cow without congestion. The LoRa device [13] will have 37 channels if the BW is narrower than 125 kHz; this will enable us to monitor 2,220 cows at the same time. Ozasa Farm generally supports 1,500 cows grazing on its pasture. As such, our system will be able to monitor them all.

VI. APPLICATION OF THE RESEARCH RESULTS

The Japanese Government is currently promoting the notion of *Society 5.0* [18], an idea that was proposed at the 5th Science and Technology Basic Plan (2016–2020) for conducting a future Japanese society. The aim of Society 5.0 is to achieve a high degree of convergence between cyberspace (virtual space) and physical (real) space. In Society 5.0, a significant amount of information from sensors in physical space is accumulated in cyberspace. In cyberspace, this big data is analyzed by AI, and the analyzed results are fed back to physical space in various forms to support society, business, and economics.

An outline of Society 5.0 for agriculture is described in Fig. 8. In order to solve problems related to agriculture and food,

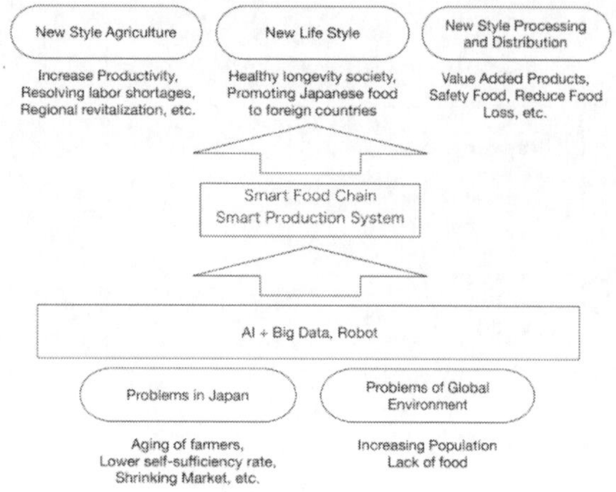

Figure 8. Agriculture in a Society 5.0 context.

Figure 9. Food-chain business model.

AI and big-data analysis technology are used to produce higher-quality primary products, such as milk, meat, and rice. Then, these high-quality products allow smart food chain and smart production systems to produce high-quality secondary and tertiary products. In addition, robots support the primary agricultural industry to solve problems such as aging among farmers. After realizing a new style of agriculture, we expect developing a new business model as illustrated in Fig. 9. Once we can produce high-quality raw milk, we will be able to produce high-quality butter and cheese and, subsequently, flavorsome sweets and dishes. The effect of such products and services is expected to promote gastronomy and health tourism.

The results of this research provide a potential platform for gathering real-time data from livestock within a wide area using LPWAs such as LoRa. Developing such a platform to gather data from sensors by LPWAs will serve as an important basis for reforming agriculture in a Society 5.0 context.

VII. Conclusion and Future Work

In this paper, we introduced our research results for developing a monitoring system that can track the behavior of cows and pH levels for grazing and an AI model to estimate the quality of raw milk. With this research ongoing, we were able to explain in detail the performance of LoRa in a real situation. Accordingly, LoRa was able to cover the entire area of farmland evaluated. Furthermore, we also briefly addressed the broader scope of a new food chain business model based on the Society 5.0 context.

We hereby plan to develop a system based on the results of this research in the second quarter of 2020 and to evaluate said system by the end of 2020.

Acknowledgment

The authors thank Mr.Aoki, who is the head of the Ozasa farm, for his support in the experiment. The part of the research results was obtained from the commissioned research by the National Institute of Information and Communications Technology (NICT), JAPAN. Also, this research is supported by JSPS KAKENHI Grant Number JP17H02249 and JP18K11849.

References

[1] S. P. Washburn, W. J. Silvia, C. H. Brown, B. T. McDaniel and A. J. McAllister, "Trends in Reproductive Performance in Southeastern Holstein and Jersey DHI Herds", J. Dairy Sci. 85, 2002, pp.244–251.

[2] M. Hirako, H. Takahashi and S. Kushibiki, "Current situation of fertility decline in dairy cattle and its relation to the uterine environment - Strategies for improving the reproductive performance in high yielding dairy cows -", Journal of Japanese Society for Clinical Infectious Disease in Farm Animals, Vol.6 No.3, 2011, pp.123-130 (in Japanese)

[3] LoRa Alliance, [Online] https://lora-alliance.org/ [Retrieved: 01, 2020]

[4] "ARIB STD-T108: 920MHz-Band Telemeter, Telecontrol and Data Transmission Radio Equipment", [Online] https://www.arib.or.jp/english/std_tr/telecommunications/std-t108.html_ [Retrieved: 01, 2020]

[5] D. Tsutsumi and Y. Kita, "Motion Tracking of Cattle with a Constrained Deformable Model" Proceedings of the 16th International Conference on Pattern Recognition (ICPR'02), 2002, DOI: 10.1109/ICPR.2002.1044728

[6] S.M.C. Porto, C. Arcidiacono, A. Giummarra, U. Anguzza and G. Cascone, "Localisation and identification performances of a real-time location system based on ultra wide band technology for monitoring and tracking dairy cow behaviour in a semi-open free-stall barn", Computers and Electronics in Agriculture, Vol. 108, October 2014, pp. 221-229.

[7] C. Arcidiacono, S.M.C. Porto, M. Mancino and G. Cascone, "Development of a threshold-based classifier for real-time recognition of cow feeding and standing behavioural activities from accelerometer data", Computers and Electronics in Agriculture, Vol. 134, March 2017, pp. 124-134.

[8] Ö. Cangara et al., "Automatic real-time monitoring of locomotion and posture behaviour of pregnant cows prior to calving using online image analysis", Computers and Electronics in Agriculture, Vol. 64, Issue 1, November 2008, pp. 53-60.

[9] Q. Li, Z. Liu and J. Xiao, "A Data Collection Collar for Vital Signs of Cows on the Grassland Based on LoRa", 2018 IEEE 15th International Conference on e-Business Engineering (ICEBE), October 2018, pp. 213-217.

[10] L. Germani, V. Mecarelli, G. Baruffa, L.a Rugini and F. Frescura, "An IoT Architecture for Continuous Livestock Monitoring Using LoRa LPWAN", MDPI Electronics 2019, 8(12), 1435; https://doi.org/10.3390/electronics8121435, December 2019

[11] "Standard for IoT", [Online] http://www.3gpp.org/news-events/3gpp-news/1805-iot_r14 [Retrieved: 01, 2020]

[12] "What is the LoRaWAN Specification?", [Online] https://lora-alliance.org/about-lorawan [Retrieved: 01, 2020]

[13] "Data sheet of ES920LR", [Online] https://easel5.com/documents/ (in Japanese) [Retrieved: 01, 2020]

[14] M. Hata, "Empirical formula for propagation loss in land mobile radio services", IEEE Trans. Veh.Tech. 29(3), 1980, pp. 317-325

[15] "Culculation tool for the Okumura-Hata Midel", [Online] http://circuitdesign-jp.check-xserver.jp/wp-pre/technical/en/technicaltool/okumura-hata-curve/ (in Japanese) [Retrieved: 01 ,2020]

[16] Akira Sasaki et al., "Experiments of LoRa to Develop Services for Tourists", Computer Aided Systems Theory – EUROCAST 2019, LNCS 12014, 2020. https://doi.org/10.1007/978-3-030-45096-0_51

[17] Jinshan Luo et al., "LoRa transmission experiment for pasturing cows", IEICE Technical Report (Network Software Research Group), October 2019 (in Japanese), pp.51-56

[18] "What is society 5.0, Cabinet Office of Japan", [Online] https://www8.cao.go.jp/cstp/english/society5_0/index.html [Retrieved: 01, 2020]

Testing Existing Prototypes of Conductivity Sensors for Monitoring the Concentration of Organic Fertilizers in Fertigation Systems

Daniel A. Basterrechea, Javier Rocher, Lorena Parra, Jaime Lloret
Research Institute for Integrated Management of Coastal Areas
Universitat Politècnica de València
Gandía, Valencia, Spain
Email: dabasche@epsg.upv.es, jarocmo@doctor.upv.es, loparbo@doctor.upv.es, jlloret@dcom.upv.es

Abstract— **Agricultural production has grown in recent years, increasing the use of Organic Fertilizers (OF). For that reason, the use of these compounds must be controlled in fertigation water. In this paper, we test three prototypes, using different combinations of coils, to determine the amount of OF in the water. A coil is powered by a sine wave of 3.3 peak-to-peak Volts for inducing another coil. The objective of this system is to detect different kinds of problems that can cause incorrect fertilization, which affects the sustainability of agriculture. We present the tests to verify the proper functioning of the prototypes. We test our prototypes by means of different dilutions of OF. The used concentrations of OF are between 0 and 20 g/l. We measure the conductivity for each concentration and the output voltage of our prototypes. The results show that prototype 3 is the one that has the best performance, obtaining 1.47 V of difference between the maximum and minimum output voltage and a good correlation coefficient. Finally, a verification test is carried out; the average error in the different samples tested is 0.2212%.**

Keywords - Coils; Conductivity; Organic Fertilizers; Fertigation.

I. Introduction

The use of fertilizer, pesticides, agriculture mechanization, and high-yielding varieties of plants have generated an increase in crop productions. This increase has produced a decrease in food prices and reduced world hunger. However, the use of fertilizer, pesticides, and large agricultural machines causes essential problems in the environment, which can cause a reduction in the production of harvest in the future.

The use of an incorrect technique of fertilizing can cause severe problems in the environment. These problems include: (i) nitrification of groundwater, (ii) pollution of surface water, (iii) transport of pollutants in soils, and accumulation of fertilizer in soils [1][2]. In addition, the excess of fertilizer causes an increment in the cost of maintenance of the crops without an increment of production. Traditionally, fertilizers are used without any control. Some farmers think that if production is poor, they need to use more fertilizer. However, the correct fertilizer is not being added even at the right points. For proper fertilization of the crops, the right quantity and type of fertilizer need to be used. If there is an excess of the fertilizer, this excess is not used by plants, and it accumulates in the soil or groundwater. In addition, the fertilizer can increment the concentration of limited nutrients in the soil. If a nutrient is limited in the soil, the plants cannot absorb the fertilizer by growing. This will cause an excess of nutrients in the soil because the nutrients are not absorbed by plants [3]. The limiting nutrient can be defined as the nutrient that is bioavailable in lower concentration than is used for growing biological organisms. This causes biological organisms to not grow even if they have sufficient concentrations of other nutrients. For this reason, it is essential that fertilization does not produce huge imbalances between the limiting nutrient and the other nutrients.

We can differentiate fertilizers using different criteria, such as: (i) Simple or multi nutrient fertilizers, depending if they are composed of one or more nutrients, (ii) Organic or inorganic, and (iii) Fast or Slow release. The use of fertilizer composed of one or more nutrients depends on the needs of the soil. Generally, it is recommended to use multi nutrient fertilizers. This is due to the fact that the increase of a single nutrient ends up creating new limiting nutrients. The fast-release fertilizers generate more pollution because they escape rapidly from the area when the plants cannot absorb them. Organic fertilizers commonly have slow release and they are multi nutrient. In addition, the use of wastewater sludge and compost of urban waste allows the recovery of waste materials. Finally, the use of organic fertilizer and water-saving politics have the potential to reduce the emission of N_2O (greenhouse gas) [4].

The use of sensors in crops has grown in the last years. Different works have been developed, such as wireless sensor networks for monitoring the state of the fruit, saving water, detecting disease, etc. [5]. This new trend is called precision agriculture and involves the inclusion of monitoring technology in agriculture (sensors, image processing, etc.).

In this paper, we propose an inductive sensor to monitor the use of organic fertilizer in irrigation. The selected prototypes have been previously used to detect the illegal dumping of wastewaters [6]. The proposed sensor is based on two copper solenoid coils. One coil is powered by alternative current and induces the other coil. We expect to have a variation on the value of the induced voltage according to the changes in the concentration of the organic fertilizer. Our sensor is located in the pipes that distribute the water in drip irrigation.

The rest of the paper is structured as follows. In Section 2, we present the related works. The methodology used in the experiment is presented in Section 3. The results of the different prototypes are presented in Section 4. Finally, Section 5 shows the conclusions and future works.

II. Related Work

In this section, we show different related work, and we explain the advantages of our system.

A solution for reducing the use of fertilizer is using a smart fertilizer. Feng et al. [7] proposed a controlled/slow-release fertilizer. This fertilizer is composed of polymer brushes of poly (N, N-dimethylaminoethyl methacrylate). Usually, slow-release fertilizers have increased discharge of nutrients with temperature and pH. This smart fertilizer has a slower release. A similar solution was proposed by Boli et al. [8]. They studied the use of slow-release fertilizer formulations basis of natural attapulgite, clay, ethylcellulose, film, and sodium carboxymethylcellu-lose/ hydroxyethylcellulose hydrogel. Their study concluded that the use of this fertilizer reduces nutrient loss, improves the use efficiency of water, and prolonges irrigation cycles. However, temperature, pH, and other soil properties can affect nutrient releasing. The paper indicated that the evaluation of soil organic matter content, soil texture, residual soil N, right irrigation strategies, and cropping systems need to be developed for reducing fertilizer use.

The use of slow-release organic fertilizers is a partial solution to the contamination problem. However, the farmers still ignore the amount of fertilizer that should be contributed to the field (except based on their own experience, without following technical criteria). To improve fertilization following technical criteria, some authors propose the use of sensors. Vijayakumar and Nelson Rosario [9] used different sensors for monitoring the water and fertilizer need. They used leaf wetness, soil moisture, soil pH, and atmospheric pressure sensors connected to 2.40 Hz MICAz mote, MDA300CA. The soil moisture sensor has been used for monitoring the water needs of the crop. For tracking the fertilizer, the system sends an SMS to the farmer with the pH value and it selects the amount of fertilizer. Zhang et al. [10] used the information of sensors in the crops and big data for determining the needs of water and fertilizer. The system is composed of 4 modules. The first one is the data acquisition system, the second one is the transmission data, the third is the big data layer, and finally, the fourth is the decision layer. The data acquisition is divided into a manual and automatic collection. The automatic collection is composed of a weather, soil, and crop growth sensors system. The manual collection used information about types of plants, the period of seedling, etc. These data are sent to a database with wireless technology. In the database, they are saved for future decisions. In the decision layer, the data are processed with irrigation and growing models for making decisions and to the historical archive of the crop data.

The use of inductive sensors has been reported in numerous scientific articles. Wood et al. [11] developed a system to measure the salinity. The system is based on two sensors: a temperature sensor, i.e., conductivity sensor, and a microcontroller. The two sensors are controlled by an Automatic Voltage Regulator (AVR) microcontroller that saves the data on a flashcard and sends the data. The conductivity sensor is composed of two coils in solenoid form (a powered and an induced coil) covered with 1-dodecanethiol protection against corrosion. The temperature sensor is used to adjust the values of conductivity to salinity. The maximum measure of the sensor is 67 g/l of table salt.

In other papers, Parra et al. [12] developed a system based on two coils for monitoring the conductivity in aquifers. They studied the different design of the coils that can be summarized in (i) changes in the number of spires maintaining the spires relationship. (ii) change the relation of spires. (iii) changes in the wire diameter (iv) change in the coil diameter. They concluded that the best prototype has 80 spires in the induced coil, 40 spires in the powered coil, a copper diameter of 0.4 mm, and 25 mm of coil diameter. Rocher et al. [13] demonstrate the use of coils for monitoring fertigation in crops. They compared the induced voltage caused by table salt and nitromagnesium (a fast release fertilizer). The different prototypes are composed of two coils (powered coil and induced coil) in a solenoid form. They concluded that prototypes with a powered coil of 40 spires and 80 spires in the induced coil are the better prototypes in the two studied salts. They found differences in the induced voltage depending on the salt that causes the conductivity. However, both papers did not study the use of organic fertilizer. It has less conductivity than inorganic salts, which can modify the behavior of the coil.

In these papers, we can observe the use of sensors based on coils for monitoring the conductivity of the water. As the inorganic fertilizer is composed of mineral salts, they suppose an increase in water conductivity. However, the OF is composed of organic components that provide less conductivity than inorganic fertilizers. Therefore, it is necessary to check if it is possible to measure the concentration of OF by using coil-based sensors.

III. Test Bench

In this section, we describe the materials used in the coils as well as the methodology used.

We created the coils with a PVC pipe, 3mm of thickness, and a diameter of 25mm. Moreover, the length of the PVC tube is 10cm. The copper used is enameled copper of 0.4 mm. We selected prototypes based on 40 spires in the Powered Coil (PC) and 80 spires in the Induced Coil (IC) from the previous works [12] and [13]. The copper is located on PVC pipe distributed in 2, 4, or 8 layers. The values of turns, layer numbers, and photography of the different prototypes are shown in Table I. Also, the copper was coiled in the clockwise direction in each one of the prototypes. This helps to maintain a similar basis for all prototypes and to obtain more relevant data. We power the coil in a clockwise direction, using the other end of the coil as a ground reference with a voltage of 3.3 Vpp, and we measure the induced voltage with an oscilloscope.

We have added a resistance of 47 Ohm in series to the PC. The induced coil has a capacitor of 10 nF in parallel. The model of the signal generator is AFG1022 [14], and the oscilloscope is TBS1104 [15]. The conductivity of the samples is measured with a conductivity model Basic 30 [16]. We tested it with concentrations of 0, 2.5, 5, 7.5, 10, 12.5, 15, 17.5, 20 g/l of organic fertilizer.

TABLE I. CHARACTERISTICS OF THE PROTOTYPES.

Prototype 1 (P1)	Prototype 2 (P2)	Prototype 3 (P3)
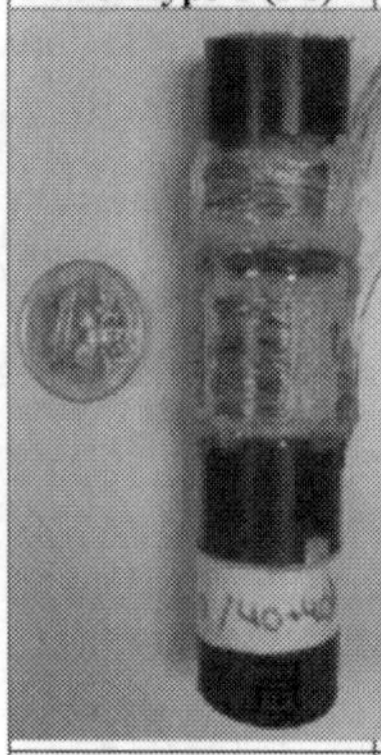	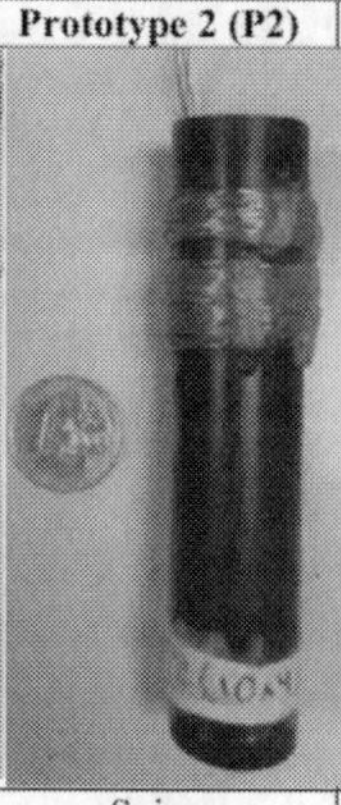	
Spire: 40 PC 80 IC Layers: 2	Spire: 40 PC 80 IC Layers: 4	Spire: 40 PC 80 IC Layers: 8

In all tests, we prepared 500 mL of the sample that was introduced in a glass. The glass has a height of 16.2 cm and 8 cm of diameter. We used 6 out of 9 samples for calibrating the sensor. The other 3 samples were used for verification of the sensor functioning. In Figure 2, we can observe the experiment being carried out.

The induced voltage measurements have been taken by varying the value of the frequency in the signal generator. They have been tested in a frequency range of 10 to 300 kHz every 10 kHz. This process has been carried out for all the samples we have mentioned above.

IV. RESULTS

In this section, we show the obtained results of the different concentrations of organic fertilizer. Firstly, we test the prototype behavior in a specific spectrum of frequency. Next, we do the calibration of the sensors to verify the best R^2 (similarity between the mathematical model and the points we are trying to predict) with the obtained data. Then, we analyze the precision and exactitude of the results. Finally, we select the best prototype.

Figure 2. Experimental setup.

A. Prototype behavior

The first step is to analyze the response of the three prototypes that we include in this test. Therefore, three samples with different concentrations of OF are used. The objective of this part of the experiment is to find the Working Frequency (WF) of the sensors to use this WF for the calibration. The WF is the frequency in which the prototype has the maximum difference in the induced voltage between the lowest and the highest concentrations of the OF.

For this test, we used three samples of 0, 5, 20 g/l, respectively. We have used a maximum concentration of 20g/l due to the fact that the level of fertilizers does not usually exceed this threshold in the irrigation of the fields. Besides, the conductivity of the samples has been measured using the EC meter model Basic 30, which is a professional conductimeter, to obtain the most exact values. The results obtained with this device are 0.37, 1.13, and 6.14 mS/cm.

The obtained results with these prototypes are shown below. Figure 3 represents the results of P1. We can see that the range, in which the Magnetic Field (MF) generated by the coil shows more significant interaction, is between 90 and 110 kHz. Even though the peak is found at 100 kHz, the maximum difference of Inductive Voltage (Vout) between the lowest and highest concentrations is obtained at 90 kHz. Next, the behavior of P2 is displayed in Figure 4. According to Figure 4, the most sensitive region of the MF is between 90 and 130 kHz, with a peak at 120 kHz. The most significant change occurs at 110 kHz. Finally, in Figure 5, we present the portion of the spectrum in which the P3 works better. This range goes between 120 and 150 kHz. The peak is located at 140 kHz, which is the working frequency.

In the case of P1 at the WF, the lowest Vout is related to the smallest conductivity and the highest output with the biggest value of conductivity. P2 shows the same behavior as P1. Besides, P3 exhibits another way to work. In this case, the lowest conductivity is related to the highest Vout in Figure 5, and the lowest Vout is for the highest conductivity.

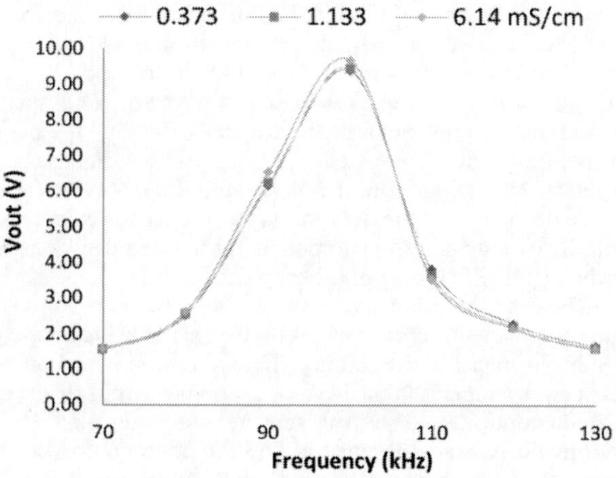

Figure 3. Representation of the frequency spectrum of P1.

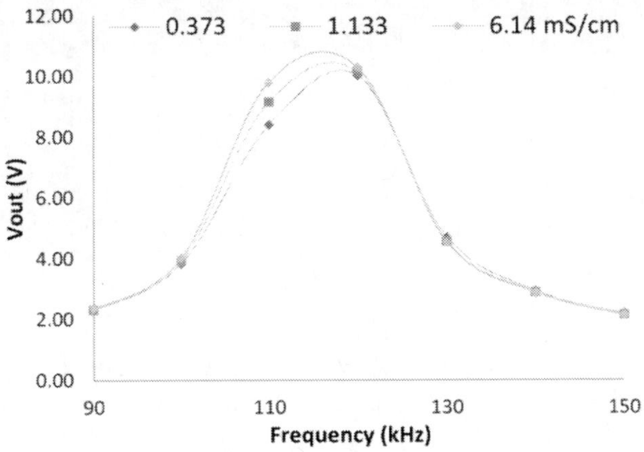

Figure 4. Representation of the frequency spectrum of P2.

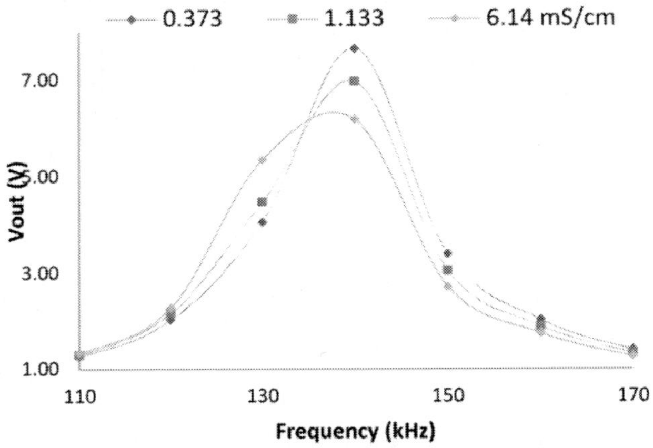

Figure 5. Representation of the frequency spectrum of P3.

All the prototypes showed a very similar range in which the generated MF and Vout are more sensitive to changes in the conductivity of the environment. Nonetheless, the way in which they respond to this change in the environment is different between them.

It will be necessary for these prototypes to perform some requirements in order to be selected as sensors:

- The Vout obtained must be as high as possible,
- The difference of Vout between the different quantities of organic fertilizer must be high (IV difference),
- The Vout for all tested dissolutions must be different, and
- The working frequency must be as low as possible (At smaller frequency cost decreases).

B. Calibration of prototypes

After scanning in a wide frequency spectrum, the results of the peaks for P1, P2, P3 have been analyzed. The highest difference of Vout between 0 and 20 g/l (IV difference) indicates the WF for each prototype, as can be seen in Table II. The three prototypes have been tested for their WF using the Statgraphics program [17]. Statgraphics is used to obtain the mathematical model for all the prototypes and observe how these adapt to the collected data. In addition, we use this program to calculate the confidence interval and the prediction interval.

The calibration of P1 is reflected in Figure 6. The best model which fits with the experimental points is the potential model. Besides, it has been realized the confidence interval and the prediction interval of the model that shows a good correlation between the *Vout* and the conductivity. Likewise, the model of P2 has been obtained. This is represented as a potential model (Figure 7). In this case, the confidence interval and the prediction interval are more separated from the model that describes the lowest correlation of the values than in the P1. Finally, the model of P3 is shown in Figure 8. The best fit model is an exponential model. In this prototype, the values of the output voltage decrease with the increase of the conductivity. The prediction interval and the confidence interval are more tithed than in the P2 ,but less than in the P1, although the correlation of the experiment point is excellent.

The *Vout* of the sensors is compared with the conductivity of the different concentrations of organic fertilizers. The mathematical models of the three kinds of prototypes are shown in (1)-(3).

TABLE II. WF AND IV DIFFERENCE IN THE PROTOTYPES.

Prototype	*Frequency(kHz)*	*IV difference*
P1	90	0.39
P2	110	1.41
P3	140	1.47

$$Vout\ (V) = \sqrt{36.1247 + 2.68502 * \sqrt{Conductivity\ \left(\frac{mS}{cm}\right)}} \quad (1)$$

$$Vout\ (V) = \sqrt{80.8549 + 9.15809 * \ln\left(Conductivity\ \left(\frac{mS}{cm}\right)\right)} \quad (2)$$

$$Vout\ (V) = e^{1.96023 - 0.0713772 * \ln\left(Conductivity\ \left(\frac{mS}{cm}\right)\right)} \quad (3)$$

The R^2 of the models are 0.9937, 0.9852, and 0.9923 for each prototype, respectively. This is a statistical parameter that indicates the adaptation of the model for each measured point.

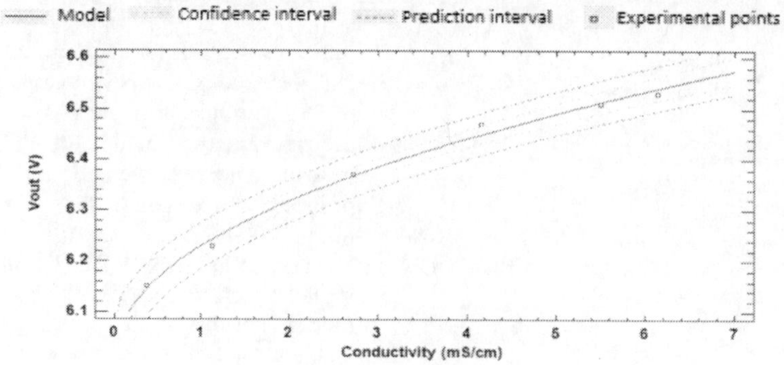

Figure 6. Tight model of P1.

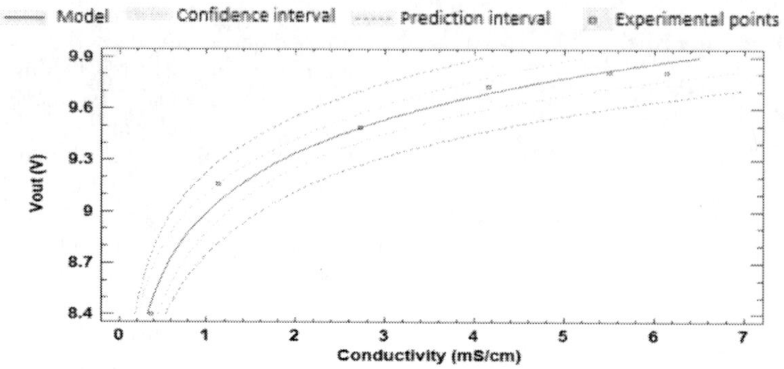

Figure 7. Tight model of P2.

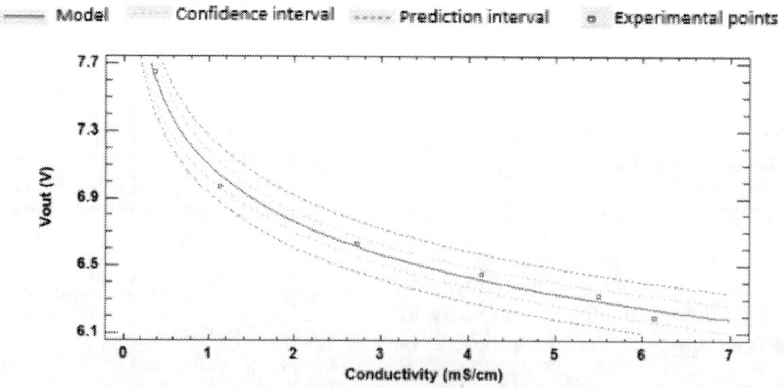

Figure 8. Tight model of P3.

C. *Accuracy of the values*

The last step is to obtain the verification of the prototypes P2 and P3. P1 has not been estimated because the difference of Vout between the lowest and highest concentration is under 1V. To obtain these results, we use the data of *Vout* and conductivity of our measurements on new samples of 5g/l, 10 g/l, and 15 g/l.

The values of Real Voltage (RV) and Model Voltage (MV) for P2 and P3 are represented in Table III. The RV is the *Vout* that was measured in the laboratory. Moreover, MV is the theoretical value according to the model of (2) for P2 and (3) for P3.

The absolute error and the relative error are calculated and represented in Table III. On the one hand, the absolute error is the difference between the Real voltage and the Model voltage. On the other hand, the relative error is the absolute value divided by the real value (in the two cases, it can be a positive or a negative value).

Our results indicated that P2 has 0.03 V of absolute error and 0.32 V of relative error. Meanwhile, P3 has 0.01 V and 0.22 V of absolute and relative error. As can be seen, the highest errors are found in P2, where the lowest error is in P3. This shows that P3 has the most significant accuracy of the values, unlike P2, which has the lowest accuracy.

V. CONCLUSION

In this paper, we presented an inductive sensor for monitoring OF in agriculture. The obtained parameters can be used to control the amount of OF that the irrigation water has.

TABLE III. ACCURACY OF THE VALUES

		P2		P3		P2		P3	
OF. (g/L)	**Conductivity (mS/cm)**	**Real (V)**	**Model (V)**	**Real (V)**	**Model (V)**	**Absolute error (V)**	**Relative error (%)**	**Absolute error (V)**	**Relative error (%)**
5.0	1.98	9.39	9.33	6.77	6.76	0.05	0.57	0.01	0.15
10.0	3.54	9.73	9.87	6.33	6.35	0.03	0.27	0.02	0.23
15.0	4.81	9.39	9.33	6.77	6.76	0.05	0.57	0.01	0.15
					AVERAGE	0.03	0.32	0.01	0.22

After we performed the measurements, we determined that the highest Vout is for P2, which shows a value of 9.81 V in the WF. P1 and P3 obtained 6.53 V and 7.65 V. Moreover, the biggest difference between 0 and 20g/l is given in P3, with 1.47V. In P1 and P2, the obtained results are 0.39 V and 1.41 V. Correspondingly, the lowest working frequency is presented in P1 in the 90 kHz, while the WF of P2 and P3 were 110 kHz and 140 kHz. Observing the absolute and relative error, the best accuracy is for P3, followed by P2.

Finally, we choose P3 as the best prototype to measure OF. Although the results of P1 are right, the difference between different concentration is very low.

In future works, we are going to study the effect of the extreme temperatures on the values of the measures. Furthermore, tests with different kinds of organic fertilizers will done.

ACKNOWLEDGMENT

This work has been partially supported by the European Union through the ERANETMED (Euromediterranean Cooperation through ERANET joint activities and beyond) project ERANETMED3-227 SMARTWATIR, by "Ministerio de Educación, Cultura y Deporte", through the "Ayudas para contratacion pre-doctoral de Formación del Profesorado Universitario FPU (Convocatoria 2016)". Grant number FPU16/05540, and by Conselleria de Educación, Cultura y Deporte with the Subvenciones para la contratación de personal investigador en fase postdoctoral, grant number APOSTD/2019/04.

REFERENCES

[1] X. T. Ju, C. L. Kou, F. S. Zhang, and P. Christie, "Nitrogen balance and groundwater nitrate contamination: comparison among three intensive cropping systems on the North China Plain," Environmental Pollution, vol. 143, no. 1, pp. 117–125, Sep. 2006.

[2] S. Savci, "An Agricultural Pollutant: Chemical Fertilizer," International Journal of Environmental Science and Development, vol. 3, no. 1, pp. 73–80, 2012.

[3] B. Q. Zhao et al., "Results from long-term fertilizer experiments in China: The risk of groundwater pollution by nitrate," NJAS - Wageningen Journal of Life Sciences, vol. 58, no. 3–4, pp. 177–183, Dec. 2011.

[4] E. Aguilera, L. Lassaletta, A. Sanz-Cobena, J. Garnier, and A. Vallejo, "The potential of organic fertilizers and water management to reduce N2O emissions in Mediterranean climate cropping systems. A review," Agriculture, Ecosystems & Environment, vol. 164, pp. 32–52, Jan. 2013.

[5] L. Parra et al., "Design of a WSN for smart irrigation in citrus plots with fault-tolerance and energy-saving algorithms," Network Protocols and Algorithms, vol. 10, no. 2, p. 95, Jun. 2018.

[6] J.Rocher, D. A. Basterrechea, M.Taha, M. Parra and J. Lloret, "Water Conductivity Sensor based on Coils to Detect Illegal Dumpings in Smart Cities," 2019 Fourth International Conference on Fog and Mobile Edge Computing (FMEC), pp. 324-329, 2019.

[7] C. Feng et al., "'Smart' Fertilizer with Temperature- and pH-Responsive Behavior via Surface-Initiated Polymerization for Controlled Release of Nutrients," ACS Sustainable Chemistry & Engineering, vol. 3, no. 12, pp. 3157–3166, Nov. 2015.

[8] B. Ni, M. Liu, S. Lü, L. Xie, and Y. Wang, "Environmentally Friendly Slow-Release Nitrogen Fertilizer," Journal of Agricultural and Food Chemistry, vol. 59, no. 18, pp. 10169–10175, Sep. 2011.

[9] S. Vijayakumar and J. Nelson Rosario, "Preliminary design for crop monitoring involving water and fertilizer conservation using wireless sensor networks," in 2011 IEEE 3rd International Conference on Communication Software and Networks (ICCSN 2011) IEEE, May, 2011, pp. 662-666, ISBN: 978-1-61284-486-2

[10] P. Zhang, Q. Zhang, F. Liu, J. Li, N. Cao, and C. Song, "The Construction of the Integration of Water and Fertilizer Smart Water Saving Irrigation System Based on Big Data," in 2017 IEEE International Conference on Computational Science and Engineering (CSE) and IEEE International Conference on Embedded and Ubiquitous Computing (EUC) IEEE, July, 2017, pp 392-397, ISBN: 978-1-5386-3221-5

[11] R. T. Wood, A. Bannazadeh, N. Q. Nguyen, and L. G. Bushnell, "A salinity sensor for long-term data collection in estuary studies," in OCEANS 2010 IEEE, Dec. 2010, ISBN: 978-1-4244-4332-1

[12] L. Parra, S. Sendra, J. Lloret, and I. Bosch, "Development of a Conductivity Sensor for Monitoring Groundwater Resources to Optimize Water Management in Smart City Environments," Sensors, vol. 15, no. 9, pp. 20990–21015, Aug. 2015.

[13] J. Rocher, D. A. Basterrechea, L. Parra, and J. Lloret, "A New Conductivity Sensor for Monitoring the Fertigation in Smart Irrigation Systems," in Advances in Intelligent Systems and Computing (ISAmI 2019), Springer, Jun. 2019, pp 136-144, ISSN: 2194-5357

[14] Tektronix. AFG1022 [Online]. Available from: https://www.tek.com/signal-generator/afg1022. 2019.11.30

[15] Tektronix. TBS1104 [Online]. Available from: https://www.tek.com/oscilloscope/tbs1104. 2019.11.30

[16] Crison. EC-Metro BASIC 30 [Online]. Available from: http://www.crisoninstruments.com/es/laboratorio/conductimetro/de-sobremesa/ec-metro-basic-30. 2019.11.30

[17] Statgraphics. Statgraphics Centurion [Online]. Available from: https://statgraphics.net/descargas-centurion-xvii/. 2019.11.30

Portable E-nose for Diagnostic of Inflammation and Diverse Variation in Health Status of Humans and Animals

Anastasiia Shuba
Physical and Analytical Chemistry Department
Voronezh State University of Engineering Technologies
Voronezh, Russia
e-mail: shuba1nastya@gmail.com

Ruslan Umarkhanov
Physical and Analytical Chemistry Department
Voronezh State University of Engineering Technologies
Voronezh, Russia
e-mail: rus_270487@mail.ru

Tatiana Kuchmenko
Physical and Analytical Chemistry Department
Voronezh State University of Engineering Technologies
Voronezh, Russia
e-mail: tak1907@mail.ru

Anton Chernitskiy
Research Center for Clinical Pharmacology and Therapy, Quality and Safety of Raw Materials and Products
All-Russian Scientific Research Veterinary Institute of Pathology, Pharmacology and Therapy
Voronezh, Russia
e-mail: cherae@mail.ru

***Abstract*—This paper discusses an application of a portable electronic nose based on an array consisting of 8 piezoelectric sensors with nanostructured solid-state coatings to detect volatile biomolecules secreted by nasal mucus and skin. A fundamentally new approach is proposed for a quick assessment of the status of the human body as a whole (normal, stress, inflammation) and the work of individual systems (reproductive, endocrine, digestive), based on the results of the assessment of the qualitative and quantitative composition of the gas mixture of biomolecules secreted by the skin in the Zakharyin-Ged zone. An algorithm is proposed for reading and visualizing signals from an array of sensors understandable to any user. Also, a portable electronic nose was applied in the veterinary field for assessment of the health status of calves' respiratory system. Unlike the traditional approach in diagnostics using sensor array, one sample of nasal mucus was monitored for 5-9 hours with an interval of 2-3 hours. The integral analytical signal of sensors, in that case, was connected to the microbiological contamination of the sample or its absence. The speed and simplicity of measurement using an electronic nose with nanostructured piezoelectric sensors allow painlessly scanning the body for metabolic disturbances and estimating the presence of certain pathologies as well as the effectiveness of treatment.**

Keywords- sensor; electronic nose; method; volatile compounds; skin; metabolism; respiratory disease; calf; non-invasive diagnostic; screening.

I. Introduction

Biosamples are complex objects to analyze. The problem of their study consists not only in the absence of a constant composition, but also in its almost instantaneous change when substances are excreted from the sample. Despite the emergence in recent years of new methods for the analysis and study of biostructures at the level of individual cells, the scheme still remains traditional: selection of biomaterial, sample preparation and detection of target components. The use of highly selective and effective methods of analysis (gas chromatography-mass spectrometry, high-pressure liquid chromatography, etc.) suggests a special sample preparation, which can change the natural profile of the biosamples. The method of sample preparation is determined by the purpose of the analysis, but the integrity of the biological object is lost. Also, the results obtained by advanced analysis methods do not reflect the complex structure and behavior of a biological object. Therefore, recently, in the analysis of complex living objects (food, environmental objects, human and animal biosamples), complex methods with a multivariate analytical signal have been used more often. Such methods, by their methodology, include systems of artificial tongues, noses, eyes [1]. The undoubted advantage of highly sensitive sensor systems with the rapid response is the ability to monitor the state of small volumes and masses of biological samples in a fairly short time (from 2 to 9 hours). Given the lack of their contact with the environment (in vitro), primarily with oxygen, small volumes of biosamples, which means fast processes of changing their properties, open up a unique opportunity to obtain information about the status of the studied object, even if the specific methods for determining individual substances or laboratory indicators (primarily microbiological) are unavailable.

A possible approach for assessing the status of the body in the absence of biomaterial selection is to analyze the chemical composition of the gas, sweat of the skin in the zones of Zakharyin-Ged. Earlier, the presence of redness, peeling, rash, temperature changes in these areas was widely used as an additional parameter to confirm the malfunction of organs corresponding to these zones. The detection limits of modern methods of analysis, the complexity of the instrumentation of the most sensitive methods do not allow non-invasive scanning and determining the chemical composition of the gas phase of secretions from the skin. Therefore, the creation of an integrated system for scanning a volatile metabolome [10] using a device with a sensitive detection from biomolecules of normal and disordered metabolism, inflammation, to microbial metabolites is actual for now.

There are some state-of-the-art approaches, including portable devices, for assessing the state of the body using electronic noses and various data processing methods: for exhaled breath air [2][4], for the analysis of biomaterials (blood, urine, secrets of the endocrine glands, etc.) [5][7]. Different approaches for assessment of health status by skin based on using electrochemical or optical methods are proposed in [8][9]. The authors did not find in the literature similar hardware solutions about the development of an electronic nose for diagnosing human health by volatile metabolites secreted by the skin.

The purpose of this paper is the development and application of a new mobile device based on piezoelectric sensors (portable electronic nose) for assessing the health status of organs and systems of humans and animals by analyzing the volatile metabolome.

We will demonstrate our approach in two ways: 1) analysis of nasal mucus samples of calves for the diagnosis of respiratory diseases and 2) characterizing of the health status of humans by skin odor in the Zakharyin-Ged zones.

In Section 2, the features of the experiment, description of biosamples and methods of analysis are presented. Section 3 contains technical characteristics of the proposed device, characteristics of the used sensors and their coatings, and a description of the procedure for obtaining and recording of output data of the sensor array. In Section 4, we show the results of the application of the proposed portable electronic nose (e-nose) for solving diagnostic problems according to the purpose of the work. Section 5 is devoted to conclusions and perspective of development.

II. Materials and Methods

A. *Diagnosis of Respiratory Diseases in Calves*

17 samples of nasal mucus from calves (10-20 days of life) both with signs of respiratory system damage and conditionally healthy were analyzed. A sampling of nasal mucus was carried out with sterile cotton swabs in individual sterile containers. The time from sampling to analyzing on e-nose was taken into account.

All calves were clinically studied in detail using a point system (WI score) developed at the University of Wisconsin-Madison (USA) [11] with mandatory laboratory control at the All-Russian Scientific Research Veterinary Institute of Pathology, Pharmacology and Therapy: bacteriological and molecular genetic (PCR) studies of nasal swabs for infectious rhinotracheitis, parainfluenza-3, viral diarrhea-disease cattle mucous membranes, rotavirus, adenovirus, chlamydia, pathogenic mycoplasmas (*M. bovis, M. bovirhinis*), hematological indicators of inflammation in the blood (leukogram, haptoglobin concentration) were determined.

For the isolation of cultures and typing of microorganisms, meat and peptone broth and agar, milk salt, enterococcal agar, Endo medium, blood agar, glucose-serum broth and agar produced by NICF (St. Petersburg, Russia) were used. The isolated Escherichia coli were typed in an agglutination reaction using O-serums.

B. *Characterizing the Some Deviation from Normal Status by Human Skin Odor*

The area of the forearm of human skin was chosen to analyze the volatile metabolome by a portable electronic nose. Over 100 conditionally healthy volunteers took part in the investigation duration for 2 years. The volunteers periodically were clinically (visits to physicians) and laboratory (general analysis of blood, urine, biochemical analysis of blood (glucose, cholesterol, some hormones)) tested to control health status. For conditionally healthy volunteers, the results of laboratory tests corresponded to the norm, and the symptoms did not match with clinically significant for illness. Clinically not diagnosed conditions, so-called descriptive states (tiredness, excitement, agitation, stress, lack of sleep, spasm, pain), were recorded from the words of the volunteers.

III. Description of Portable E-nose and Measurement Technique

A. *Making of Piezoelectric Sensors*

We used piezoelectric quartz resonators (PQR) with a natural frequency of 14 MHz with an established linear response with a film mass on its electrodes up to 20 μg/cm^2. The array contained 8 piezoelectric sensors with electrodes covered by films of carbon nanomaterial, biohydroxyapatite, zirconium salts of different mass (1-5 μg) (NANO-BIO array).

1) *Characteristics of the Used Sorbents*

Hydroxyapatite $Ca_5(PO_4)_3OH$ was obtained by the sol-gel method developed at Nizhny Novgorod State University named after N.I. Lobachevsky and optimized by us to obtain nanostructured coatings with good sorption properties.

The reaction was carried out according to the following equation:

$5Ca(NO_3)_2\cdot 4H_2O + 3H_3PO_4 + 10NaOH \rightarrow Ca_5(PO_4)_3OH + 10NaNO_3 + 29H_2O$

To a solution of calcium nitrate (2 mol/dm^3) prepared from $Ca(NO_3)_2 4H_2O$ in bidistilled water has added a solution of H_3PO_4 in the amount necessary to maintain the ratio Ca/P = 5/3. The resulting solution was thermostated for one hour at 37 °C, then its pH was adjusted to 7-8 using a NaOH solution with a concentration of 2 mol/dm^3. At pH = 4, a $Ca_5(PO_4)_3OH$ sol began to form. The reaction mixture was kept at this temperature for 1 hour. Then, the resulting gel was centrifuged and dried in air. The obtained sorbent can be stored for at least 0.5 years in airtight conditions. Multi-walled carbon nanotubes were obtained by gas-phase chemical deposition during ethanol pyrolysis. Nickel was used as a catalyst; the temperature of deposition was 450-500 °C. Then nanotubes were washed with HNO_3 concentrated (Institute for Extra Pure Materials of the Russian Academy of Sciences, Chernogolovka). The solvent for the suspension of hydroxyapatite and carbon nanotubes was chloroform. Zirconium nitrate ($ZrO(NO_3)_2 \cdot 2H_2O$), (chemically pure) was obtained from aqueous solutions containing zirconium and nitrate ions (Reachem, Russia). The solvent for the suspension of zirconium nitrate was acetone. These sorbents are selective and sensitive to volatile metabolites of bacteria and inflammation according to the results of a preliminary experiment [12].

2) The Method of Forming Films on the Surface of the Piezoelectric Quartz Resonator

To change and control the sensitivity and selectivity of micro-weighing of vapors of organic substances, thin films were uniformly deposited to the electrodes of piezoelectric quartz resonators, fat-free with acetone or chloroform, by immersion in solutions of sorbents suspended by ultrasound.

The hydroxyapatite, as well as carbon nanotubes and zirconium nitrate, formed the sensors using the following procedure:

Step 1 – the measurement of the initial oscillation frequency of the piezoelectric resonator (10 or 14 MHz) *F0*, Hz with an accurate record, for example, 9999280 Hz;

Step 2 – suspension was prepared in the beaker as dissolution of sorbent (0.5 g) in 10 ml of solvent;

Step 3 – processing in an ultrasonic bath for 15 minutes at a power of 90 W;

Step 4 – exposure of the quartz piezoelectric resonator in suspension for 15 s;

Step 5 – drying the coating in an oven (40 minutes at a temperature from 50 ° C) in the holder vertically;

Step 6 – the measurement of the oscillation frequency of the sensor, calculation of the coating mass (Δm) according to the Sauerbrey equation [13]:

$$\Delta m = \frac{\Delta F \cdot 0.2}{2.27 \cdot 10^{-6} \cdot F_0^2} \quad (1)$$

where ΔF is the change in the oscillation frequency of the quartz plate of the resonator after film deposition and removal of an unbound solvent, MHz;

$2.27 \cdot 10^{-6}$ – calibration constant of piezoelectric quartz resonator at normal condition, cm^2/g;

F_0 — base oscillation frequency of the PQR, MHz;

0.2 – the area of electrodes of PQR, cm^2.

B. Characteristic of Portable E-nose

The portable device for diagnosing the status of humans and animals is a miniature case, consisting of two functional parts (Figure 1): head 1 and the protective part of the body 6, a microprocessor 2 with terminals for sensor mount sockets, a block for fixing and transmitting information 3 to the recording device of any type (laptop, tablet, PC); the sockets are located in the cover 4, into which removable sensors 5 are mounted on the outside, separated from the environment by the protective part of the body 6, which is tightly attached to the head 1. Optionally e-nose is supplemented by an internal gas-permeable gasket 7, which separates the sensor region and the free air region of the body 6.

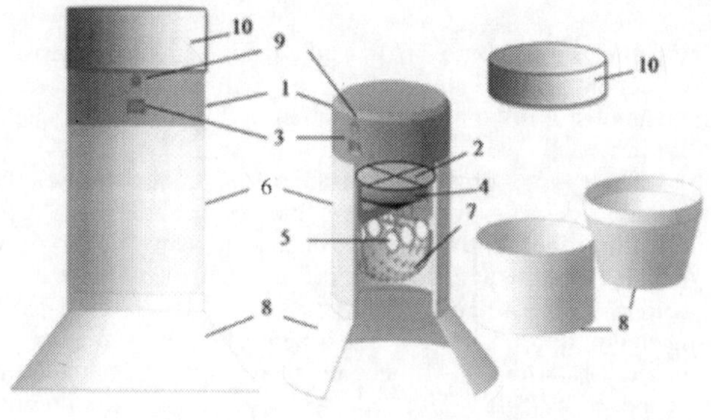

Figure 1. General view of the 3D model of the portable e-nose for diagnostics: 1 – head; 2 – microprocessor with terminals for sensor mount sockets; 3 – block recording and transmitting information to a recording device of any type; 4 – cover; 5 – removable sensors; 6 – protective part of the body; 7 – internal gas-permeable gasket; 8 – nozzles; 9 – power supply from the electricity; 10 – removable battery.

To reduce interfering factors (external fluctuation in airflow, temperature, air composition in the near-sensor space), protective nozzles of various types 8 from inert materials (fluoroplastic) are used in accordance with the nature of the analyzed sample. The e-nose is powered by either an electronic device, with which is combined via a USB cable, either from electricity 9 or a removable battery 10.

The developed portable device is an electronically counting frequency meter with 8 channels for measuring the oscillation frequency of BAW-type piezoelectric quartz resonators with a base oscillation frequency of 5 to 20 MHz with a resolution of 1 Hz and a time interval (step) of 1 second. The electronic counting frequency meter is switched on in the network (220 V); it warms up for 10-15 minutes. In this case, to reduce measurement errors, the sensors should be in the device. But their subsequent inclusion is also possible. It takes about 5-10 minutes to stabilize the baseline of the oscillation frequency of the quartz plate.

To simultaneously record (read) the oscillation frequency of each sensor independently of each other every second for a certain time interval (from 1 s to a maximum of 6000 s), the device is connected to a computer via USB cable, and other connection options are possible (via Wi-Fi, Bluetooth).

Operating conditions and technical specifications of E-nose:

- Ambient temperature from +15 to +35 ° C.
- Increased humidity up to 98% at temperatures up to 308 K (+35 °C).
- The device is powered by an alternating current with a voltage of 220 ± 22 V and a frequency of 50 ± 0.5 Hz.
- Frequency range 4 MHz – 20 MHz.
- Reference frequency oscillator is 4 MHz.
- Overall dimensions – 38x120x170 mm.
- Weight with a cover – 0.40 kg.

C. *Specification of Software*

The responses are recorded in the instrument software, which not only saves the current measurement but also converts it into analytical information a change in the oscillation frequency of each resonator individually without load or with load at each measurement moment relative to the starting point of measurement ($-\Delta F$, Hz). The full output curve is displayed in the form of a set of chronograms for all resonators installed in the e-nose (Figure 2). During the interaction of vapors with the surface of the piezoelectric sensors, sorption occurs on the films or electrodes, as a result of which the frequency changes. Individual colors reflect a change in time of the base oscillation frequency of each of the 8 piezoelectric sensors (Figure 2). In the developed software based on chronograms, the "visual print" is constructed using different algorithms depending on the purpose of analysis. The quantitative characteristic of "visual prints", therefore, the total amount of volatile substances excreted by samples and sorbed by piezoelectric sensors, is the area of "visual print" (*S*v.p., Hz's). The area of "visual print" is calculated in software as a sum of definite integrals of time dependence the signals of sensors during measurement (chronograms).

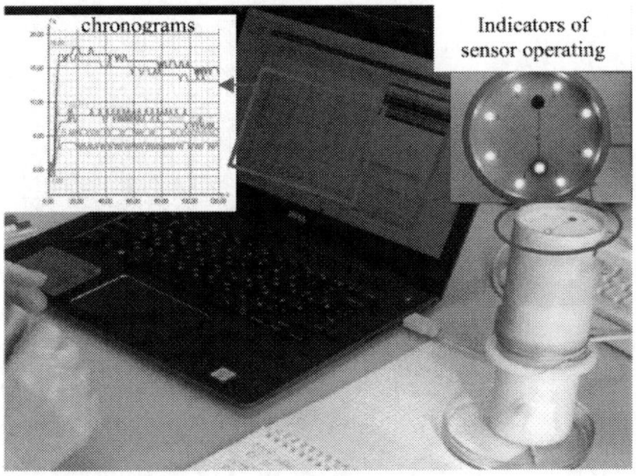

Figure 2. E-nose connected with the laptop when measuring the sample of nasal mucus.

Additionally, in software, the parameters of sorption (A(i/j)) are calculated, which can be used for the identification of volatile substances in the gas phase over samples [14] or to describe additional analytical information about sample characteristics.

D. *Technique of Measurement*

The gas phases over nasal mucus samples were studied with the front input method into the detection cell. For analyzing the volatile substances excreted by the skin on the forearm area (20 cm^2) the open detection cell of device contacted with this area. The registration time of the sorption of volatile substances excreted by the skin and nasal mucus was 80 s, the registration of desorption was 120 s. Thus, the full time of one measurement was 200 s.

IV. RESULTS AND DISCUSSION

A. *Diagnosis of Respiratory Diseases in Calves*

Based on the results of clinical studies, the determination of hematological and biochemical markers of inflammation (leukocytosis, an increase in the concentration of haptoglobin in the blood serum), pathogens of viral and bacterial infections accompanied by damage to the respiratory system of calves, we selected three groups: "healthy respiratory system" (n=4), "with the subclinical course of respiratory diseases" (n=8), "early signs of respiratory disease" (n=5).

A natural change in the composition of the mucus taken at a weekly interval can reflect only significant changes in the condition - for example, a vivid manifestation of the inflammatory process. Unlike state-of-the-art approaches to the diagnosis of respiratory diseases by one measurement of biosamples [5-7], for the first time, it has been proposed monitoring one sample for 5-9 hours with an interval of 2-3 hours. It allows recording changes in the state at the micro-level associated with microbiological contamination of the sample or its absence. The areas of "visual prints" were calculated for all samples of nasal mucus. Early it was shown that the values of the area of "visual prints" correlate with biochemical indicators of inflammation characterizing the disease of respiratory organs in calves [15].

All results of one-day monitoring of nasal mucus biosamples can be divided into three groups (Figure 3).

1) Positive (increasing) dynamics of changes in the value of the integral analytical signal of the sensor array (area of "visual print") - indicates the destruction of nasal mucus and production of a large number of volatile compounds including microorganisms metabolites.

2) The negative (decreasing) dynamics of the change in the value of the analytical signal of the sensor array indicates the decreasing of volatile substances excreted from nasal mucus due to increasing of its viscosity by the high level of proteins, mucin, which is observed in the acute phase of respiratory disease [16].

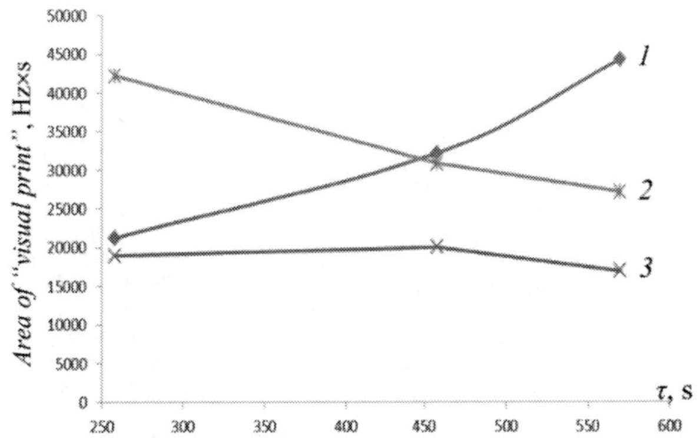

Figure 3. Total "visual prints" area of signals of the sensor array in vapors of nasal mucus of calves with different diagnoses: 1 –healthy respiratory system, 2- early signs of respiratory disease, 3 - with the subclinical course of respiratory disease.

3) The almost constant value of the integral signal from the array of sensors, which is observed at the first sign of respiratory disease (subclinical course), indicates that the excretion of substances at the destruction of nasal mucus and the production of metabolites by microorganisms are not so active. If one takes another sample of nasal mucus from an animal with the subclinical course of the respiratory disease within 5 minutes after the first selection, then the time dependence of area of "visual print" for this sample will be like for conditionally healthy (curve 1, Figure 3). It is in good agreement with the data on the formation of local protection of the respiratory tract of calves [16]. Thus, several measurements of one biosample during the day allow easy clarifying the diagnosis without multivariate analysis of sensor signals unlike modern approaches [3][5].

B. Characterizing the Some Deviation from Normal Health Status by Human Skin Odor

A forearm zone of skin was chosen for scanning the health status of the whole organism according to information about the diagnostic significance of the Zakharyin-Ged zone.

The primary database contained the responses of 8 sensors in 200 seconds of measurement (1590-1600 signals). Based on the analysis of the skin odor of 100 volunteers in various states according to their words and the results of laboratory tests, a primary algorithm of "visual print" construction has been developed for linking the features of the forms of "visual prints" with the human condition and possible causes of deviation (Table 1, Figure 4). The proposed algorithm is different from the traditional approach to visualize the sensor signals, used in the state-of-the-art methods [3]. Moreover, such visualization is simpler and clearer for the user.

TABLE I. ALGORITHM FOR CONSTRUCTING "VISUAL PRINTS" OF SIGNALS FROM AN ARRAY OF 8 SENSORS FOR ASSESSING THE HEALTH STATUS OF PEOPLE

Name of an algorithm of "visual print" construction (characteristic)	**Time of recording the sensor responses, s / number of sensors used to build a "visual print"**
"General state" (the most complete information about reproductive, digestive systems)	30, 45, 60, 80, 100, 120, 180 / 8
"Energy" (reflects the strength and intensity of the metabolome part, which shows the ability of the body to act)	110, 120, 130, 140, 150 / 3
"Endocrine system" (reflects malfunctions of the endocrine glands, primarily the pancreas)	10 20 30 60 / 4 Additionally, the parameter is calculated: $\gamma = \Delta F_4(60\ s)/\Delta F_4(20\ s)$. At $\gamma \leq 2$ pathology occurs
"Negative" (the severity of destructive processes in the body)	20, 30, 170, 180 / 8 Additionally, parameters are calculated: $\beta_1 = \Delta F_4(20\ s)/\Delta F_4(170\ s)$. $= \Delta F_4(30\ s)/\Delta F_4(180\ s)$. At β_1, $\beta_2 \leq 2.5$ pathology occurs

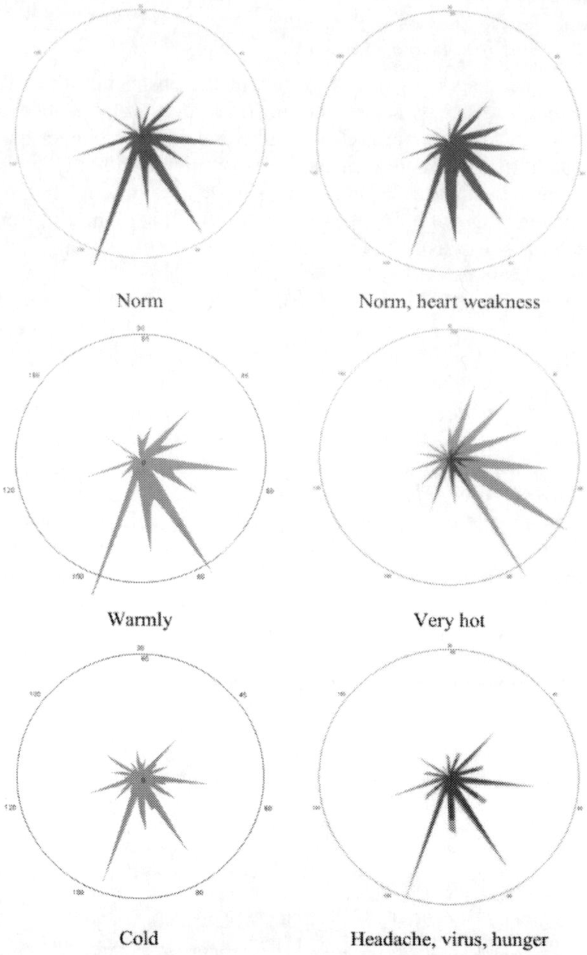

Figure 4. Statistically significant typical changes in the shape of the integral signals of the sensor array of the portable e-nose for different conditions of one person (for left forearm – the blue color and for right – red color).

Figure 4 shows the comparison of "visual prints" forms for left and right hands, which used for visual assessment of descriptive states. As a result, statistically reliable responses and smell trace forms were determined, what correspond to the physically normal functioning of the body (norm), stress, tiredness, inflammation, headache, and weakness, in total no less than 17 states (some of them are shown in Figure 4). This is more than in other research [4][5]. Besides, reference limits for the degree of its severity have been established for each state, for example, the low level of tiredness, the middle level of tiredness, the high level of tiredness and the critical level of tiredness. It is established that the geometric shape of the "visual print" is strictly individual for each person and the calculated parameters (A(i/j)) – for health status (Figure 4, Table 2). The shape of "visual print" is influenced to a greater extent by the health of the body, by the psycho-emotional state during measurement, by gender, and to a lesser extent by age. If we normalize for one person the average quantitative parameter of the smell trace (area of "visual print") according to the results of not less than 500 measurements in different periods for 2 years, then the general nature of the displacement of this indicator will obey the laws presented in Table 3.

TABLE II. THE VALUE OF SOME PARAMETERS OF SORPTION A(I/J) IN VARIOUS STATES

Parameter A(i/j)	**The numerical range of parameter values**			
	Norm	***Description of the deviation state***		
Sector color	green	yellow	red	burgundy
A(1/5)	< 0.75	0.75-0.94 Stress, body weakness	> 0.90 Hormone imbalance	> 0.81 Stress, weakness, severe inflammation
A(1/7)	≤ 1.90	> 1.9	> 2.3 Adrenaline, severe stress	-
A(1/2)	> 1.15	0.90 – 1.14 Inflammation, very hot	< 0.9 Alcohol, Ketones	-
A(2/4)	≤ 0.1	-	0.25-0.30 Ketones, sugar is above normal, hormones are very unbalanced	0.16-0.24 Weakness, exhaustion

TABLE III. THE MOST TYPICAL EXAMPLES OF CHANGES IN THE AREA OF THE "VISUAL PRINTS" WITH SOME CHANGES IN HEALTH STATUS

Person's state	**The trend of changing and the relative difference in the parameter $S_{v.p.}$,%**
Norm	Differences between the left and right hands - 5-10%, for the left more than for the right
Norm, after eat	11-30% more for the right hand than for the left one
Norm, easy hunger	For the right hand less than for the left one by 11-25%
Norm, severe hunger	If the gallbladder is malfunctioning, a response increase of 15-20% for the right hand is observed due to the excreted of propandial
Cold, temperature for a long time 15-20°C	20% (before meals) – 10% (after meals), the shape of "visual prints" changes
Headache, toothache, other pain, spasm	10-35%, the shape of "visual prints" changes
Increase the air temperature up to 26-30°C	10-30%, at perspiration till 500%
Virus, malaise without fever	Decrease on the right hand to 38-40%
Menstruation	An increase in the side of the working ovary by 15-25%.
Fatigue, heart failure	The left side is smaller than the right in normal to 12-20%, the shape of "visual prints" changes
Bronchitis, inflammation	The difference between left and right Zakharyin-Ged zone of bronchi for acute bronchitis - 40 %, recovery – up to 15 %, healthy lung and bronchi – up to 5 %

The electronic nose was trained by 45 individual substances of normal and pathogenic metabolism: C1-C5 alcohols, ketones, C5-C7 cyclic ketones, aldehydes, N-, S-containing aldehydes, C1-C5 carboxylic acids; primary, tertiary, cyclic amines, O-containing amines. Therefore, it is possible to evaluate the appearance of these substances in the descriptive states (Table 2). Thereby, using portable e-nose for scanning volatilome secreted by the skin allows determining the diverse variation in health status, including the descriptive states, the presence of 45 individual volatile substances at ppm-ppb level [14] in comparison with state-of-the-art methods [4][5][8][9].

For the convenience of deciding the health status of the organism, the state sphere is constructed using parameters A(i/j) (Figure 5), while the color of the sector corresponding to a certain parameter, which is determined by its numerical value in Table 2.

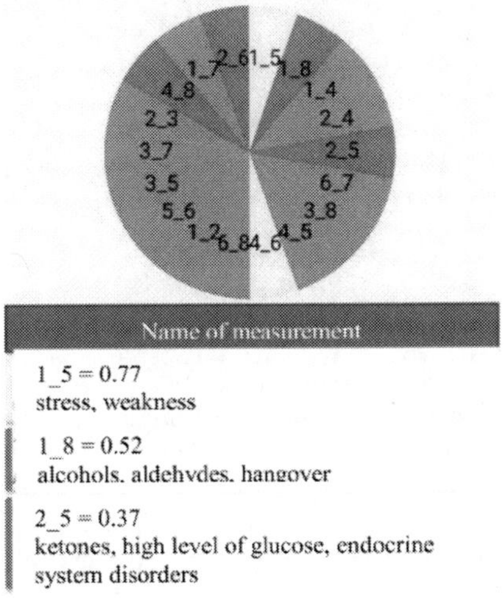

Figure 5. Example of the sphere for human health status on parameter A(i/j) in the dialogue window of the software.

The greener the sectors in the health status sphere, the closer it is to normal. For instance, in Figure 5 the value of parameter A(2/6) is in the red zone accordingly to the results of clinical and laboratory tests which are confirmed as an inflammatory process in the digestive and respiratory tracts. Thus, according to the parameters of sensor signals, one can easily and quickly obtain extended information about the work of both individual organs and the deviation of the health status from the average norm.

V. CONCLUSION AND FUTURE WORK

According to the responses of the electronic nose, when monitoring biosamples of nasal mucus from 17 calves during 5-9 hours, with an interval of 2-3 hours, it is possible to assess changes in the qualitative composition of biosamples gas phase in an atraumatic way, in place.

For the first time, a fundamentally new approach is proposed for a quick assessment of the health status of the human body as a whole (normal, stress, inflammation) and the work of individual systems (reproductive, endocrine, digestive), based on the results of an integrated assessment of the qualitative and quantitative composition of the gas mixture of biomolecules secreted by the skin in the Zakharyin-Ged zone.

The correct interpretation and prediction of the status of biosamples and a person's state have been proved by traditional diagnostic and analysis methods (leukogram, biochemical, microbiological, molecular genetic analysis). An algorithm is proposed for reading and visualizing signals from an array of sensors understandable to any user. More information about data processing for e-nose implementation will be in this paper [17].

The time of one analysis of volatile substances excreted by the biosamples or skin using portable e-nose, including visualization and processing, is up to 5 min, which is faster than that described in works [2][5] and without any sample preparation unlike other modern research works [2][7][8].

We believe that the approach proposed in this work for the analysis by sensor array is appropriate for other biosamples, such as blood, cervical mucus, exhaled breath condensate, and urine.

ACKNOWLEDGMENT

This work was financially supported by Russian Scientific Found (grant number 18-76-10015).

REFERENCES

[1] A. D. Wilson and M. Baietto, "Advances in Electronic-Nose Technologies Developed for Biomedical Applications", Sensors, vol. 11, pp. 1105-1176, Jan. 2011, doi: 10.3390/s110101105.

[2] A. T. Güntner, S. Abegg, K. Königstein, P. A. Gerber, A. Schmidt-Trucksäss and S. E. Pratsinis, "Breath Sensors for Health Monitoring", ACS Sens., pp. 268-280, Jan. 2019, doi: 10.1021/acssensors.8b00937.

[3] M. Yakob, D. Mustika, R. I. Nila and R. A. Putra, "Design of E-nose as an Instrument Identification of Diseases Through the Respiratory Tract", Journal of Physics: Conference Series (The 4th International Conf. on Applied Physics and Materials Application), IOP Publ., Feb. 2020, vol. 1428, 012062, doi:10.1088/1742-6596/1428/1/012062.

[4] E. Kabir, N. Raza, V. Kumar, J. Singh, Y. F. Tsang, D. K. Lim, J. E. Szulejko and Ki-H. Kim, "Recent Advances in Nanomaterial-Based Human Breath Analytical Technology for Clinical Diagnosis and the Way Forward", Chem, vol. 12, pp. 3020-3057, Dec. 2019, doi:10.1016/j.chempr.2019.08.004

[5] Y. Y. Broza, Xi Zhou, M. Yuan, D. Qu, Y. Zheng, R. Vishinkin, M. Khatib, W. Wu and H. Haick, "Disease Detection with Molecular Biomarkers: From Chemistry of Body Fluids to Nature-Inspired Chemical Sensors", Chem. Rev., vol. 119, pp. 11761-11817, Nov. 2019, doi:10.1021/acs.chemrev.9b00437.

[6] T. A. Kuchmenko, A. A. Shuba, V. V. Bityukova and N. A. Matveeva, "Application of a Chemical Sensor Array to Assessing the Presence of Neoplasms by Blood Smell", Journal of Analytical Chemistry, vol. 73, pp. 91-101, Jan. 2018, doi: 10.1134/S1061934817110053.

[7] Q. Gao and W.-Y. Lee, "Urinary Metabolites for Urological Cancer Detection: a Review on the Application of Volatile Organic Compounds for Cancers", Am J Clin Exp Urol, vol. 7, pp. 232–248, Aug. 2019; ISSN:2330-1910/AJCEU0101247.

[8] G. E. Bergdahl, T. Andersson, M. Allhorn, S. Yngman, R. Timm and R. Lood, "In Vivo Detection and Absolute Quantification of a Secreted Bacterial Factor from Skin Using Molecularly Imprinted Polymers in a Surface Plasmon Resonance Biosensor for Improved Diagnostic Abilities", ACS Sens., vol. 4, pp. 717-725, Mar. 2019, doi:10.1021/acssensors.8b01642.

[9] S. Zhang, S. Li, Z. Xia and K. Cai, "A Review of Electronic Skin: Soft Electronics and Sensors for Human Health", J. Mater. Chem. B, vol. 8, pp. 852-862, Dec. 2019, doi:10.1039/C9TB02531F.

[10] A. Amann and D. Smith "Volatile Biomarkers. Non-invasive Diagnosis in Physiology and Medicine", Amsterdam: Elsevier, 2013. p. 568.

[11] S. M. McGuirk "Disease Management of Dairy Calves and Heifers", Veterinary Clinics of North America: Food Animal Practice, vol. 24, pp. 139-153, April 2008, doi: 10.1016/j.cvfa.2007.10.003.

[12] T. A. Kuchmenko and L. B. Lvova "A Perspective on Recent Advances in Piezoelectric Chemical Sensors for Environmental Monitoring and Foodstuffs Analysis", Chemosensors, vol. 7, pp. 39-45, Aug. 2019, doi: 10.3390/chemosensors7030039.

[13] G. Sayerbrey "Messung Von Plattenschwingungen Sehr Kleiner Amplitude Durch Lichtstrommodulation", Zeitschrift Fuer Physik, vol. 178, pp. 457-471, 1964.

[14] T. A. Kuchmenko and A. A. Shuba, "Informative Nature of the Electronic Nose Output Signals Based on the Piezoelectric Sensors", Analitika i kontrol' [Analytics and Control], vol. 21, pp. 72-84, June 2017, doi: 10.15826/analitika.2017.21.2.001 (in Russian).

[15] T. A. Kuchmenko, A. A. Shuba, R. U. Umarkhanov and A. E. Chernitskii "Electronic Nose Signals Correlation Evaluation for Nasal Mucus and Exhaled Breath Condensate of Calves with the Clinical and Laboratory Indicators", Analitika i kontrol' [Analytics and Control], vol. 23, pp. 557-562, Dec. 2019, doi: 10.15826/analitika.2019.23.4.014 (in Russian).

[16] Yu. Alekhin, M. Zhukov, V. Morgunova, G. Chusova and I. Klement'eva "Formation of Local Protection of the Respiratory Tract in Holstein Calves", Turk. J. Vet. Anim. Sci., pp. 656-661, Oct. 2019, doi:10.3906/vet-1903-73.

[17] T. Kuchmenko, I. Murakhovskiy, R. Umarkhanov and D. Kuchmenko, "Development of a Program for Analytical Systems of Personal Diagnostics of People and Animals on the Basis of Array of Piezosensors", Proc. of Conf. "The Twelfth International Conference on eHealth, Telemedicine, and Social Medicine", IARIA Publ., Mar. 2020, in press.

Detection and Classification of Obstacles Using a 2D LiDAR Sensor

Alejandro Olivas González

Group of Automation, Robotics
and Computer Vision (AUROVA)
University of Alicante
Alicante, Spain
Email: alejandro.olivas@ua.es

Fernando Torres Medina

Group of Automation, Robotics
and Computer Vision (AUROVA)
University of Alicante
Alicante, Spain
Email: fernando.torres@ua.es

***Abstract*—Detecting and mapping obstacles is an important component in mobile robots. In this paper, we use only an economic 2D Light Detection and Ranging (LiDAR) sensor to make a 3D map of the scene, classifying the scanned data into ground, obstacles and potholes. To do this, the points from the LiDAR are clustered in segments, and then they are classified depending of their height. The method successfully classifies in low dynamic structured environments, and generates compact 3D map that represents the scene with a few points.**

Keywords–Mobile robots; LiDAR; 3D map; Low-cost.

I. INTRODUCTION

In this paper, we present a novel method to generate a 3D map from the data of a 2D downward looking LiDAR. This map has enough information to identify the ground, obstacles and potholes, but it is also cost efficient in terms of memory. This information will help the robot to decide where it can go and where not. The importance of this method is that only a low-cost sensor is used, so economic mobile robots can be produced in the future.

To generate the map, each scan is segmented into lines and then they are classified as ground, obstacle or pothole using the line height. Therefore, the map is made up of few points which represent the lines.

The rest of this paper is organized as follows. Section II describes work that is related to this research. Section III describes the algorithm that does the detection and classification of the lines. Section IV presents the experimental results of this method. Finally, in Section V, the conclusions are exposed and future work lines are introduced.

II. RELATED WORK

The 2D LiDAR sensor can be used in two ways. On the one hand, it can be placed horizontally, so the sensor only detects obstacles with the same height as the sensor or higher. On the other hand, the sensor can be put downward looking, enabling the detection of short obstacles and potholes. However, this way has more difficulty to detect dynamic objects as a drawback. In the last case, the scanned points can be divided in segments searching consecutive points with a difference in height greater that the a given threshold [1]. From this division, the segments can be classified into ground, obstacles or potholes.

Recently, methods based on neuronal networks have been used to classify the data from LiDAR sensors. Wang *et al.* [2] propose the use of a 3D LiDAR and a camera to determine the class of the points by projecting the points in the image and classifying the objects of the image using a You Only Look Once (YOLO) network. In a different way, VoxelNet [3] is a neural network that uses the points as input and classifies them by dividing the point cloud in uniform voxels. Kružić *et al.* [4] use the data from a 2D LiDAR in networks trained by simulation to avoid collisions. In this case, it is not used for the classification, but to directly avoid the obstacles.

In 2D images, the optical flow has been used to determine dynamic objects by analysing the movement of the point between frames. This method can be applied to the points scanned by a LiDAR. In the case of 2D LiDAR placed horizontally, the method can be used to detect and track the trajectory of dynamic objects [5]. By using multiple sensors, the system is more robust and safe. This method is difficult to apply in a downward looking LiDAR in movement because the sensor captures different points constantly. To determine the optical flow in 3D LiDAR, Vaquero *et al.* [6] have proposed a Convolutional Neural Network (CNN), which obtains the optical flow from the data of the sensor.

III. METHODOLOGY

In this research, the acquisition of the data from the LiDAR, the creation of the 3D map and the detection of obstacles are implemented using Robotic Operative System (ROS) nodes. This makes it possible to obtain a modular software that can be easily customized for other mobile robots with other features and sensors.

Next, we explain how the data is obtained and is transformed into a point cloud in a global coordinate system. Then, the line detection will be explained, and how the lines are added to the map. At the end of the section, the line classification will be presented.

A. *Data acquisition*

In this research, the Hokuyo UBG-04LX-F01 sensor, a 2D LiDAR sensor, has been used. Since the objective is to detect obstacles or potholes in the ground, the sensor is placed with an inclination of 15º with respect to the horizontal axis. Data needs to be obtained from approximately 2 meters in front of the robot so that it has enough time to change the trajectory, a sufficient distance if the maximum speed is considered 1 m/s. With the distance and the inclination, it was determined that the sensor has to be placed at a height of 55 cm. Besides, higher heights were tried, but higher the sensor is placed, the more noise it is seen in the data, so the previous height was chosen.

The Hokuyo sensor reads the distances in a range of 270º. To use the sensor in ROS, the node urg_node was used with a median filter of 5 samples to reduce the noise in the data.

B. Point cloud map

The data is represented in a 3D map where the origin of coordinates of the global axis are in the ground. At the start of the program, they are just below the sensor. The global and local axis are represented in Figure 1. Next, the transformation of the scanned points from local axis to global will be explained.

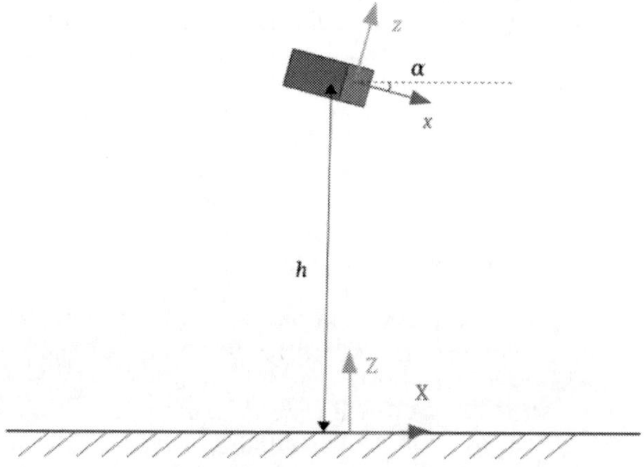

Figure 1. Global and local coordinates systems.

First, the obtained data is transformed to a point cloud. It is a simple transformation from polar coordinates to Cartesian. Then, a rotation in the Y axis of α degrees and a translation in the Z axis of h meters are made. With this, the height and inclination of the sensor are taken into account. In our case, $\alpha = 15°$ and $h = 0.55$. So, the following transformation matrix is applied to every point:

$$\begin{bmatrix} cos(\alpha) & 0 & sen(\alpha) & 0 \\ 0 & 1 & 0 & 0 \\ -sen(\alpha) & 0 & cos(\alpha) & h \\ 0 & 0 & 0 & 1 \end{bmatrix}$$

Finally, another transformation is made to obtain the points in the global coordinate system. For this purpose, the robot's position is obtained from a message, which is published from other nodes of ROS, like an odometry node. The robot's position is represented by the values x, y y z; and the orientation is determined by a quaternion $Q = [q1, q2, q3, q0]$. So, the transformation matrix is:

$$\begin{bmatrix} 1-2q2^2-2q3^2 & 2q1q2+2q0q3 & 2q1q3-2q0q2 & x \\ 2q1q2-2q0q3 & 1-2q1^2-2q3^2 & 2q2q3-2q0q1 & y \\ 2q1q3+2q0q2 & 2q2q3-2q0q1 & 1-2q1^2-2q2^2 & z \\ 0 & 0 & 0 & 1 \end{bmatrix}$$

C. Line detection

To detect the obstacles, the point cloud will be segmented in lines, which will be classified as ground or obstacle. A threshold δ around the first point of the line will determine if a point belongs to the line or not. If the distance in Z axis between the first point and the new point is lower than δ, then the point belongs to the line. This is done because big changes in this axis means the existence of an obstacle or pothole.

Furthermore, it should be considered the distance between points, because if the sensor does not detect points in a zone, there will be big distances between points. For this reason, the euclidean distance between consecutive points cannot be greater than a maximum distance d. Both conditions are represented in 2D in Figure 2. In addition, a minimum number of points n is needed to consider a line. With this, the number of little lines is reduced.

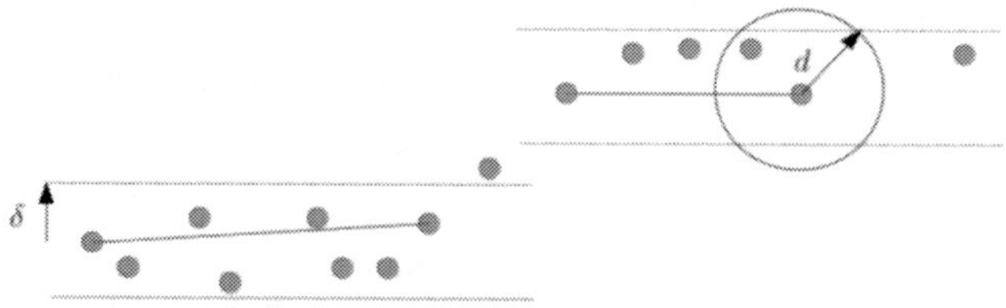

Figure 2. Diagram of the detection of lines.

Then, the lines are refined because there are a lot of lines that were segmented because of the height difference with the first point. This occurs frequently in the lateral walls.

If the normalized vector from the first point to the last point of a line is equal to the normalized vector of the next line and to the vector from the first point of the first line to the last point of the second line, both lines are grouped into one line because they belong to the same straight. In Figure 3, these vectors and the result of the refinement can be observed. In this refinement, a slight error γ in the equality of vectors is allowed. The different parameters of the detection of lines will be determined during the experimentation.

D. Map of lines

The map of the segmented lines has been divided into cells called submaps. The submaps will have the lines that are between the limits in the X and Y axis. So, the map will be a vector of submaps that will add dynamically new submaps when they are needed. This allows to reduce the time of computation in different functions because it is not necessary to search in all the lines of the map. When a line is added to the map, Figure 4 is used.

The lines are defined by two points, the first and the last. Firstly, we search the submap where the first point is. If it does

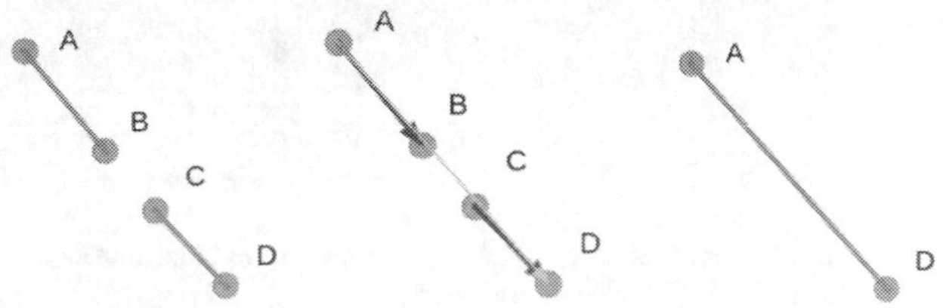

(a) Initial lines A-B and C-D. (b) Unnormalised vectors A-B, C-D y A-D. (c) Final line A-D.

Figure 3. Since the normalized vectors are sufficiently similar, the two lines have been joined into one.

Data: map,line
submap = searchSubmap(map, line.first);
updateSubmap(submap, line);
if not *submap.is_in_submap(line.last)* **then**
  submap = searchSubmap(map, line.last);
  updateSubmap(submap, line);
  vector = line.last-line.first;
  if *A point of the line is not in the submaps* **then**
    submap = searchSubmap(map, point);
    updateSubmap(submap, line);
  end
end

Figure 4. Add a line to the vector of submaps.

not exist in the map, a new submap is created and it is added to the vector. Then, the submap is updated. In this function, the nearest line to the new one is searched. If the distance is smaller than a threshold, then the old line is replaced by the new one. Otherwise, the line is added to the submap. Doing this, the submap doesn't accumulate lines that were detected, saving the most recent information.

Lastly, we check if the last point of the line is in the same submap. If it is in another, the other submap is also updated so that the line is considered in searches in both submaps. Furthermore, in this last case, it is possible that the line goes through a third submap (when the line is near the corners of submaps).

The size of the submaps is customizable. In this research, it has been decided to use square submaps with the side of 10 m. It is considered large enough that there will not be an excessive number of submaps and also small enough that the search of lines is done in the required time. Moreover, as the sensor has a range of 4 meters, a line can be in a maximum of three sub-maps of this size.

E. Line classification

The lines are classified depending on the mean heigh of the line. If the height is in a threshold ζ around the actual height of the robot, the line is considered as ground. If the height is greater, the line is classified as obstacle, otherwise the line is a pothole. The classification is done continuously because, depending the height of the robot, some lines that were classified as obstacles can be ground, like on the ramps

IV. Experimental results

In this section, the results will be shown. During the experimentation, a mobile robot was not used, the sensor was moved manually and a ROS node changed the position of the X axis constantly.

In Table I, the values of the different parameters are shown. In this research, the parameter settings indicated in Table I produced good results.

TABLE I. Parameters obtained experimentally.

Parameter	Description	Value
δ	Threshold in the Z axis to consider a point in a line.	0.05
d	DMaximum distance between two consecutive points of line.	0.2
n	Minimum number of points in a line	10
ζ	Threshold in the Z axis around the robot to consider a line as ground.	0.05
γ	Maximum allowed difference during the line refinement.	0.04

In the visualization of the results, the ground lines are represented in green, the obstacles in red and the potholes in yellow. In Figure 5, the generated lines can be compared with the point cloud of the scene. There were not obstacles, so the ground and the walls were detected.

During the experimentation, a video was also recorded. The detected lines can be projected in the video to see the correspondences of the lines with the real world. In Figure 6, the projection in a scene with obstacles can be observed.

The detection of potholes can be observed in Figure 7. The scene shows a flight of stairs from the top,, but there was not enough space to detect the first steps, so the potholes have to be seen from far. However, in the absence of ground lines, the robot should avoid the pothole.

TABLE II. Line classification results.

		Predicted class		
		Ground	Obstacle	Pothole
True class	Ground	3633	0	90
	Obstacle	0	29415	0
	Pothole	0	0	107

Table II shows the results of the line classification in approximately 7 minutes of experiments. The ground sometimes is confused with potholes due to the sensor error. Also, it can be observed that there are many obstacle's lines, because there is an oversegmentation in the obstacles. The tests were done in an indoor environment, so there were no potholes, except in the case of Figure 7.

V. Conclusion and future work

To conclude, we have presented a method that segments the data of a 2D LiDAR sensor in lines and classifies them. We

(a) Point cloud

(b) Lines

Figure 5. Comparison between the point cloud and the lines.

Figure 6. Lines projection.

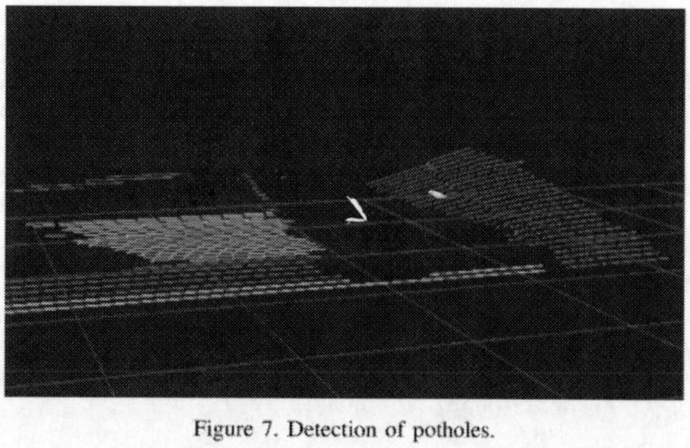

Figure 7. Detection of potholes.

demonstrated that this approach detects correctly the obstacles and potholes in a structural environment. However, the point cloud is segmented in more lines than necessary, but it could be improved changing the parameter of line refinement.The algorithm is less restrictive when grouping lines if the parameter value is higher.

Moreover, it is necessary to address the issue of dynamic objects in future works, analysing the movement in the lines. In the great majority of scenes, there are some dynamic changes that should be considered to improve the control of the robot.

ACKNOWLEDGEMENT

This work was funded by the Spanish Government's Ministry of Science and Innovation through the research project RTI2018-094279-B-100.

REFERENCES

[1] O. Yalcin, A. Sayar, O. Arar, S. Akpinar, and S. Kosunalp, "Approaches of road boundary and obstacle detection using lidar," in IFAC Proc, vol. 46, no. 25, 2013, pp. 211–215.

[2] H. Wang, X. Lou, Y. Cai, Y. Li, and L. Chen, "Real-time vehicle detection algorithm based on vision and lidar point cloud fusion," Journal of Sensors, vol. 2019, 2019, pp. 1–9. [Online]. Available: https://dx.doi.org/10.1155/2019/8473980

[3] Y. Zhou and O. Tuzel, "Voxelnet: End-to-end learning for point cloud based 3d object detection," in 2018 IEEE/CVF Conference on Computer Vision and Pattern Recognition, 2018, pp. 4490–4499.

[4] S. Kružić, J. Music, M. Bonković, and F. Duchonň, "Crash course learning: an automated approach to simulation-driven lidar-based training of neural networks for obstacle avoidance in mobile robotics," Turkish Journal of Electrical Engineering & Computer Sciences, vol. 28, 2020, pp. 1107–1120.

[5] V. Vaquero, E. Repiso, and A. Sanfeliu, "Robust and real-time detection and tracking of moving objects with minimum 2d lidar information to advance autonomous cargo handling in ports," Sensors, vol. 19, no. 1, 2018, pp. 107–132. [Online]. Available: https://dx.doi.org/10.3390/s19010107

[6] V. Vaquero, A. Sanfeliu, and F. Moreno-Noguer, "Hallucinating dense optical flow from sparse lidar for autonomous vehicles," in 2018 24th International Conference on Pattern Recognition (ICPR), 2018, pp. 1959–1964.

A Novel Low-concentration Isopropanol Gas Sensor Based on Fe-doped ZnO Nanoneedles

Yifan Luo[1,3], Ahmadou Ly[2], Marc Debliquy[1], Driss Lahem[2]
[1]Materials Sciences Department, University of Mons
[2] Material Science Department, Materia Nova
Mons, Belgium
Yifan.LUO@umons.ac.be
Ahmadou.Ly@materianova.be
Marc.Debliquy@umons.ac.be
Driss.Lahem@materianova.be

Chao Zhang[3]
[3]College of College of Mechanical Engineering
Yangzhou University
Yangzhou, China
zhangc@yzu.edu.cn

***Abstract*—This work reports a highly sensitive Fe doped ZnO nanoneedles based gas sensor for detection at low concentrations. Pure and Fe doped ZnO were synthesized via a hydrothermal method and spray-coated onto an alumina substrates. The sensing properties were investigated under different temperatures and concentrations. Fe doping significantly increased the sensing performance of ZnO nanoneedles. The 5 at% Fe doped sensor showed the best response to isopropanol and the optimal working temperature is 275°C. The sensor showed a high response to 250 ppb isopropanol, together with high stability under different humidity levels.**

Keywords- ZnO; Fe doping; gas sensor; isopropanol; lung cancer.

I. INTRODUCTION

To realize the early detection of lung cancer via e-nose, sensors with high response to low concentrations of Volatile Organic Compounds (VOCs) biomarkers are necessary. Metal oxide sensor is a good candidate for the sensors in e-nose [1][2]. Isopropanol is one of the important biomarkers of lung cancer. The concentration of isopropanol in the breath of lung cancer patients can come up to over 270 ppb, with an average concentration of 438 ppb [3]. In this work, we present a sensor that can detect ppb level isopropanol as low as to 250 ppb with good stability in humidity.

In Section II, we will introduce the method we use to synthesize the sensing materials, characterizing the as-synthesized powders and making the sensing test. In Section III, the results of characterization and sensing test are shown. We conclude our work in Section IV.

II. MATERIALS AND METHODS

The ZnO nanoneedles are synthesized via a simple hydrothermal method. 3×10^{-3} mol of $Zn(NO_3)\cdot 2H_2O$ were dissolved into 44 ml of deionized water. Meanwhile, 1 g of Cetyltrimethylammonium Bromide (CTAB) was dissolved in 22 ml of ethanol. After that, 3×10^{-2} mol of NaOH was added into the $Zn(NO_3)_2$ solution, then the two different solutions were mixed, followed with the addition of 10 ml ethylenediamine. The solution was treated at 100°C for 2 h in an oven. The obtained powder was washed and dried in an oven overnight. To prepare the Fe-doped ZnO needles, $Fe(NO_3)_3$ solutions with different concentrations were slowly added into the $Zn(NO_3)_2$ solution before the addition of NaOH. The doping contents of Fe were 1%, 3% and 5% by atom ratio, which are written as 1 at%, 3 at% and 5 at% Fe-ZnO. The sensors are prepared on alumina substrate with gold interdigitated electrodes by spraying.

The as-synthesized powders are characterized by Scanning Electron microscopy (SEM) [4], Energy-dispersive X-ray spectroscopy (EDS) [5] and X-ray diffraction (XRD) [6]. The gas sensing test is carried out in a home-made system. The gas flow is controlled at 1 L/min by 3 flow meters. Before the sensing test, all the sensors were pre-heated at 350°C for 1 week. The response of the sensors was defined as $S=(R_a-R_g)/R_g$. In the equation, S refers to the response of the sensor, Ra represents the electrical resistance in air, R_g represents the electrical resistance the target gas. The response and recovery time were respectively defined as the time needed to reach 90% of the maximum response and the time needed to recover to 110% of the baseline.

III. RESULTS AND DISCUSSION

The XRD of the samples indicated that all the samples are ZnO or Fe-doped ZnO without any other impurities. The main peak of Fe-ZnO has a small shifting to the left with the increase of the amount of Fe, indicating that the Fe^{3+} was doped into the ZnO. The SEM picture of pure and different Fe-doped ZnO are shown in Figure 1. All the samples have needle like nanostructure. The Fe doping changed the structure of ZnO, making the needles become smaller.

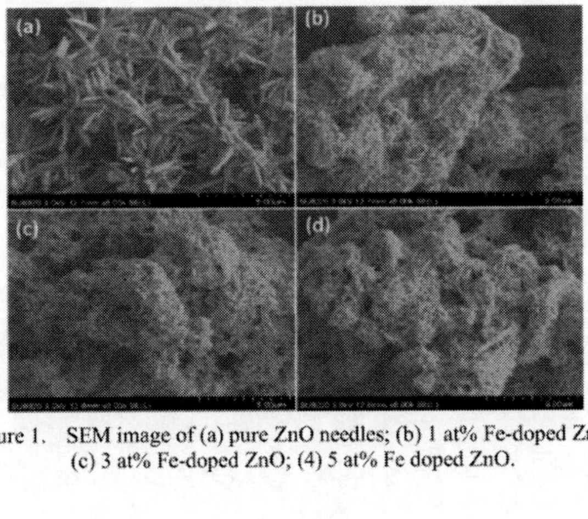

Figure 1. SEM image of (a) pure ZnO needles; (b) 1 at% Fe-doped ZnO; (c) 3 at% Fe-doped ZnO; (4) 5 at% Fe doped ZnO.

Fig. 2 (a) and (b) exhibited the resistance change and gas sensing performance of Fe-ZnO to different concentrations of isopropanol at 275°C with 50% Relative Humidity (RH). The resistance of the four sensors decreased significantly with the presence of isopropanol, which indicated that the Fe-doped ZnO remains n-type. The response of 5 at% Fe-doped ZnO nanoneedles can reach 23.6 when the concentration of isopropanol is 5 ppm. When the concentration of isopropanol decreased to 250 ppb, the response still can reach around 4.7. The response and recovery time of 5 at% Fe-doped ZnO to 5 ppm ZnO is calculated as 51 s and 762 s respectively. Fig. 2 (c) shows the response to 5 ppm isopropanol at different temperature. It can be seen that the Fe doping not only increases the response, but also decreases the optimal operating temperature. Fig. 2 (d) is the response to 5 ppm isopropanol under different RH. From 25% to 100%, the response of 5 at% Fe-ZnO is not affected by RH a lot. In Table 1, we compared the results with some other works.

For the gas sensing mechanism, we consider that the isopropanol reacted with both the adsorbed oxygen ions and the Fe^{3+} doped in the ZnO.

IV. CONCLUSION

ZnO and Fe-doped ZnO nanoneedles were synthesized via a simple one-step hydrothermal method. The Fe doping changed the morphology of ZnO. The Fe-doped ZnO retains the n-type semiconductor property. The 5 at% Fe-doped ZnO showed the best sensing performance to isopropanol at 275°C with fast response. The improvement of sensing properties is considered as the adjustment of the band structure by the doping of Fe.

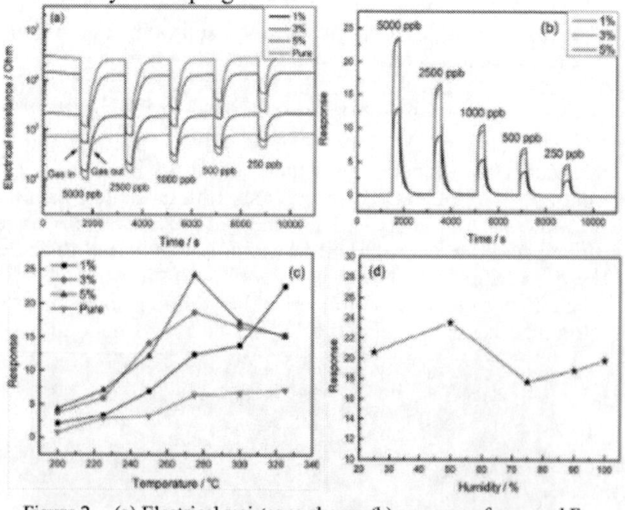

Figure 2. (a) Electrical resistance change (b) response of pure and Fe doped ZnO nanoneedles to isopropanol. (c) Response to 5 ppm isopropanol under different operating temperature (d) Response of 5 at% Fe-doped ZnO under different RH%

TABLE I. COMPARISON OF THE GAS SENSING RESULT OF ISOPROPANOL SENSORS BETWEEN THIS WORK AND SOME PREVIOUS WORKS

Material	Temperature (°C)	Concentration (ppm)	Response	Ref
CdO-ZnO	248°C	1000	174.8	[4]
$ZnO-ZrO_2$	350°C	100	33.4	[5]
$Pd@Co_3O_4$-ZnO	240°C	1	1.8	[6]
Fe-ZnO	275°C	5	23.6	This work

ACKNOWLEDGMENT

The authors acknowledge Mr. Yoann Paint from Materianova for his contribution to the characterization part.

REFERENCES

[1] J. Kaur, K. Anand, K. Anand and R. Singh, "WO_3 nanolamellae/reduced graphene oxide nanocomposites for highly sensitive and selective acetone sensing." J Mater Sci, vol. 53, pp. 12894-12907, 2018.

[2] H. Duan et al., "Controllable synthesis of Ho-doped In_2O_3 porous nanotubes by electrospinning and their application as an ethanol gas sensor." J Mater Sci, vol. 53, pp. 3267–3279, 2018.

[3] R. Machado et al., "Detection of Lung Cancer by Sensor Array Analyses of Exhaled Breath." American Journal of Respiratory and Critical Care Medicine, vol. 171, pp. 1286-1291, 2005.

[4] X. Geng, C. Zhang, Y. Luo and M. Debliquy, "Flexible NO_2 gas sensors based on sheet-like hierarchical ZnO_{1-x} coatings deposited on polypropylene papers by suspension flame spraying." Journal of the Taiwan Institute of Chemical Engineers, vol. 75, pp. 280-286, 2017.

[5] C. Zhang, X. Geng, H. Liao, C. Li and M. Debliquy, "Room-temperature nitrogen-dioxide sensors based on ZnO_{1-x} coatings deposited by solution precursor plasma spray. Sensors and Actuators B: Chemical, vol 242, pp. 102-111, 2017.

[6] Y. Luo, C. Zhang, B. Zheng, X. Geng and M. Debliquy, "Hydrogen sensors based on noble metal doped metal-oxide semiconductor: A review." International Journal of Hydrogen Energy, vol 42, pp. 20386-20397, 2017,

[7] X. Cai et al., "Isopropanol sensing properties of coral-like ZnO–CdO composites by flash preparation via self-sustained decomposition of metal-organic complexes." Sensors and Actuators B: Chemical, vol. 198, pp. 402-410, 2014.

[8] Q. Jin, W. Wen, S. Zheng and J. Wu, "Enhanced isopropanol sensing of coral-like $ZnO–ZrO_2$ composites." Nanotechnology, vol. 31, pp. 402-410, 2014.

[9] Y. Sun et al., "Electrospinning preparation of $Pd@Co_3O_4$-ZnO composite nanofibers and their highly enhanced VOC sensing properties." Materials Research Bulletin, vol. 109, pp. 255-264, 2019.

Normal Distributions Transform-Based Mapping Using Scanning LiDAR Mounted on Motorcycle

Kota Matsuo, Akihiko Yoshida
Graduate School of Science and Engineering
Doshisha University
Kyotanabe, Kyoto, Japan
e-mail: {ctwd0130, ctwf0158}@mail4.doshisha.ac.jp

Masafumi Hashimoto, Kazuhiko Takahashi
Faculty of Science and Engineering
Doshisha University
Kyotanabe, Kyoto, Japan
e-mail: {mhashimo, katakaha}@mail.doshisha.ac.jp

Abstract—**This paper presents a 3D point cloud mapping method for Global Navigation Satellite Systems (GNSS)-denied and dynamic environments using a scanning multilayer Light Detection And Ranging (LiDAR) mounted on a motorcycle. The distortion in the scan data from the LiDAR is corrected by estimating the motorcycle's pose (3D positions and attitude angles) in a period shorter than the LiDAR scan period based on the information from Normal Distributions Transform (NDT) scan matching and an Inertial Measurement Unit (IMU). The corrected scan data are mapped onto an elevation map. The static and moving scan data, which originate from static and moving objects in the environments, respectively, are classified using the occupancy grid method. Only the static scan data are applied to generate a point cloud map using NDT-based Simultaneous Localization And Mapping (SLAM). The experimental results obtained in an urban road environment demonstrate the qualitative effectiveness of the proposed method.**

Keywords—motorcycle; LiDAR; NDT-based SLAM; distortion correction; dynamic environment.

I. Introduction

In recent years, numerous studies were conducted on the active safety and autonomous driving of vehicles and personal mobility devices, while many also focused on last-mile automation by delivery robots. Important technologies from these studies include environmental map generation (mapping) [1]–[3]. In this study, we focus on mapping with a Light Detection And Ranging (LiDAR) mounted on a vehicle.

Within the domain of Intelligent Transportation Systems (ITS), maps are generated using mobile mapping systems [4]. These maps are applied to the areas of autonomous driving and active safety for automobiles in wide road environments, such as highways and motorways. In this study, we focus on environment maps for the active safety and autonomous driving of personal mobility devices and delivery robots as well as for various social services such as disaster prevention and mitigation [5][6].

In the process, we address generating 3D point cloud maps for narrow road environments, such as community roads and scenic roads in urban and mountainous areas, using LiDAR mounted on two-wheeled vehicles (e.g., bicycles and motorcycles) with higher maneuverability than four-wheeled vehicles (e.g., cars and buses). To generate 3D point cloud maps using LiDAR-based Simultaneous Localization And Mapping (SLAM), the LiDAR data captured in the sensor coordinate frame must be accurately mapped onto the world coordinate frame using the pose (i.e., position and attitude angle) information of the vehicle. Since LiDAR generally obtains data via laser scanning, all the scan data within one scan cannot be obtained at the same time when a vehicle is moving or is changing its attitude. Therefore, if such data are transformed based on the vehicle's pose at the same time, distortion appears on the environmental maps.

To reduce the distortion in the scan data, several methods were proposed [7]–[10]. Most conventional methods were aimed at correcting the distortion in the scan data from a LiDAR mounted on four-wheeled vehicles moving on flat road surfaces. To the best of our knowledge, very few studies exist that addressed distortion correction when vehicles change their poses drastically.

Thus, we proposed a Normal Distributions Transform (NDT)-based SLAM for application in Global Navigation Satellite Systems (GNSS)-denied environments using a scanning LiDAR mounted on two-wheeled vehicle that change their pose drastically [11]. The pose of the two-wheeled vehicle was calculated via NDT scan matching [12] using the LiDAR scan data obtained for each scan period. By estimating the vehicle's pose in a period shorter than the scan period via an Inertial Measurement Unit (IMU), the distortion in the scan data was corrected. The corrected scan data were applied to 3D point cloud maps. The experimental results of the road-environment mapping by a scanning LiDAR mounted on a bicycle under a zigzag motion validated the efficacy of the proposed method.

However, further improvement to our NDT-based SLAM is needed. While it was designed to be used in static environments, moving objects such as cars, buses, two-wheeled vehicles, and pedestrians exist in practical environments. The presence of moving objects in practical dynamic environments deteriorates the mapping performance. This problem can be addressed by integrating SLAM with moving-object detection. Many SLAM methods were presented for use in dynamic environments [2][13]–[15]. However, most of the methods were based on the use of a sensor mounted on a four-wheeled vehicle. SLAM with a sensor mounted on a two-wheeled vehicle in dynamic environments remains a challenging issue.

Thus, in this paper, we present an NDT-based SLAM using a scanning LiDAR mounted on a motorcycle in GNSS-denied and dynamic environments. This paper is an extension of our previous paper [15] on NDT-based SLAM, which used a scanning LiDAR mounted on a four-wheeled vehicle within

Figure 1. Overview of experimental bicycle.

similar environments. The rest of this paper is organized as follows. Section II describes the experimental system. Section III summarizes the scan-data mapping based on the NDT scan matching. Section IV explains the distortion correction method for the LiDAR scan data, and Section V presents the extraction method for the static scan data from the LiDAR. Section VI explains the experiments conducted to verify the proposed method, followed by the conclusions and future work in Section VII.

II. Experimental System

Figure 1 shows the overview of the motorcycle (Honda Gyro Canopy). A scanning 32-layer LiDAR (Velodyne HDL-32E) and an IMU (Xsens MTi-300) are mounted on the upper part of the motorcycle. The maximum range of the LiDAR is 70 m, the horizontal viewing angle is 360° with a resolution of 0.16°, and the vertical viewing angle is 41.34° with a resolution of 1.33°. The LiDAR provides 384 measurements (the object's 3D position and reflection intensity) every 0.55 ms (at 2° horizontal angle increments). The time that the LiDAR beam takes to complete one rotation (360°) in the horizontal direction is 100 ms, and 70,000 measurements are obtained in one rotation.

The IMU provides the attitude angles (roll and pitch angles) and the angular velocities (roll, pitch, and yaw velocities) every 10 ms with an attitude angle error of ±0.3° (typ.) and an angular velocity error of ±0.2 °/s (typ.).

In this paper, one rotation of the LiDAR beam in the horizontal direction (360°) is referred to as one scan, while the data obtained from this scan is referred to as scan data. The LiDAR's scan period (100 ms) is denoted as τ and the scan data observation period (0.55 ms) as $\Delta\tau$. The observation period (10 ms) of the IMU is denoted as $\Delta\tau_{IMU}$, which means the IMU data are obtained 10 times in one scan of the LiDAR ($\tau = 10\Delta\tau_{IMU}$), while the LiDAR scan data are obtained 18 times within the observation period of the IMU ($\Delta\tau_{IMU} = 18\Delta\tau$).

III. Normal Distributions Transform Scan Matching

The scan data mapping is based on NDT scan matching [12]. For clarity, we explain the NDT scan matching using the LiDAR scan data in which the distortion is corrected. The distortion correction method is detailed in the following section.

A voxel grid filter is applied to downsize the scan data. The voxel used for the filter is a tetrahedron with a side length of 0.2 m. In the world coordinate frame, Σ_W, a voxel map with a voxel size of 1 m is used for NDT scan matching. For the i-th (i = 1, 2, …n) measurement in the scan data, the position vector in Σ_b is defined as $\boldsymbol{p}_{bi}$ and that in Σ_W as $\boldsymbol{p}_i$. Thus, the relation is given by the following homogeneous form:

$$\begin{pmatrix} \boldsymbol{p}_i \\ 1 \end{pmatrix} = \boldsymbol{T}(\boldsymbol{X}) \begin{pmatrix} \boldsymbol{p}_{bi} \\ 1 \end{pmatrix} \tag{1}$$

where $\boldsymbol{X} = (x, y, z, \phi, \theta, \psi)^T$ is the motorcycle's pose, $(x, y, z)^T$ and $(\phi, \theta, \psi)^T$ are the 3D position and attitude angle (roll, pitch, and yaw angles) of the motorcycle, respectively, in Σ_W. $\boldsymbol{T}(\boldsymbol{X})$ is the following homogeneous transformation matrix:

$$T(\boldsymbol{X}) = \begin{pmatrix} \cos\theta\cos\psi & \sin\phi\sin\theta\cos\psi - \cos\phi\sin\psi & \cos\phi\sin\theta\cos\psi + \sin\phi\sin\psi & x \\ \cos\theta\sin\psi & \sin\phi\sin\theta\sin\psi + \cos\phi\cos\psi & \cos\phi\sin\theta\sin\psi - \sin\phi\cos\psi & y \\ -\sin\theta & \sin\phi\cos\theta & \cos\phi\cos\theta & z \\ 0 & 0 & 0 & 1 \end{pmatrix}$$

The scan data obtained at the current time $t\tau$ (t = 0, 1, 2, …), $\boldsymbol{P}_{b(t)} = \{\boldsymbol{p}_{b1(t)}, \boldsymbol{p}_{b2(t)}, \cdots, \boldsymbol{p}_{bn(t)}\}$ or $\boldsymbol{P}_{(t)} = \{\boldsymbol{p}_{1(t)}, \boldsymbol{p}_{2(t)}, \cdots, \boldsymbol{p}_{n(t)}\}$, are referred to as the new input scan, and the scan data obtained in the previous time before $(t-1)\tau$, $\boldsymbol{P} = \{\boldsymbol{P}_{(0)}, \boldsymbol{P}_{(1)}, \cdots, \boldsymbol{P}_{(t-1)}\}$, are referred to as the reference scan.

NDT scan matching involves conducting an NDT for the reference scan data in each grid on a voxel map and calculating the mean and covariance of the LiDAR measurement positions. By matching the new input scan at $t\tau$ with the reference scan data obtained prior to $(t-1)\tau$, the motorcycle's pose $\boldsymbol{X}_{(t)}$ at $t\tau$ can be determined. The motorcycle's pose is used for conducting a coordinate transform with (1), the new input scan can then be mapped to Σ_W, and the reference scan is updated.

In this study, we use the point cloud library for the NDT scan matching [16].

IV. Distortion Correction of LiDAR Scan Data

A. Motion and Measurement Models

As shown in Figure 2, the linear velocity of the motorcycle in Σ_b is denoted as V_b (the velocity in the x_b-axis direction), and the angular velocities around the x_b-, y_b-, and z_b-axes are denoted as $\dot{\phi}_b$, $\dot{\theta}_b$, and $\dot{\psi}_b$, respectively.

If the motorcycle is assumed to move at nearly constant linear and angular velocities, a motion model can be derived as (A.1) in the Appendix. We express (A.1) in the following vector form:

$$\boldsymbol{\xi}_{(t+1)} = \boldsymbol{f}[\boldsymbol{\xi}_{(t)}, \boldsymbol{w}, \tau] \tag{2}$$

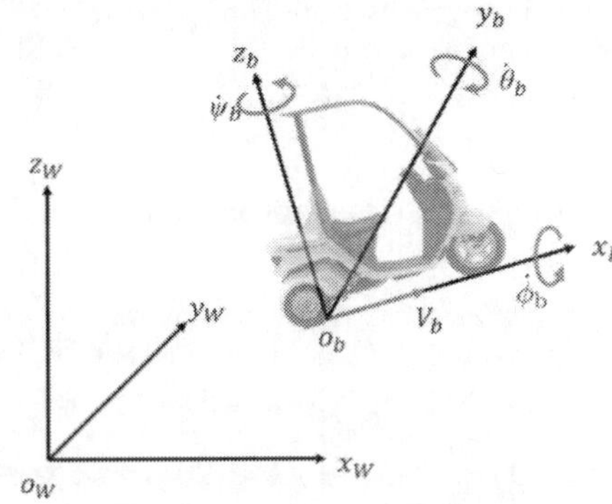

Figure 2. Notation related to motorcycle motion.

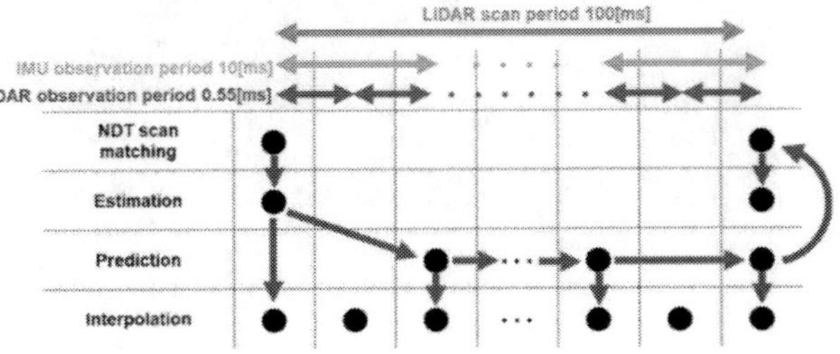

Figure 3. Flow of distortion correction.

The attitude angle and angular velocity of the motorcycle obtained at time $t\tau_{IMU}$ by the IMU is denoted as $z_{IMU}(t)$. The measurement model is then

$$z_{IMU}(t) = H_{IMU}\xi(t) + \Delta z_{IMU}(t) \quad (3)$$

where Δz_{IMU} is sensor noise, and H_{IMU} is a measurement matrix.

The motorcycle's pose obtained at $t\tau$ using the NDT scan matching is denoted as $z_{NDT(t)} \equiv X_{(t)}$. The measurement model is then

$$z_{NDT}(t) = H_{NDT}\xi(t) + \Delta z_{NDT}(t) \quad (4)$$

where Δz_{NDT} is the measurement noise, and H_{NDT} is the measurement matrix.

B. Distrotion Correction

Figure 3 shows the correction flow of the LiDAR scan data [11]. The LiDAR's scan period τ is 100 ms, the observation period $\Delta\tau_{IMU}$ of the IMU is 10 ms, and the scan data observation period $\Delta\tau$ is 0.55 ms. When the scan data are mapped onto Σ_W using the motorcycle's pose, which is calculated for every LiDAR scan period, distortion appears on the environmental map. Therefore, the distortion in the LiDAR scan data is corrected by estimating the motorcycle's pose using the Extended Kalman Filter (EKF) for every scan data observation period $\Delta\tau$.

The IMU data are obtained 10 times per LiDAR scan ($\tau = 10\Delta\tau_{IMU}$). The state estimate of the motorcycle and its error covariance obtained at the time $(t-1)\tau+(k-1)\Delta\tau_{IMU}$, where k =1–10, using EKF are denoted as $\hat\xi^{(k-1)}{}_{(t-1)}$ and $\Gamma^{(k-1)}{}_{(t-1)}$, respectively. From these estimates, the EKF prediction algorithm gives the state prediction $\hat\xi^{(k/k-1)}{}_{(t-1)}$ and the error covariance $\Gamma^{(k/k-1)}{}_{(t-1)}$ at $(t-1)\tau+k\Delta\tau_{IMU}$ by

$$\left.\begin{aligned}\hat\xi^{(k/k-1)}(t-1) &= f[\hat\xi^{(k-1)}(t-1), 0, \Delta\tau_{IMU}]\\ \Gamma^{(k/k-1)}(t-1) &= F(t-1)\Gamma^{(k-1)}(t-1)F(t-1)^T + G(t-1)QG(t-1)^T\end{aligned}\right\} \quad (5)$$

where $F = \partial f/\partial\hat\xi$, $G = \partial f/\partial w$, and Q is the covariance matrix of the plant noise w.

At $(t-1)\tau+k\Delta\tau_{IMU}$, the attitude angle and angular velocity z_{IMU} of the motorcycle are observed with the IMU. Then, the EKF estimation algorithm gives the state estimate $\hat\xi^{(k)}{}_{(t-1)}$ and its error covariance $\Gamma^{(k)}{}_{(t-1)}$ as follows:

$$\left.\begin{aligned}\hat\xi^{(k)}(t-1) &= \hat\xi^{(k/k-1)}(t-1) + K\{z_{IMU} - H_{IMU}\hat\xi^{(k/k-1)}(t-1)\}\\ \Gamma^{(k)}(t-1) &= \Gamma^{(k/k-1)}(t-1) - KH_{IMU}\Gamma^{(k/k-1)}(t-1)\end{aligned}\right\} \quad (6)$$

where $K = \Gamma^{(k/k-1)}{}_{(t-1)}H^T_{IMU}S^{-1}{}_{(t-1)}$ and $S = H_{IMU}\Gamma^{(k/k-1)}{}_{(t-1)}H^T_{IMU} + R_{IMU}$. R_{IMU} is the covariance matrix of the sensor noise Δz_{IMU}.

In the state estimate $\hat\xi^{(k)}{}_{(t-1)}$, the elements related to the motorcycle's pose (x,y,z,ϕ,θ,ψ) are denoted as $\hat X^{(k)}{}_{(t-1)}$. Since the observation period $\Delta\tau_{IMU}$ of the IMU is 10 ms, and the scan data observation period $\Delta\tau$ is 0.55 ms, the LiDAR scan data are obtained 18 times within the IMU observation period ($\Delta\tau_{IMU} = 18\Delta\tau$). Using the pose estimates $\hat X^{(k-1)}{}_{(t-1)}$ and $\hat X^{(k)}{}_{(t-1)}$ obtained at $(t-1)\tau+(k-1)\Delta\tau_{IMU}$ and $(t-1)\tau + k\Delta\tau_{IMU}$, respectively, the motorcycle's pose $\hat X^{(k-1)}{}_{(t-1,j)}$ at $(t-1)\tau+(k-1)\Delta\tau_{IMU}+j\Delta\tau$, where j = 1–18, can be interpolated by

$$\hat X^{(k-1)}(t-1,j) = \hat X^{(k-1)}(t-1) + \frac{\hat X^{(k)}(t-1) - \hat X^{(k-1)}(t-1)}{\Delta\tau_{IMU}} j\Delta\tau \quad (7)$$

Using (1) and the pose prediction $\hat X^{(k-1)}{}_{(t-1,j)}$, the scan data $p^{(k-1)}_{bi}{}_{(t-1,j)}$ in Σ_b obtained at $(t-1)\tau+(k-1)\Delta\tau_{IMU}+j\Delta\tau$ can be transformed to $p^{(k-1)}_i{}_{(t-1,j)}$ in Σ_W as follows:

$$\begin{pmatrix} p_i^{(k-1)}(t-1,j) \\ 1 \end{pmatrix} = T(\hat X^{(k-1)}(t-1,j))\begin{pmatrix} p_{bi}^{(k-1)}(t-1,j) \\ 1 \end{pmatrix} \quad (8)$$

Since the IMU data are obtained 10 times per LiDAR scan ($\tau = 10\Delta\tau_{IMU}$), the time $t\tau$ is equal to $(t\text{-}1)\,\tau+10\Delta\tau_{IMU}$. Using the motorcycle's pose estimate $\hat X^{(10)}{}_{(t-1)}$ at $t\tau$, the scan data $p^{(k-1)}_i{}_{(t-1,j)}$ in Σ_W at $(t-1)\tau + (k-1)\Delta\tau_{IMU} + j\Delta\tau$ are transformed to the scan data $P^*_{bi(t)}$ in Σ_b at $t\tau$ by

$$\begin{pmatrix} p^*_{bi}(t) \\ 1 \end{pmatrix} = T(\hat X^{(10)}(t-1))^{-1}\begin{pmatrix} p_i^{(k-1)}(t-1,j) \\ 1 \end{pmatrix} \quad (9)$$

In such way, the corrected scan data $P^*_{b(t)} = \{p^*_{b1(t)}, p^*_{b2(t)}, \cdots, p^*_{bn(t)}\}$ within one scan (LiDAR beam rotation of 360° in a horizontal plane) are obtained and used as the new input scan for the scan matching to calculate the pose z_{NDT} of the motorcycle at $t\tau$. Then, the EKF estimation algorithm is used to calculate the state estimate $\hat{\xi}_{(t)}$ and its error covariance $\Gamma_{(t)}$ of the motorcycle at $t\tau$ as follows:

$$\left.\begin{aligned} \hat{\xi}(t) &= \hat{\xi}^{(10)}(t-1) + K(t)\{z_{NDT}(t) - H_{NDT}\hat{\xi}^{(10)}(t-1)\} \\ \Gamma(t) &= \Gamma^{(10)}(t-1) - K(t)H_{NDT}\Gamma^{(10)}(t-1) \end{aligned}\right\} \quad (10)$$

where, $K_{(t)} = \Gamma^{(10)}{}_{(t-1)} H^{T}_{NDT} S^{-1}{}_{(t)}$, $S_{(t)} = H_{NDT}\Gamma^{(10)}{}_{(t-1)} H^{T}_{NDT} + R_{NDT}$, and R_{NDT} is the covariance matrix of Δz_{NDT}.

The corrected scan data $P^{*}_{b}{}_{(t)}$ are mapped onto Σ_W using the pose estimate calculated by (10), and the distortion in the environmental maps can then be removed.

V. Removal of Moving Scan Data

In dynamic environments where moving objects such as cars, motorcycles, and pedestrians exist, the LiDAR scan data related to moving objects (referred to as moving scan data) must be removed from the entire scan data, and only the scan data related to static objects (static scan data), such as buildings and trees, have to be utilized for the mapping.

We previously studied moving-object detection and tracking in crowded environments [17][18]. This method is applied to extract the static scan data from the LiDAR scan data.

To extract the static scan data, the LiDAR scan data are first classified into two types, scan data originating from road surfaces (road-surface scan data) and scan data originating from objects (object scan data), according to a rule-based method. The object scan data obtained in Σ_b are mapped onto an elevation map represented in Σ_W using the motorcycle's pose calculated by (1). In this study, the cell of the elevation map is a square with a side length of 0.3 m.

A cell containing scan data is referred to as an occupied cell. For moving scan data, the time to occupy the same cell is short, while for static scan data, the time is long. Therefore, using the occupancy grid method based on the cell occupancy time [17], the occupied cells are classified into two types of cell, moving and static, which are occupied by the moving and static scan data, respectively. Cells that the LiDAR cannot identify due to obstructions are defined as unknown cells, and their cell occupancy time is not counted.

Since the scan data related to an object generally occupy multiple cells, adjacent occupied cells are clustered. Then, the scan data in clustered static cells are applied to the mapping.

When moving objects such as vehicles pause (e.g., at a red light), the occupancy grid-based method often misidentifies their scan data as static scan data. To address this problem, the road-surface scan data are mapped onto the elevation map, and the cells in which the road-surface scan data are occupied for a while are regarded as the road-surface cells. If the road-surface cells contain the object scan data, the object scan data are always determined as moving scan data and are removed from the entire scan data.

VI. Experimental Results

Mapping experiments were conducted within road traffic environments (Figure 4). Figure 5 shows photos of areas 1 and 2, which are shown in Figure 4. The traveled distance of the motorcycle was around 2,886 m, while its maximum speed was 30 km/h. The motorcycle turned left six times and then tilted approximately 10° in a roll direction.

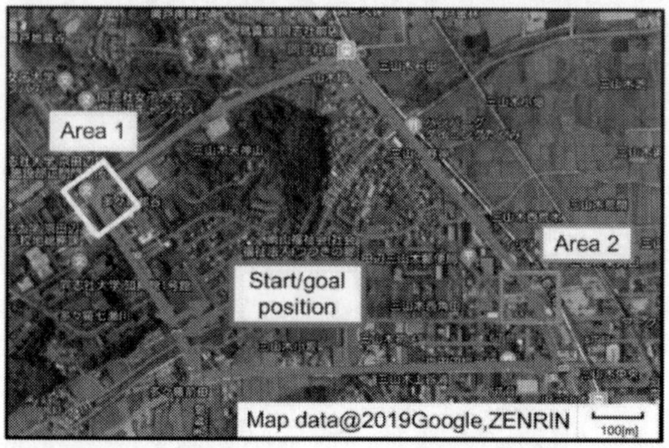

Figure 4. Moved path of vehicle (top view).

(a) Area 1

(b) Area 2

Figure 5. Photo of environment.

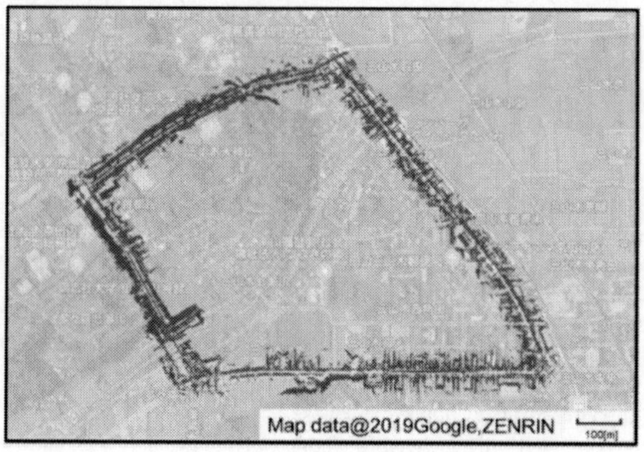

Figure 6. Mapping result (top view).

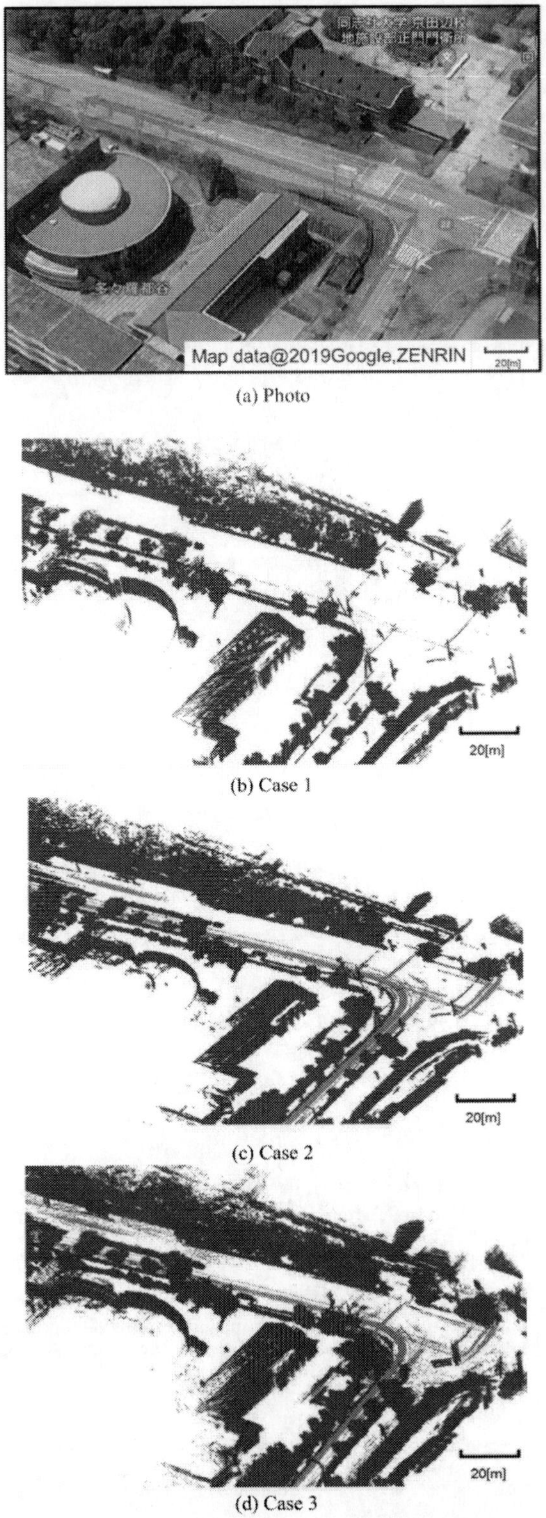

(a) Photo

(b) Case 1

(c) Case 2

(d) Case 3

Figure 7. Mapping result of area 1 (bird's-eye view). The red line in (a) indicates the movement path of the motorcycle. The blue and red dots in (b)–(d) indicate the static and moving scan data, respectively.

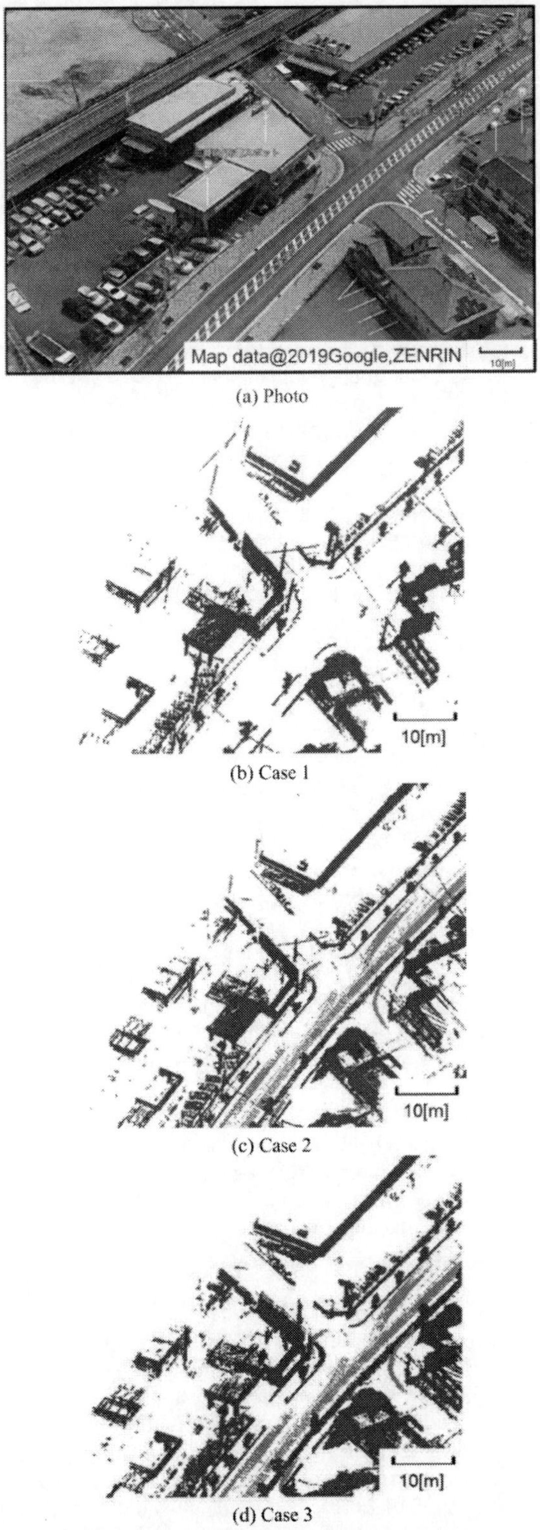

(a) Photo

(b) Case 1

(c) Case 2

(d) Case 3

Figure 8. Mapping result of area 2 (bird's-eye view). The red line in (a) indicates the movement path of the motorcycle. The blue and red dots in (b)–(d) indicate the static and moving scan data, respectively.

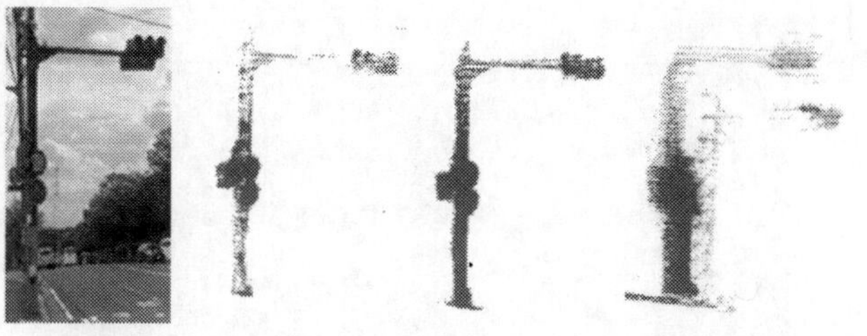

Figure 9. Mapping result of a traffic signal in area 1.

Figure 6 shows the mapping result using NDT-based SLAM in conjunction with distortion correction of the LiDAR scan data and the extraction of the static scan data.

To evaluate the mapping performance in detail, enlarged maps of areas 1 and 2 in Figure 4 are compiled, as shown in Figures 7 and 8. Figure 7 presents the map when the motorcycle is turning left, while Figure 8 presents the map when the motorcycle is going straight. Figure 9 also shows the mapping result of a traffic sign in area 1, in which the motorcycle is turning left. In area 1, there are four cars and four pedestrians, and in area 2, there are four cars and three pedestrians.

For comparison purposes, the maps were generated in terms of the following cases:

Case 1: Mapping by the proposed method: NDT-based SLAM with the distortion correction of the LiDAR scan data and the extraction of the static scan data from the entire LiDAR scan data.

Case 2: NDT-based SLAM with the distortion correction but without the extraction of the static scan data.

Case 3: NDT-based SLAM without either method.

As Figures 7 and 8 show, case 1 (proposed method) removes the track (red dots) of any moving objects (cars and pedestrians) more than cases 2 and 3. Meanwhile, as Figure 9 shows, the mapping results obtained in case 1 are more crisp than those obtained in case 3. Thus, the conclusion exists that the proposed method provides a better mapping result than cases 2 and 3.

However, our method of moving-object detection exhibits one drawback. When, for example, cars slow down at an intersection, stop at a red light, or pause to turn left (or right), they are sometimes determined as static objects. Then, the LiDAR scan data that relate to cars partially remain on the mapping.

VII. Conclusions and Future Work

This paper presented NDT-based mapping using a scanning LiDAR mounted on a motorcycle in GNSS-denied and dynamic environments. The distortion in the LiDAR scan data was corrected based on the information from the NDT scan matching and the IMU via EKF. The moving scan data were removed from the entire LiDAR scan data using the occupancy grid-based method, and the static scan data were applied to 3D point cloud maps using the NDT scan matching. The efficacy of the mapping was qualitatively demonstrated through experimental results obtained in road environments. We are currently conducting quantitative evaluations of the presented method in various environments.

Some improvements to the presented method are required. Since the distortion correction of the LiDAR scan data requires a great deal of computational time, Graphical Processing Unit (GPU) must be utilized in real-time operations. NDT-based SLAM degrades the mapping accuracy over time due to the accumulation error and must be integrated with Graph-based SLAM to reduce the drift. In addition, NDT-based SLAM with moving-object detection should be extended to SLAM with Detection And Tracking of Moving Objects (DATMO) for advanced rider assist systems. The SLAM DATMO approach will improve the mapping performance of both the mapping and the moving-object tracking.

Appendix: Motion Model of Motorcycle

$$\begin{pmatrix} x_{(t+1)} \\ y_{(t+1)} \\ z_{(t+1)} \\ \phi_{(t+1)} \\ \theta_{(t+1)} \\ \psi_{(t+1)} \\ V_{b(t+1)} \\ \dot{\phi}_{b(t+1)} \\ \dot{\theta}_{b(t+1)} \\ \dot{\psi}_{b(t+1)} \end{pmatrix} = \begin{pmatrix} x_{(t)} + a_{1(t)} \cos\theta_{(t)} \cos\psi_{(t)} \\ y_{(t)} + a_{1(t)} \cos\theta_{(t)} \sin\psi_{(t)} \\ z_{(t)} - a_{1(t)} \sin\theta_{(t)} \\ \phi(t) + a_2(t) + \{a_3(t)\sin\phi(t) + a_4(t)\cos\phi(t)\}\tan\theta(t) \\ \theta(t) + \{a_3(t)\cos\phi(t) - a_4(t)\sin\phi(t)\} \\ \psi(t) + \{a_3(t)\sin\phi(t) + a_4(t)\cos\phi(t)\}\dfrac{1}{\cos\theta(t)} \\ V_{b(t)} + \tau w_{\dot{V}_b} \\ \dot{\phi}_{b(t)} + \tau w_{\ddot{\phi}_b} \\ \dot{\theta}_{b(t)} + \tau w_{\ddot{\theta}_b} \\ \dot{\psi}_{b(t)} + \tau w_{\ddot{\psi}_b} \end{pmatrix} \tag{A.1}$$

where (x, y, z) and (ϕ, θ, ψ) are the 3D position and attitude angle (roll, pitch, and yaw angles) of the motorcycle, ($\dot{\phi}_b$, $\dot{\theta}_b$, $\dot{\psi}_b$) are the angular velocities (roll, pitch, and yaw velocities) of the motorcycle, and ($w_{\dot{V}_b}, w_{\ddot{\phi}_b}, w_{\ddot{\theta}_b}, w_{\ddot{\psi}_b}$) are the acceleration disturbances. $a_1 = V_b\tau + \tau^2 w_{\dot{V}_b}/2$, $a_2 = \dot{\phi}_b\tau + \tau^2 w_{\ddot{\phi}_b}/2$, $a_3 = \dot{\theta}_b\tau + \tau^2 w_{\ddot{\theta}_b}/2$, and $a_4 = \dot{\psi}_b\tau + \tau^2 w_{\ddot{\psi}_b}/2$.

Acknowledgment

This study was partially supported by the KAKENHI Grant #18K04062, the Japan Society for the Promotion of Science (JSPS).

References

[1] C. Cadena et al., "Past, Present, and Future of Simultaneous Localization and Mapping: Toward the Robust-Perception Age," IEEE Trans. on Robotics, vol. 32, pp. 1309–1332, Dec. 2016, doi: 10.1109/TRO.2016.2624754.

[2] G. Bresson, Z. Alsayed, L. Yu, and S. Glaser, "Simultaneous Localization And Mapping: A Survey of Current Trends in Autonomous Driving," IEEE Trans. on Intelligent Vehicles, vol. 2, pp. 194–220, Sept. 2017, doi: 10.1109/TIV.2017.2749181.

[3] B. Huang, J. Zhao, and J. Liu, "A Survey of Simultaneous Localization and Mapping," eprint arXiv:1909.05214, 2019.

[4] H. G. Seif and X. Hu, "Autonomous Driving in the iCity—HD Maps as a Key Challenge of the Automotive Industry," Engineering, vol. 2, pp.159–162, June 2016, doi:10.1016/J.ENG.2016.02.010.

[5] K. Morita, M. Hashimoto, and K. Takahashi, "Point-Cloud Mapping and Merging using Mobile Laser Scanner," Proc. of the third IEEE Int. Conf. on Robotic Computing (IRC 2019), pp.417–418, March 2019, doi: 10.1109/IRC.2019.00078.

[6] D. Schwesinger, A. Shariati, C. Montella, and J. Spletzer, "A Smart Wheelchair Ecosystem for Autonomous Navigation in Urban Environments," Autonomous Robot, vol. 41, pp. 519–538, March 2017, doi: 10.1007/s10514-016-9549-1.

[7] S. Hong, H. Ko, and J. Kim, "VICP: Velocity Updating Iterative Closest Point Algorithm," Proc. of 2010 IEEE Int. Conf. on Robotics and Automation (ICRA 2010), pp. 1893–1898, May 2010, doi: 10.1109/ROBOT.2010.5509312.

[8] F. Moosmann and C. Stiller, "Velodyne SLAM," Proc. of IEEE Intelligent Vehicles Symp. (IV2011), pp. 393–398, July 2011, doi: 10.1109/IVS.2011.5940396.

[9] J. Zhang and A. Singh, "LOAM: Lidar Odometry and Mapping in Real-time," Proc. of Robotics: Science and Systems, Jan. 2014.

[10] K. Inui, M. Morikawa, M. Hashimoto, and K. Takahashi, "Distortion Correction of Laser Scan Data from In-Vehicle Laser Scanner Based on Kalman Filter and NDT Scan Matching," Proc. of the 14th Int. Conf. on Informatics in Control, Automation and Robotics (ICINCO), pp. 329–334, 2017, doi: 10.5220/0006422303290334.

[11] K. Tokorodani, M. Hashimoto, Y. Aihara, and K. Takahashi, "Point-Cloud Mapping Using Lidar Mounted on Two-Wheeled Vehicle Based on NDT Scan Matching," Proc. of the 18th Int. Conf. on Informatics in Control, Automation and Robotics (ICINCO), pp. 446–452, 2019, doi: 10.5220/ 0007946204460452.

[12] P. Biber and W. Strasser, "The Normal Distributions Transform: A New Approach to Laser Scan Matching," Proc. of IEEE/RSJ Int. Conf. on Intelligent Robots and Systems (IROS 2003), pp. 2743–2748, Oct. 2003, doi: 10.1109/IROS.2003.1249285.

[13] J. P. Saarinen, H. Andreasson, T. Stoyanov, and A. J. Lilienthal, "3D Normal Distributions Transform Occupancy Maps: An Efficient Representation for Mapping in Dynamic Environments," Int. J. of Robotics Research, vol.32, pp.1627–1644, Sept. 2013, doi:10.1177/0278364913499415.

[14] X. Ding, Y. Wang, H. Yin, L. Tang, and R. Xiong, "Multi-Session Map Construction in Outdoor Dynamic Environment," Proc. of the 2018 IEEE Int. Conf. on Real-time Computing and Robotics (IRC2018), pp. 384–389, Aug. 2018, doi: 10.1109/RCAR.2018.8621770.

[15] M. Yamaji, S. Tanaka, M. Hashimoto, and K. Takahashi, "Point Cloud Mapping Using Only Onboard Lidar in GNSS Denied and Dynamic Environments," Proc. of the Fifteenth Int. Conf. on Systems (ICONS 2020), Feb. 2020.

[16] R. B. Rusu and S. Cousins, "3D is Here: Point Cloud Library (PCL)," Proc. of 2011 IEEE Int. Conf. on Robotics and Automation (ICRA 2011), 2011.

[17] S. Sato, M. Hashimoto, M. Takita, K. Takagi, and T. Ogawa, "Multilayer Lidar-Based Pedestrian Tracking in Urban Environments," Proc. of IEEE Intelligent Vehicles Symp. (IV2010), pp. 849–854, June 2010, doi: 10.1109/IVS.2010.5548135.

[18] S. Kanaki et al., "Cooperative Moving-Object Tracking with Multiple Mobile Sensor Nodes -Size and Posture Estimation of Moving Objects using In-Vehicle Multilayer Laser Scanner-," Proc. of 2016 IEEE Int. Conf. on Industrial Technology (ICIT 2016), pp. 59–64, March 2016, doi: 10.1109/ICIT.2016.7474726.

Design of an Acoustic Transducer Structure for Biosensing

Emmanuel Attal
MN2S Department
FEMTO-ST Institute
UMR 6174 CNRS
Besançon, France
email: emmanuel.attal@hotmail.fr

Sophie Sok
MN2S Department
FEMTO-ST Institute
UMR 6174 CNRS
Besançon, France
email: sok.sophie.m@gmail.com

Thérèse Leblois
MN2S Department
FEMTO-ST Institute
UMR 6174 CNRS
Besançon, France
email: therese.leblois@femto-st.fr

***Abstract*—In a biomedical context linked to the detection of biological particles in a liquid by a biosensor, we have modeled a piezoelectric transducer based on Gallium Arsenide. The future application will enable to evaluate the mass of biological specific elements present in a complex fluid. The multiphysics simulations of this transducer allowed us to identify a quasi-transverse thickness mode at around 2 MHz. For this mode, the out-of-plane displacement is low, which is a prerequisite to keep the performance when immersed in a liquid medium. In this study, we demonstrated the effect of holes distributed over the structure on the in-plane/out-of-plane displacement ratio and on its resonance frequency.**

Keywords-Gallium Arsenide; Acoustic transducer; Holes numbers.

I. Introduction

In the medical field, the growing need to provide real-time information on the presence of a specific biological element in a complex environment has motivated the development of a multitude of detection technologies [1][2]. Nevertheless, it is important to mention that many methods of detection still use culture processes before measurement because their limit of detection is too high. The culture of biological elements requires a lot of time and does not allow a real time monitoring of the biological liquid. The objective of this study is to design a transducer whose sensitivity and limit of detection in liquid media are at the state of the art [3][4].

For this purpose, we propose an original acoustic transduction microdevice to detect the immobilization of specific analytes. The challenge of this type of transducer is to maintain its quality factor Q at the value in air when it is immersed in a liquid medium, especially in a viscous medium such as blood. To get close to this result, we must cancel as much as possible the out-of-plane components of the vibration.

Previous works [5][6] on wave propagation in clamped plates have demonstrated the strong attenuation that these embedding could generate on these waves, making measurements difficult when the plate is immersed in a liquid medium. To avoid signal losses when the plate is in contact of a fluid, two alternatives are studied: (1) to clamp the plate along two sides rather than four, and (2) to add holes so as to soften the structure in the plane of the plate.

II. Experiment

In this study, the considered transducer structure is a rectangular thin plate in the plane (x, y) made of piezoelectric gallium arsenide (GaAs) which size is 3000x2000x50 μm^3 (Figure 1(a)). GaAs was chosen because of its pure crystallinity and its knowledge in terms of microfabrication. The generation of the elastic wave in the structure is ensured by means of three gold electrodes deposited by sputtering on the upper surface. These electrodes are oriented along the plate width and separated equidistantly. The structure is clamped along x direction. All the numeric simulation are performed using COMSOL Multiphysics© software.

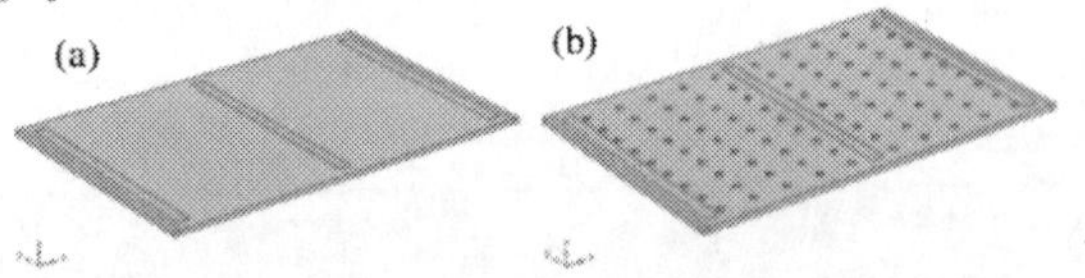

Figure 1. Clamped structure in (100) GaAs crystal (a) without circular holes and (b) with circular holes

The considered mode of vibration (Figure 2) is a quasi-thickness shear mode at a resonance frequency close to 2MHz

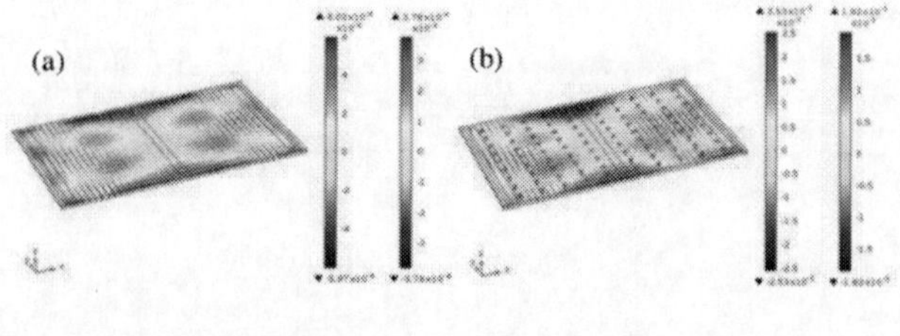

Figure 2. Quasi-thickness shear mode at a resonance frequency of 2 MHz. (a) without circular holes and (b) with circular holes

With this configuration, the attenuation due to the fluid in contact with the membrane is minimized, but not negligible. In order to increase the in-plane amplitude of the acoustic wave in the GaAs crystal, we generate several circular holes in the plate (Figure 1(b)). The objective of these holes distributed over the plate is to increase the elasticity of the plate and then to improve the electrical response of the transducer. In this study, the effect of a circular holes array evenly distributed between each electrode is presented. The simulated results shown in Figure 3(a) and 3(b) highlight the impact of the size and number of holes on the in-plane/out-of plane displacements ratio. As seen in this figure, the displacement ratios X/Z and Y/Z have the same trend. Because of the orientation of electrodes toward Y axis, the ratio X/Z is higher than Y/Z. The most important displacement ratio (in the two directions) is obtained for a holes number equal to 90 and a hole diameter equal to 50 µm. Other recent simulations on equivalent models prove that the frequency step of the model is a significant parameter and impact on the displacement ratios. The apparent plateau observable in displacement ratio of Figure 3(a) is due to a lack of simulation points for a given holes configuration.

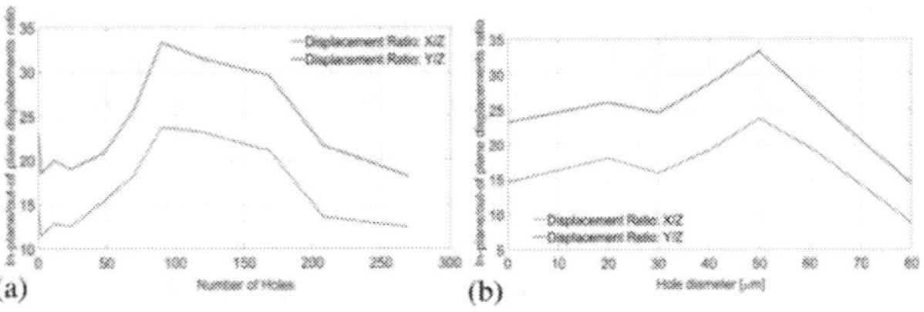

Figure 3. Impact of a) the holes numbers (for a given hole diameter of 50 µm) and b) holes diameters (holes array in the plate considered: 10x9) on the X/Z and Y/Z displacement ratios.

Figure 4(a) displays the resonance frequency evolution with the number of holes for a hole diameter equal to 50 µm. The resonance frequency shift vs the number of holes behaves as a linear curve. Figure 4(b) shows that for two different sizes of holes the behavior of resonance frequency with the hole diameters is non linear.

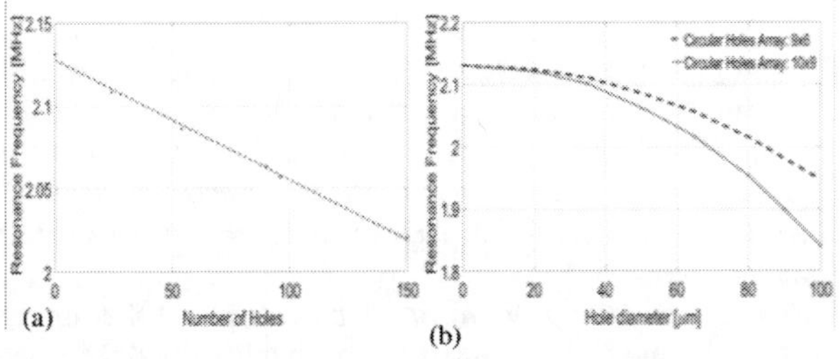

Figure 4. Quasi-thickness shear mode at a resonance frequency of 2 MHz (a) without circular holes and (b) with circular holes.

III. CONCLUSION

A plate mode (including clamped), with few displacement, depending on the thickness, and, therefore, having small attenuation in contact with the fluid, has been identified around 2 MHz. The addition of holes has the effect of shifting this mode towards lower frequencies. The displacement ratio gives better results for a holes number equal to 90 and a hole diameter equal to 50 µm. Future work will focus on the validation of this model with different fluid media: air, water, ionic solution and a biological fluid. For this purpose, several steps will be undertaken:

- Finite Element Method (FEM) simulation of the electrical impedance as a function of the size and the number of holes in the plate.
- Microfabrication of the GaAs / electrode structures by wet chemical etching and measurement of the acoustic impedance at the resonance frequency of the device placed in air and in liquid. The goal is to validate experimentally the previous results. The experimental study will focus on the "solid" structure and then on structures with holes. Some of the different tests that can be performed include:
    - The electrical impedance measurement with impedance analyzer enables to check the resonance frequency value of the mode and provides the quality factor of the resonators.
    - The 3D vibration measurements enable to conclude on the evolution of the out of plane displacement of the structure according to the holes parameters.

These experimental validations aim to conclude on the relevance of these microstructured devices for biosensing in liquid.

REFERENCES

[1] V. Lacour and T. Leblois, "Thermal and conductivity dependence of GaAs based acoustic biosensors," IEEE Ultrasonics Symp, pp. 1-4, Sept 2016.

[2] M. E. E. Alahi and S. C. Khopadhyay, "Detection methodologies for pathogen and toxins: a review," *Sensors*, vol. *17*(8), pp. 1885-1905, 2017.

[3] E. Nazemi, W. M. Hassen, E. H. Frost, and J. J. Dubowski, "Growth of Escherichia coli on the GaAs (001) surface," Talanta, vol. 178, pp. 69-77, 2018.

[4] J. Chawich, P. Boiteux, T. Leblois, and C. Elie-Caille, "Specificity and sensitivity characterization of a gallium arsenide resonant bio-sensor", *IEEE International Ultrasonics Symp*, pp. 1-9, Oct 2018.

[5] A. Bienaimé, "*Microcapteur en arséniure de gallium pour la détection de molécules dans un fluide*, Doctoral dissertation, Besançon, 2012.

[6] V. Lacour, A. Bienaime, J. F. Manceau, T. Leblois, and J. Dubowski, "Design and experimental studies of Gallium Arsenide bulk acoustic wave transducer under lateral field excitation", *European Frequency and Time Forum (EFTF)*, pp. 163-166, Jun 2014.

Non-Linear Modeling and Sensitive Analysis of a Magnetostrictive Force Sensor

Mojtaba Ghodsi
School of Energy and Electronic Engineering
University of Portsmouth
Portsmouth, UK
e-mail: mojtaba.ghodsi@port.ac.uk

Morteza Mohammadzaheri
Mechanical and Industrial Engineering Department,
Sultan Qaboos University,
Muscat, Oman
e-mail: morteza@squ.edu.om

Payam Soltani
School of Mechanical,
Aerospace and Automatic Engineering
Coventry University, UK
e-mail: payam.soltani@coventry.ac.uk

***Abstract*— In this paper, a non-linear model is presented for a magnetostrictive force sensor and the effective parameters in the sensor are highlighted. It was found that pre-stress and bias magnetic fields are the most significant parameters. It was observed that the presented force sensor has linear behavior for an applied force range from 100 to 1700 N. Response Surface Method (RSM) was employed to analyze the sensitivity of the sensor against the effective parameters. It was found that the pre-stress and bias magnetic field and their interactions play a significant role in the sensitivity of the force sensor. Furthermore, it was manifested that the linearity can be enhanced by increasing the pre-stress. On the other hand, the sensitivity of the sensor will be sacrificed by increasing the pre-stress. Bias magnetic field plays the same role. The sensor's sensitivity can be enhanced by increasing the bias magnetic field. Conversely, the sensor loses its linearity in a higher magnetic field. Therefore, there is a trade-off between sensor sensitivity and nonlinearity and both are adjustable by both, pre-stress and magnetic bias.**

Keywords- Force Sensor; Non-Linear Model; Sensitivity; Non-linearity; Pre-steers; Magnetic Bias.

I. INTRODUCTION

Nowadays, the force sensing element is an inevitable feedback element in many control systems in industries. Warning alarms of the seat belt in automobiles, manipulators of robots, and oil/gas monitoring systems are highly dependent on the force/pressure sensing elements. Compared to the traditional force sensors using strain gages, smart materials are promising better static and dynamic characteristics. Piezoelectric elements have been employed as smart sensors for many years [1][2]. However, the piezoelectric element is brittle and its output signal transmission cannot be wireless. On the other hand, a magnetostrictive force sensor has some outstanding merits in comparison with the other force sensors such as machinability [3]-[6], high coupling factor between elastic and magnetic states (about 0.7), heavy loads withstanding [7], adaptive with a harsh environment [8], low response time (about a few microseconds), zero-energy consumption [9] and is suitable for wireless applications [10]. It is required to mention that magnetostrictive materials suffer from some disadvantages such as Hysteresis behavior, Eddy current loss, and thermal instability. Talebian presented a good enough model for Hysteresis [11] and Eddy current loss [12]. Furthermore, Ghodsi et al. employed a thermoelectric cooler to remove heat generated by the excitation coil [13][14]. Magnetostrictive force sensors are based on the Villari effect [15]. Therefore, when subjected to a mechanical force, their magnetization varies and we can measure the variation of magnetic field density passing through the magnetostrictive bar. This variation can be proportional to the applied mechanical load. Calkins et al. and Stachowiak investigated the effects of pre-stress on the dynamic performance of Terfenol-D transducers/actuators [16][17]. Many researchers developed various types of magnetostrictive force sensors. Zhu et al. proposed a model for a giant magnetostrictive force sensor and investigated the effect of frequency on the output voltage of the sensor [18]. A precise impact force sensor using Galfenol has been developed by Shu et al. They showed that the cantilever type is more sensitive than the rod type [19]. Galfenol was employed to develop a high sensitivity and linearity tactile magnetostrictive force sensor in 2019 [20]. Despite high linearity, this cantilever force sensor is suitable for a low range of force detection less than 5 N.

In this paper, after presenting the principle of the sensor in Section 2, a non-linear magneto-mechanical model for giant magnetostrictive force is combined with Faraday's law to predict the generated voltage by a search coil. Furthermore, the sensitive analysis of the sensor and the effects of parameters on the sensor's performance will be discussed in Section 3.

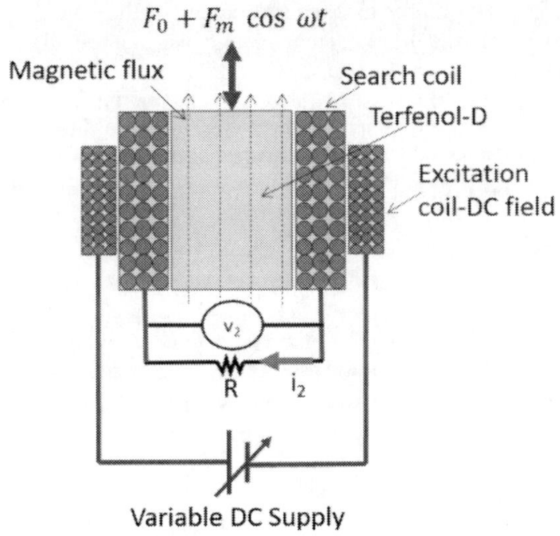

Figure1. Schematic of the force sensor

II. Principle and Modeling of Force Sensor

A. Principle of Operation

The proposed force sensor consists of a core made of Giant Magnetostrictive Material (GMM) which is in the presence of a bias magnetic field, a search coil, and an excitation coil to generate a bias magnetic field (Figure 1). The bias magnetic field can be generated by permanent magnets or a coil energized by a variable DC power supply. Applied force changes the magnetic flux density pass through the Terfenol-D. Based on Faraday's law, the variation of magnetic flux can be detected by the generated voltage across the resistive load connected to the ends of the search coil. The amplitude of the generated voltage (V_2) is proportional to the amplitude of the applied force (F_m). The proportional relationship can be changed to an equal relationship by (1).

$$V_2 = k\,(H_0, F_0)\,F_m \tag{1}$$

k is the coefficient, which is dependent on the magnetic bias and pre-stress applied to the Terfenol-D. The effect of magnetic bias and pre-stress will be examined in the next section.

B. Non-linear Analytical Modeling

This section aims to find a relationship between the amplitude of the applied force and the amplitude of the induced voltage. By applying axial harmonic force consists of bias force to the magnetostrictive bar, Terfenol-D, the sensitive part of the sensor is subjected to tensile and compressive normal stresses. By assuming the vibration as the axial harmonic force, the non-linear magneto-mechanical relation of Terfenol-D can be presented in (2) [21].

$$\begin{cases} \varepsilon = \dfrac{\sigma}{E} - \dfrac{M_s}{\gamma}\left[\dfrac{\gamma H}{\sigma}\tanh\left(\dfrac{\gamma H}{\sigma}\right) - \ln\left(\cosh\left(\dfrac{\gamma H}{\sigma}\right)\right)\right] \\ B = \mu_0 H + M_s \tanh(\dfrac{\gamma H}{\sigma}) \end{cases} \tag{2}$$

where B is magnetic flux density, H is the magnetic field ε , and σ are strain and the applied stress, respectively. For Terfenol-D, the best value of γ and M_s are -347 and 0.8, respectively [12][22]. The magnetic field consists of two components of (a) magnetic field bias, H_0, (b) magnetic field caused by generated current, $\widehat{H}$. Using Ampere's law, the magnetic field can be concluded as (3).

$$H = H_0 + \widehat{H} = H_0 + \frac{Ni_2}{l_0} \tag{3}$$

where N is the number of turns of the search coil, i_2 is induced current due to the applied force and l_0 is the length of the Terfenol-D bar. Based on Faraday's law, the relationship between magnetic flux and generated voltage can be written as follow:

$$\varphi = BA = -\frac{1}{N}\int v_2 dt \tag{4}$$

By substituting (3) and (4) into (2) and considering $F=\sigma A$ and $v_2=Ri_2$ the induced current can be derived by solving differential (5).

$$-\frac{R}{L_0}\int_0^{\tau} i_2\,dt = i_2 + \frac{NAM_s}{L_0}\tanh\left(\frac{\frac{\gamma ANi_2}{l_0} + \gamma AH_0}{F_0 + F_m\cos\omega t}\right) + \frac{NA\mu_0}{L_0}H_0 \tag{5}$$

To solve this non-linear differential equation, we employed the Simulink of MATLAB (Appendix A). The parameters of the force sensor are shown in Table I. The sample of output voltage calculated by Simulink is shown in Figure 2 while the sensor is under harmonic force. Figure 3 shows the simulated relationship between applied force and output voltage when the magnetostrictive force sensor is under various magnetic fields from 100 to 20 kA/m, and constant bias compressive force is about 1000 N. It is obvious that the force sensor has a linear behavior in the range from 100 to 1700 N. Furthermore, magnetic bias has a positive effect on the sensitivity of the sensor while its nonlinearity is magnified for force amplitude larger than 1700 N. The effect of bias force (pre-stress) is simulated in Figure 4. It is found that higher pre-stress causes lower sensitivity. However, pre-stress is helpful to enhance the linearity of the sensor in a force range higher than 1700 N.

TABLE I. FORCE SENSOR PARAMETERS

Terms	Values
Cross-section of Terfenol-D, A	78.5 (mm^2)
Young Modulus, E	45 (GPa)
Terfenol-D density, ρ	9200 (kg/m^3)
External Resistor	0.3 Ω
Number of turns in pickup coil, N	300
Length of the Terfenol-D and search coil, l_0	50 (mm)
Relative magnetic permeability, μ_r	12-25

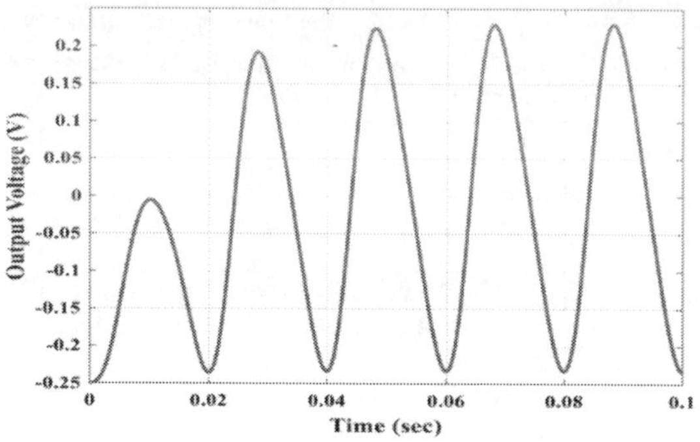

Figure 2. Output voltage of search coil, , R=0.3 Ω, H_0=5 kA/m, F_0= -1060 N, F_m= 1000 N, f= 50 Hz (simulated results)

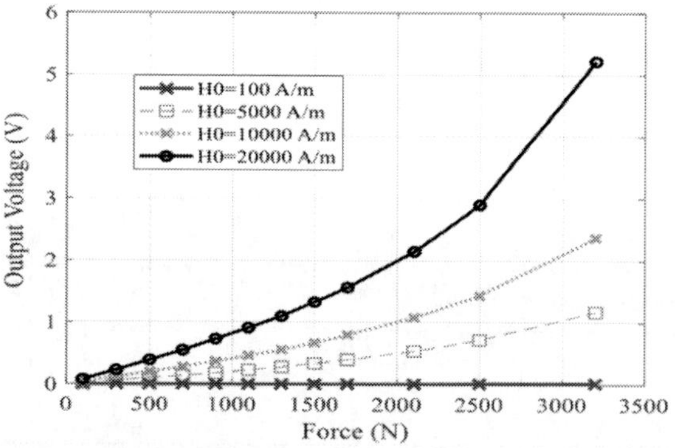

Figure 3. Output voltage of force sensor (V_{pp}); R=0.3 Ω ; F_0 = -1000 N (simulated results)

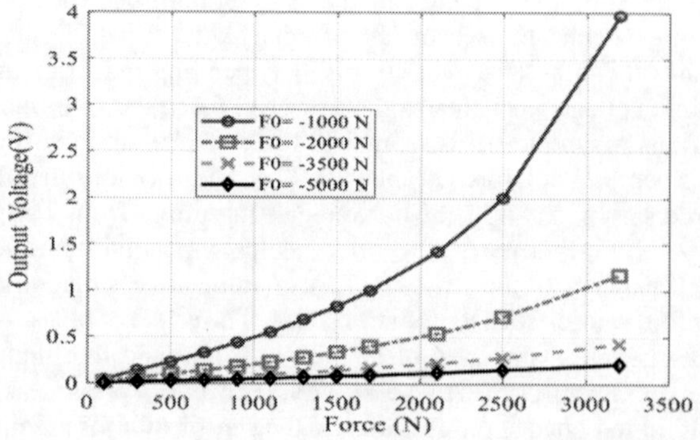

Figure 4. Output voltage of force sensor (V_{pp}); R=0.3 Ω ; H_0 = 5000 A/m (simulated results)

III. SENSITIVITY ANALYSIS OF THE FORCE SENSOR

Referring to the (5), and the sample of the voltage output shown in Figures 2 to 4, the magnetic bias and pre-stress seem to be effective on the measured voltage across the search coil. To examine this assumption, the Design Of Experiments (DOE) was exploited [23][24]. The goal of this part is to determine the optimum operating conditions while the pre-stress and bias magnetic fields are assumed adjustable. The variable factors in this force sensor are F_0 and H_0. To maximize the output voltage, the Response Surface Method (RSM) is employed to find proper values for each factor to have optimum output voltage [25][26]. To specify a regression equation between the amplitude of output voltage and pre-stress and magnetic bias, Minitab 17 software is used. Table II shows two factors with five levels for each. Based on the design proposed by RSM and selection of $\alpha = 1.44$, it is found that nine simulation results including one center point are required (Table III). Table IV shows the P_{value} and the coefficients of each factor. Since the P_{value} of $H_0 \times H_0$ is greater than 0.05, the effect of this term, $H_0 \times H_0$, is ignorable on the output voltage. However, F_0, H_0, and their interaction are effective, since their P_{value} is smaller than 0.05. R-Sq = 98.38% shows the goodness of the model represented by RSM.

TABLE II. CODED INPUT VARIABLES

Factors	- α	-1	0	1	+ α
F_0	-3940	-3500	-2500	-1500	-1060
H_0	1400	2500	5000	7500	8600

TABLE III. ANALYTICAL RESULTS USED IN RSM

Order	F_o (N)	H_o (A/m)	V_m (v)
1	-3500	2500	0.023
2	-1500	2500	0.075
3	-3500	7500	0.07
4	-1500	7500	0.225
5	-3940	5000	0.038
6	-1060	5000	0.23
7	-2500	1400	0.0215
8	-2500	8600	0.13
9	-2500	5000	0.075

TABLE IV. COEFFICIENT OF REGRESSION EQUATION AND P_{VALUE} IN INITIAL AND MODIFIED MODELS

Terms	Initial Model		Modified Model	
	Reg. Eq. Coefficient	P_{value}	Reg. Eq. Coefficient	P_{value}
Constant	0.075	0.00	0.07411	0.00
F_0	0.5982	0.00	0.05982	0.00
H_0	0.04381	0.00	0.04381	0.00
$F_0 \times H_0$	0.02575	0.002	0.02575	0.001
$F_0 \times F_0$	0.02784	0.000	0.02801	0.000
$H_0 \times H_0$	-0.00128	0.767	---------	------

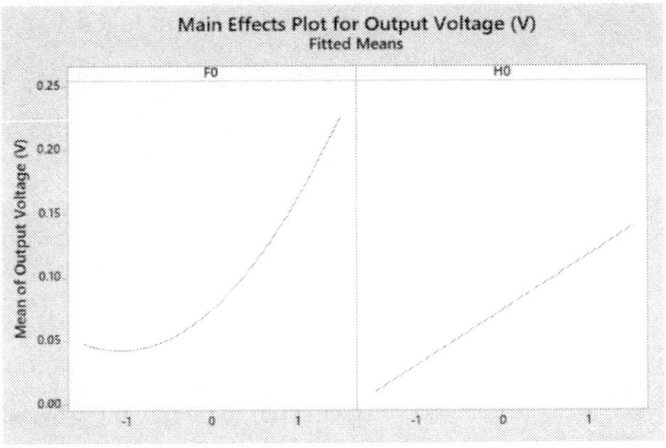

Figure 5. Relationship between the output voltage and main effects, F_0 and H_0

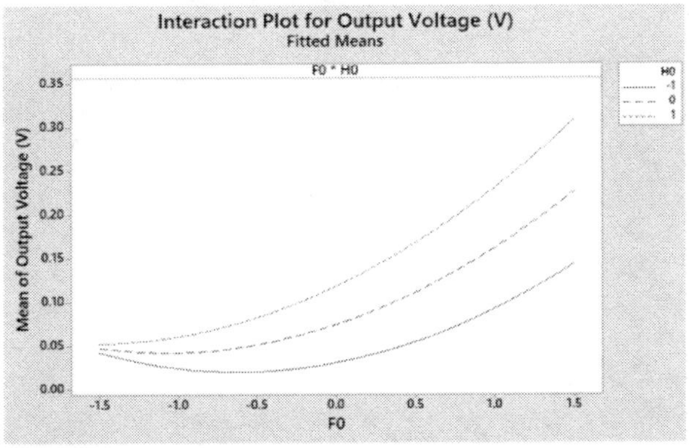

Figure 6. Interaction between F_0 and H_0

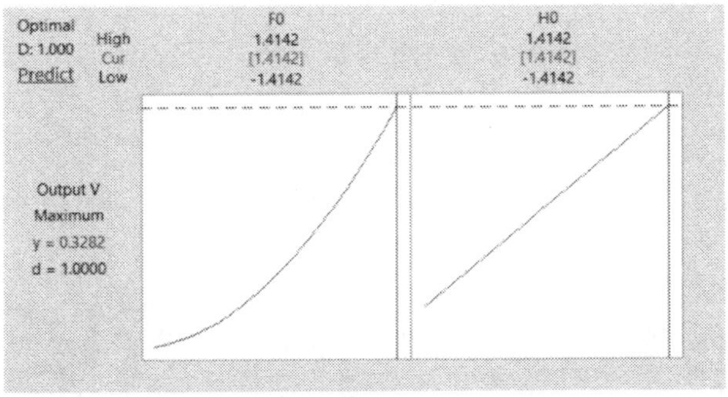

Figure 7. RSM optimizer to predict the maximum output

Based on the coefficients presented in Table IV, the output voltage can be modeled by (6):

$$V_2\,(v) = 0.07411 + 0.05982\,F_0 + 0.04381\,H_0 + 0.02801\,F_0 \times F_0 + 0.02575\,F_0 \times H_0 \quad (6)$$

Therefore, among the factors and their interactions, F_0 has the highest effect since its coefficient is the largest. Figures 5 and 6 show the main effects and interactions between the main factors. One of the biggest advantages of RSM is determining the maximum output voltage. Figure 7 predicts that the maximum amplitude of output voltage (V_m) can be enhanced to 0.32 V, when both F_0 and H_0 are 1060 N and 8.6 kA/m, respectively. This prediction is confirmed when these values are substituted in (5) and the amplitude of output voltage (V_m) reaches 0.4 V.

IV. Conclusion

A magnetostrictive force sensor was modeled using non-linear magneto-mechanical coupling equations. The effect of the pre-stress and bias magnetic field was investigated on the sensitivity and nonlinearity of the force sensors. It was highlighted that the presented applied force has linear behavior for the applied force range from 100 to 1700 N. Response Surface Method (RSM) was employed to analyze the sensitivity of the sensor against the effective parameters. It was found that the pre-stress and bias magnetic fields and their interactions play a significant role in the sensitivity of the force sensor. Furthermore, it was manifested that the linearity can be enhanced by increasing the pre-stress. On the other hand, the sensitivity of the sensor will be sacrificed by increasing the pre-stress. Bias magnetic field plays the same role. The sensor's sensitivity can be enhanced by increasing the bias magnetic field. Conversely, the sensor loses its linearity in a higher magnetic field. Consequently, there is a trade-off between sensor sensitivity and nonlinearity and both are adjustable by both, pre-stress and magnetic bias.

References

[1] H. Hoshyarmanesh, A. Abbasi, P. Moein, M. Ghodsi, and K. Zareinia, "Design and Implementation of an Accurate, Portable, and Time-Efficient Impedance-Based Transceiver for Structural Health Monitoring," *IEEE/ASME Transactions on Mechatronics*, vol. 22, pp. 2809-2814, 2017.

[2] H. Hoshyarmanesh, M. Ghodsi, M. Kim, H. H. Cho, and H.-H. Park, "Temperature Effects on Electromechanical Response of Deposited Piezoelectric Sensors Used in Structural Health Monitoring of Aerospace Structures," *Sensors*, vol. 19, p. 2805, 2019.

[3] M. Ghodsi, T. Ueno, and T. Higuchi, "Novel Magnetostrictive Bimetal Actuator Using Permendur," *Advanced Materials Research*, vol. 47-50, pp. 262-265, 2008.

[4] A. Saleem, M. Ghodsi, M. Mesbah, and A. Ozer, "Model identification of terfenol-D magnetostrictive actuator for precise positioning control," in *Active and Passive Smart Structures and Integrated Systems 2016*, 2016, p. 97992J.

[5] M. Sheykholeslami, Y. Hojjat, M. Ghodsi, M. Zeighami, and K. Kakavand, "Effect of magnetic field on mechanical properties in Permendur," *Materials Science and Engineering: A*, vol. 651, pp. 598-603, 2016.

[6] M. R. Sheykholeslami, Y. Hojjat, S. Cinquemani, M. Ghodsi, and M. Karafi, "An approach to design and fabrication of resonant giant magnetostrictive transducer," *Smart Structures and Systems*, vol. 17, pp. 313-325, 2016.

[7] M. Ghodsi, S. Mirzamohamadi, S. Talebian, Y. Hojjat, and M. Sheikhi, "Analytical, numerical and experimental investigation of a giant magnetostrictive (GM) force sensor," *Sensor Review*, vol. 35, pp. 357-365, 2015.

[8] M. Ghodsi and M. Modabberifar, "Quality factor, static and dynamic responses of miniature galfenol actuator at wide range of temperature," *International Journal of Physical Sciences*, vol. 6, pp. 8143-8150, 2011.

[9] M. Ghodsi, T. Ueno, H. Teshima, H. Hirano, T. Higuchi, and E. Summers, "“Zero-power” positioning actuator for cryogenic environments by combining magnetostrictive bimetal and HTS," *Sensors and Actuators A: Physical*, vol. 135, pp. 787-791, 2007.

[10] N. Adelsberg, Y. Weber, A. Yoffe, and D. Shilo, "Wireless thin layer force sensor based on a magnetostrictive composite material," *Smart Materials and Structures*, vol. 26, p. 065013, 2017.

[11] S. Talebian, Y. Hojjat, M. Ghodsi, M. R. Karafi, and S. Mirzamohammadi, "A combined Preisach–Hyperbolic Tangent model for magnetic hysteresis of Terfenol-D," *Journal of Magnetism Magnetic Materials*, vol. 396, pp. 38-47, 2015.

[12] S. Talebian, Y. Hojjat, M. Ghodsi, and M. R. Karafi, "Study on classical and excess eddy currents losses of Terfenol-D," *Journal of Magnetism and Magnetic Materials*, vol. 388, pp. 150-159, 2015.

[13] M. Ahanpanjeh, M. Ghodsi, and Y. Hojjat, "Precise Positioning of Terfenol-D Actuator Eliminiating the Heat Generated by Coil," *Modern Applied Science*, vol. 10, pp. 232-244, 2016.

[14] M. Ghodsi, A. Saleem, A. Özer, I. Bahadur, K. Alam, A. Al-Yahmadi, *et al.*, "Elimination of thermal instability in precise positioning of Galfenol actuators," in *Behavior and Mechanics of Multifunctional Materials and Composites 2016*, 2016, p. 980008.

[15] M. Ghodsi, H. Ziaiefar, M. Mohammadzaheri, and A. Al-Yahmedi, "Modeling and Characterization of Permendur Cantilever Beam for Energy Harvesting," *Energy*, vol. 176, pp. 561-569, 2019.

[16] F. T. Calkins, M. J. Dapino, and A. B. Flatau, "Effect of prestress on the dynamic performace of a Terfenol-D transducer," in *Smart Structures and Materials 1997: Smart Structures and Integrated Systems*, 1997, pp. 293-304.

[17] D. Stachowiak, "The influence of magnetic bias and prestress on magnetostriction characteristics of a giant magnetostrictive actuator," *Przegląd Elektrotechniczny*, vol. 89, pp. 233-236, 2013.

[18] Z. Zhu, F. Liu, X. Zhu, H. Wang, and J. Xu, "Vibration analysis and experiment of giant magnetostrictive force sensor," *IOP Conference Series: Materials Science and Engineering*, vol. 274, p. 012071, 2017.

[19] L. Shu, J. Yang, B. Li, Z. Deng, and M. J. Dapino, "Impact force sensing with magnetostrictive Fe-Ga alloys," *Mechanical Systems and Signal Processing*, vol. 139, p. 106418, 2020.

[20] Y. Li, B. Wang, Y. Li, B. Zhang, L. Weng, W. Huang, *et al.*, "Design and output characteristics of magnetostrictive tactile sensor for detecting force and stiffness of manipulated objects," *IEEE Transactions on Industrial Informatics*, vol. 15, pp. 1219-1225, 2018.

[21] C. S. Clemente and D. Davino, "Modeling and characterization of a kinetic energy harvesting device based on galfenol," *Materials*, vol. 12, p. 3199, 2019.

[22] S. Talebian, Y. Hojjat, M. Ghodsi, S. Mirzamoha, and S. Mirzamohammadi, "Study of effects of bias magnetic field and mechanical pre-stress on sensitivity and linear measurement range of Terfonel-D force sensor," *Modares Mechanical Engineering* vol. 13, pp. 46-55, 2013.

[23] M. Ghodsi, "Optimization of mover acceleration in DC tubular linear direct-drive machine using response surface method," *International Review of Electrical Engineering*, vol. 10, pp. 492-500, 2015.

[24] M. Ghodsi, H. Ziaiefar, M. Mohammadzaheri, F. K. Omar, and I. Bahadur, "Dynamic analysis and performance optimization of permendur cantilevered energy harvester," *Smart Structures and Systems*, vol. 23, pp. 421-428, 2019.

[25] M. Ghodsi, H. Ziaifar, M. Mohammadzaheri, and P. Soltani, "Effect of Damping on Performance of Magnetostrictive Vibration Energy Harvester," *International Journal of Mechanical and Mechatronics Engineering*, vol. 14, pp. 147-151, 2020.

[26] M. Ghodsi, H. Ziaifar, M. M. Mohammadzaheri, and P. Soltani, "Effect of inductance ratio on operating frequencies of a hybrid resonant inverter," *International Journal of Energy and Power Engineering*, vol. 14, pp. 123-128, 2020.

Appendix A

Figure A1 shows the Simulink program used to solve the (5).

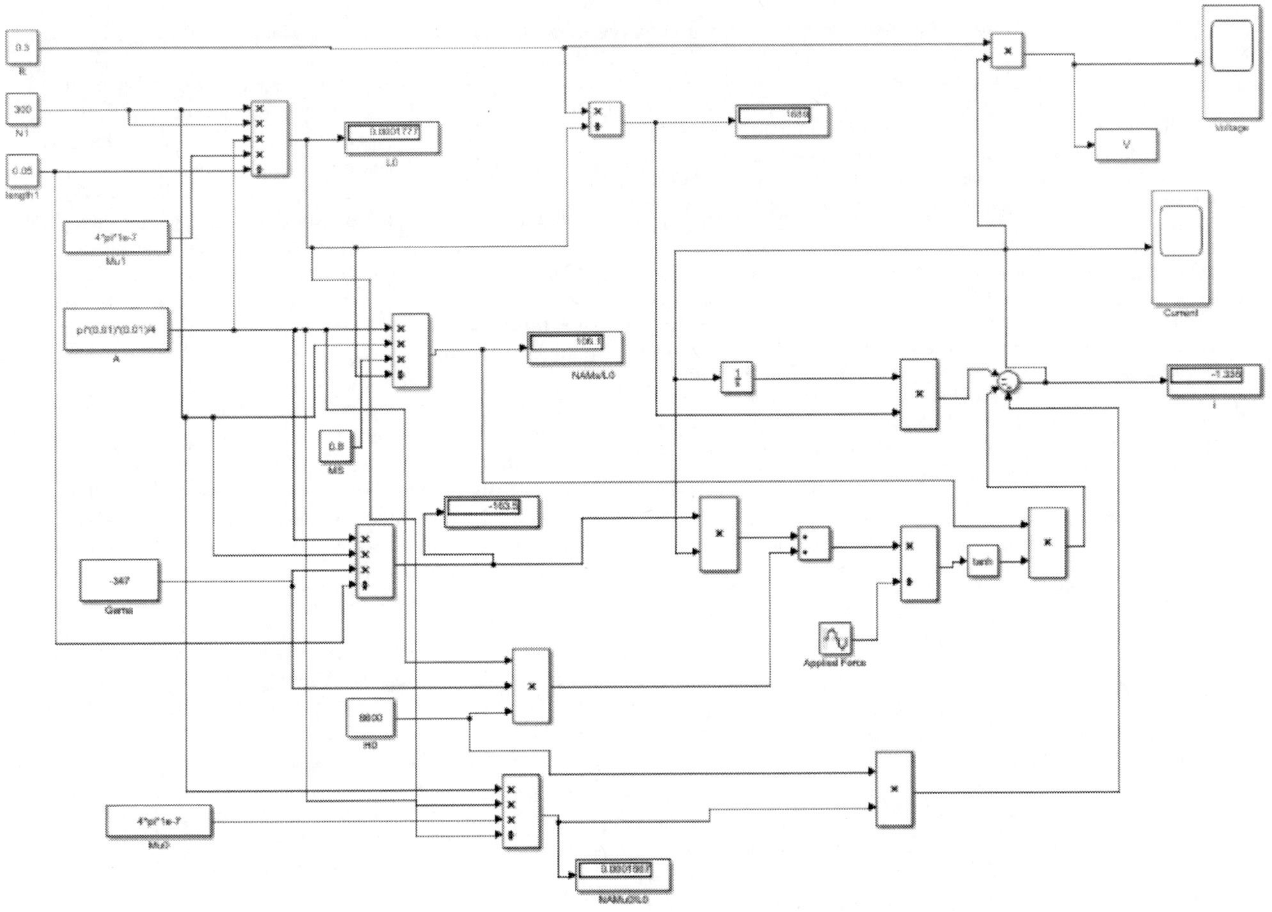

Figure A1. Simulink program to calculate the output voltage

Near-Ground Wireless Coverage Design in Rural Environments

Marta Botella-Campos[1], José Miguel Jiménez[1], Sandra Sendra[1,2], Jaime Lloret[1]
[1]*Instituto de Investigación para la Gestión Integrada de zonas Costeras (IGIC)*
Universitat Politècnica de València, València, Spain
[2]*Departamento de Teoría de la Señal, Telemática y Comunicaciones (TSTC)*
Universidad de Granada, Granada, Spain
emails: marbocam@etsid.upv.es, jojiher@dcom.upv.es, ssendra@ugr.es, jlloret@dcom.upv.es

Abstract—**Due to the broad range of options that wireless systems offer, Wi-Fi products are increasingly being used in agriculture environments to improve farming practices and better control the output of the production. However, the foliage has proven to harm radio-frequency propagation as well as decreasing the coverage area of Wireless Sensor Networks (WSNs). Therefore, near-ground channel characterization can help in avoiding high antennas and vegetation. Nevertheless, theoretical models tend to fail when forecasting near-ground path losses. This paper aims at determining how the field components such as soil, grass and, trunks affect radio-links in near-ground scenarios. To do this, we measure the Received Signal Strength (RSSI), the Signal to Interference Ratio (SIR) and the Round-Trip Time (RTT) of a Wireless Local Area Network (WLAN), at different distances, and the results are compared with 3 prediction models: the Free-Space Propagation Model, Two-Ray Ground Reflection Model and, One-Slope Log-Normal Model. The experiment was carried out by collecting experimental data at two different locations, i.e., an orange tree plantation and a field without vegetation, taking measurements every meter. A comprehensive analysis of the influence of rural environments can help to obtain better near-ground WSN performance and coverage in precision agriculture.**

Keywords—Wireless network coverage; IEEE 802.11; Precision agriculture; Propagation Losses; Free-Space Propagation Model; Two-Ray Ground Reflection Model, One-Slope Log-Normal Model.

I. Introduction

Smart Farming (SF) emphasizes the use of Information and Communication Technologies (ICTs) to leverage the farm management cycle. Improving the production capacity does not only enhance business efficiency but increases production and reduces the environmental impact. Since the United Nations expects the world population to reach 9.8 billion by 2050, human societies are facing the challenge of providing nourishment and livelihoods, while addressing the effects of climate change [1]. As it is, smart farming applies measures ecologically meaningful and site-specific, focusing on implementing auto-piloted harvesters and other farm machinery to achieve the smartest treatment [2].

The Internet of Things (IoT) and Cloud Computing are expected to move forward in farming management development by introducing these technologies into machinery and production systems [3]. The gathered information will then be sent via different technologies such as IEEE 802.11 standards, Bluetooth, Zigbee, LoRa, 6LoWPAN, 3G, 4G, etc., depending on the amount of data to be transmitted and the distance [4]. Nevertheless, IoT systems usually deal with small amounts of data to be transmitted through short distances. The two main storage systems used to save the gathered information from the sensors are traditional databases or clouds. The most used databases are MySQL and SQL, while the Thingspeak platform is the most used in cloud systems [4].

Wireless Sensor Networks (WSNs) are needed to monitor environmental conditions and provide decision-making information. This type of networks is composed of a group of spatially dispersed sensors to monitor and record environmental conditions such as humidity, temperature, soil moisture, etc. WSNs are made up of four parts: a wireless sensor node, a gateway node, a wireless communication network, and a server [5]. With the evolution of microelectronic technology, sensor nodes have evolved to be small devices with sensing, communication and computing devices. However, each node can only monitor a specific part of the field. Thus, the coverage area is a key problem since all nodes among a WSN must be autonomous to cooperatively pass data through the network to a main location. Moreover, its topology can vary enormously depending on the field.

Whatever WSN application may be, IEEE 802.11 g/n standard is generally used in WSN because it allows distances up to approximately 300 meters in outdoor environments (when there is free space between devices) [5]. This allows a maximum raw data throughput of 54 Mbps or 600 Mbps, depending on the standard used. Likewise, the radio-frequency band can vary from 2.4 GHz to 5 GHz using Modulation Code Keying (CCK), Direct-sequence Spread Spectrum (DSSS) or Orthogonal Frequency-Division Multiplexing (OFDM) modulation schemes.

In 2019, Bacco et al. [7] conducted a survey on SF research activities to state the achieved results and current investigations within EU territory. As a result, challenges impeding the adoption of recent technologies and techniques were highlighted. Although the current use of sensor nodes and analytic techniques is boosting Decision Support Systems (DSSs) in farms the lack of diffusion programs is preventing areas affected by the digital divide from incorporating ICTs. Nevertheless, technology is expected to have an increasing role in agriculture so that operations, such as planting and harvesting, may be automatized. Moreover, the availability of real-time data will allow finer control of pesticides and other chemicals. However, none of these will be possible without supporting policies to address poor telecommunication infrastructures and reduced digital skills.

As for Precision Agriculture (PA), Lindblom et al. [8] conducted a review on agricultural DSSs within the frame of the ongoing Swedish project. This project intends to identify the scientific disciplines and other competences that need to work together in developing technology for agricultural DSS. Therefore, the discussion is focused on the importance of considering in-land processes to design suitable WSNs. However, the lack of active participation in agricultural research and development processes is preventing the development of new practices and behaviours for more sustainable farming.

This paper aims to study near-ground wireless coverage in rural environments to ease multi-hop routing design. To this end, the Received Signal Strength Indicator (RSSI), the Signal to Interference Ratio (SIR) and the Round-Trip Time (RTT) of a wireless signal were measured at an orange field. This study aims to determine how near-ground radio-links are affected by field components such as grass, soil, trunks, etc. In this experiment, measurements were made at two different scenarios: one without vegetation and one at an orange tree plantation. In both cases, we used an access point and a laptop to take measurements at different distances, 30 cm above the ground.

The rest of this paper is structured as follows. Section II presents some related works. In Section III, the most popular propagation models are explained. The methodology and materials used in the experiment are presented in Section IV. In Section V, the experimental results are analysed. Finally, the main conclusions and future work are exposed in Section VI.

II. RELATED WORKS

Few technical works characterize near-ground radio-frequency propagation. In this section, some of the related works are discussed.

In 2011, Lloret et al. [9] presented a WSN that uses image processing to detect bad leaves in vineyards and sends an alarm to the farmer. In this case, wireless communications are made through IEEE 802.11 a/b/g/n standard to allow long-distance connections. Although the proposed system does not identify the cause of the deficiency, it detects bad leaves and notifies it to the farmer who can then decide what actions need to be taken. This solution provides a cost-effective sensor based on IP routers that have been adapted to fulfil this purpose. The designed WSN takes into account both sensing and radio coverage areas to allow low bandwidth consumption and higher scalability. The system to detect bad leaves goes through a 5-stage process before the node decides whether an alarm needs to be sent.

In [10], Wang et al. depicted a statistical model for near-ground channels based on experimental data collected through three different scenarios at 2.4 GHz. The main objective of this study was to develop a WSN to collect data in military explosive research. To do this, sensor nodes were fixed on the ground and had an antenna height of 3 cm to resist damages from detonations. Different propagation models were applied to predict path loss and compare the results with the performance of the obtained model. The main conclusion of this research was that antenna height determines the breakpoint distance of the nodes.

Luciani et al. [11] described a study done on near-ground node range at different heights in Wi-Fi crowded environments. The designed WSN used IEEE 802.15.4 standard to avoid direct Wi-Fi interference. Signal quality and range were determined by collecting RSSI data of three nodes at increasing node separation distance until signal loss. To perform the tests, measures were taken at three different heights: 15 cm, 30 cm, and 100 cm, at three different scenarios. The results of this experiment showed that prediction models failed to accurately forecast path loss. Moreover, ground-loss proved to be a major issue that determines node range and thus, must be taken into account when designing WSNs.

In 2015, Szajna et al. [12] characterized path loss and near-ground channels at 2.45 GHz on forested areas covered by snow. This study aimed to investigate the impact of antenna height and distance between nodes on path loss and special correlation. To do this, measurements were carried out in two different scenarios: a multi-purpose sports facility and a forested area covered by 15 cm of snow. In this case, antenna heights varied from 0 to 130.8 cm and the distance between the nodes varied in steps of 15.24 m and up to 79.2 m. The analysis of the results showed that reducing antenna heights increased path loss and reduced spatial correlation.

In [13], Torabi et al. proposed a near-ground prediction model to facilitate accurate WSN simulations using the principles of the Fresnel zones. In this study, the effects of antenna height, frequency, polarization, and electrical and geometrical properties of the terrain were studied. The accuracy of the proposed model was verified by comparing the theoretical results with near-ground measurements carried out in outdoor open areas. The results of this study showed that antenna height was by far the most influential parameter on network connectivity. Moreover, the wireless connection was proven to be fairly sensitive to the reflection coefficient in near-ground situations.

Sangodoyin et al. [14] presented a near-ground channel model to achieve precision ranging and localization of ultrawideband (UWB) propagation channels. This experiment was performed using a self-built channel sounder with an arbitrary waveform generator and a high-bandwidth sampling oscilloscope. In this case, antenna heights ranged from 10 cm up to 2 m above ground to determine its effects on signal strength. The results showed that the distance-dependent path loss was highly dependent on antenna heights. Moreover, under near-ground situations, frequency-dependent path loss exponent and shadowing variance increased.

In 2017, Klaina et al. [15] presented a narrowband radio channel model operating under near-ground conditions [15]. To do this, a WSN based on ZigBee was designed to analyse the effects caused by soil and grass fields. In this case, radio communications were made at 868 MHz, 2.4 GHz and, 5.8 GHz. In order to estimate signal quality, RSSI was measured and compared to path loss. Finally, they concluded that the ground has no effects on RF propagation except in the cases where antenna heights were 40 cm or less. However, signal levels decreased in the presence of grass fields and soil.

Tang et al. [16] studied a near-ground WSN at 470 MHz in four different scenarios to obtain the corresponding path loss models. To do this, measurements were taken on a flat concrete road, flat grass and two derived scenarios placing the transmitter directly on the ground. Three different antenna heights were used: 5 cm, 50 cm and, 1 m, and the RSSI was measured every meter at a distance up to 10 m, every 2 m at a distance of up to 20 m and every 5 m at a distance of up to 50 m. The results showed that when antenna height is lower than 50 cm, prediction models tend to inaccurately forecast path loss and thus, network connectivity.

After analysing previous works, we can conclude that near-ground wireless systems are difficult to characterize. In [9], the presented solution did manage to detect bad leaves. However, in this case, vegetation loss was not introduced into the power balance formula. The statistical model described in [10] demonstrated that antenna height determines coverage area and that propagation models fail to accurately forecast path loss. Moreover, the study depicted in [11] demonstrated that ground-loss is a major issue when determining node range. Nevertheless, this experiment was performed in Wi-Fi crowded environments. The study performed in [12] concluded that reducing antenna heights increased path loss, though this investigation was carried out in forested areas covered by snow. The research in [13] demonstrated that wireless connections were fairly sensitive to the reflection coefficient in near-ground situations. The experiment performed in [14] to characterize near-ground UWB propagation channels showed that the node range is highly dependent on antenna heights. Furthermore, the study carried in [15] to design a WSN based on ZigBee under near-ground conditions showed that grass fields and soil affect signal strength. Finally, in [16], a near-ground WSN where a transmitter was placed directly on the ground was presented, showing that prediction models fail to forecast path loss when antenna heights are lower than 50 cm.

For the reasons stated above, in this work, we present a site-specific study to guarantee the performance of near-ground radio-links in orange tree plantations.

III. ANALYTICAL STUDY

In this section, three propagation models are presented to predict the average signal strength drop and assess the level of accuracy that can be achieved in near-ground WSN scenarios. Thus, this section is divided into three different subsections.

A. *Free-Space Model*

The Free-space propagation model is the simplest way to calculate radio-signals propagation. From [17], we can extract the Free-Space propagation model based on Friis Transmission Formula. This equation is usually used when there are no obstacles in the line-of-sight, and it is given by equation (1).

$$P_r = \frac{P_t G_t G_r \lambda^2}{(4\pi)^2 d^2} \tag{1}$$

where:

P_t: transmitter power, in watts.

G_t: transmitter antenna gain.

G_r: receiver antenna gain.

λ: wavelength.

d: distance, in meters, between transmitter and receiver.

However, it is possible to calculate the losses between a transmitter (Tx) and a receiver (Rx) in terms of the frequency with equation (2).

$$FSPL\,(dB) = 20\log\left(\frac{4\pi\, d\, f}{c}\right) - G_T - G_R \tag{2}$$

where:

d: distance, in meters, between transmitter and receiver.

f: frequency in Hz.

c: speed of light in the vacuum (meters per second).

G_T: transmitter antenna gain, in dBi.

G_R: receiver antenna gain, in dBi.

B. *Two-Ray Ground Reflection Model*

The Two-Ray Ground Reflection Model predicts path losses between a Tx and a Rx when they are both in line-of-sight but have different antenna heights. This way, the received signal has two components: the line-of-sight component and the multipath component which is given by ground reflected waves. From [17], the given equation for the Two-Ray Model can be expressed by equation (3).

$$P_r = P_t G_t G_r \frac{h_t^2 h_r^2}{d^4} \tag{3}$$

where:

P_t: transmitter power, in watts.

G_t: transmitter antenna gain.

G_r: receiver antenna gain.

h_t: transmitter antenna height, in meters.

h_r: receiver antenna height, in meters.

d: distance, in meters, between transmitter and receiver.

Nevertheless, from the work in [16], we can tell that when radio-waves propagate near-ground in line-of-sight conditions, the path loss can be described by the plane-earth path loss formula, given by equation (4).

$$PL(dB) = 40\log(d) - 20\log(h_r) - 20\log(h_t) \tag{4}$$

where:

d: distance, in meters, between transmitter and receiver.

h_t: transmitter antenna height, in meters.

h_r: receiver antenna height, in meters.

C. *One-Slope Log-Normal Model*

The log-distance path loss model is a statistical model that takes into consideration object blockage, environmental clutter, and other changes to predict path loss. From [17], the log-normal model can be described by equation (5).

$$PL\,(d) = PL(d_0) + 10n\log\left(\frac{d}{d_0}\right) + X_\sigma \tag{5}$$

where:

PL (d): path loss at distance d, in dB.

PL (d_0): path loss, in dB, at reference distance of 1 meter (FSPL at 1 meter).

n: path loss factor (n = 2).

X_σ: zero mean Gaussian distributed variable with standard deviation σ.

σ: linear regression of measured data.

However, from reference [18] we can express One-Slope Log-Normal Model by equation (6).

$$PL\,(d) = FSPL(f, 1\,m) + 10n\log\left(\frac{d}{1\,m}\right) \qquad (6)$$

where:

PL (d): path loss at distance d, in dB.

FSPL (f, 1 m): free space path loss, in dB, at a reference distance of 1 meter.

n: path loss factor (n = 2).

d: distance, in meters, between transmitter and receiver.

Other studies have determined that, when antenna heights are lower than 50 cm, the One-Slope Model tends to estimate path losses better than other models [16]. However, other researches state that the use of these theoretical models can lead to overestimations of the networking capacities and should be avoided [17]. In the following sections, we will compare these three models with collated data to evaluate their performance and verify their accuracy in near-ground scenarios.

IV. Scenario Description and Tools Used

This section describes the devices used to perform the experiments, as well as the setup. Therefore, this section is segmented in four different subdivisions.

A. *Place of measurement*

In order to evaluate the path loss in near-ground radio wave signals, we sought out an orange tree plantation with an area of 1.775 m^2, with a length and a width of 71 m by 25 m, with no walls.

B. *Hardware used*

To perform this experiment, we used Linksys WRT320N-EZ router as a Tx configured to work at 2.4GHz with IEEE 802.11 b/g/n standard [19]. This router has three internal antennas with 1.5 dBi of antenna gain and an RF power of 17 dBm. The Rx was ASUS Gaming Notebook GL753V, which has a 2.8 GHz Intel Core i7-7700 HQ processor, 16 GB of memory. Wireless connections are made with Intel Dual Band Wireless Wifi Bluetooth Card 7265NGW that uses the IEEE 802.11 ac standard and has two antennas of 5 dBi of gain.

C. *Software used*

The measurements were made using the software Vistumbler [20] to scan the wireless network and measure both the SIR and the RSSI. As for the latency of the connection, it was measured by sending a ping signal through MS-DOS commands to the gateway.

D. *Set-up of the experiment*

Both Tx and Rx were positioned along the same line, 30 cm above the floor to measure the SIR and the RSSI. The evaluation of the path loss of RF signals was made by taking measurements in two different scenarios.

- Scenario 1: Measurements were made at an orange tree plantation, with data being collected every meter 30 cm above the ground.
- Scenario 2: Measurements were made on a field with no vegetation, collecting data every meter 30 cm above the ground.

Fig. 1 illustrates the set-up of the experiment at the orange tree plantation. In order to be able to perform comparisons of the signal strength, measurements were made at the same distances in both scenarios. Fig. 2 shows the set-up in Scenario 1. The noise floor in both cases was 80 dBm. Measurements were taken three times at each point.

V. Experimental Results

In this section, the accuracy of the chosen prediction models will be verified by comparing them to near-ground measurements. First, the measured data will be examined and then prediction models will be discussed and compared to collated data.

Fig. 3 shows the RSSI levels measured in the chosen scenarios. The RSSI from Scenario 1 fluctuates much more than the one from Scenario 2. This can be due to the random distribution of vegetation, as well as the presence of trunks. Moreover, the absorption of energy in Scenario 1 may be caused by the presence of grass.

Fig. 4 shows the SIR measured in both scenarios. It can be inferred that the presence of vegetation has little effect on the quality of the signal, though the reflection on the ground may cause errors depending on the modulation used.

Fig. 5 shows the RTT measured during the experiment. In this case, the time delays vary far more in Scenario 1 than in Scenario 2. This agrees with the observed fluctuations of RSSI in Scenario 1.

In Fig. 6, One-Slope Model was plotted as a function of the logarithm of the distance, in meters. The accuracy of this model was validated by performing its trend line and the related R-squared value. As Fig. 6 shows, the trend line that best fits the plotted data has a linear tendency and an R-squared value of 1.

Finally, we compared the selected prediction models by plotting them together with the collected data from both scenarios in Fig. 7. In this figure, One-Slope Model overlaps Free-Space Model. Attending to the collected data curves, the path loss is higher in Scenario 1. However, the Two-ray Model failed to predict the attenuation correctly. Furthermore, the collected data from Scenario 2 shows a greater path loss than one the predicted by the Free-Space Model and the One-Slope Model.

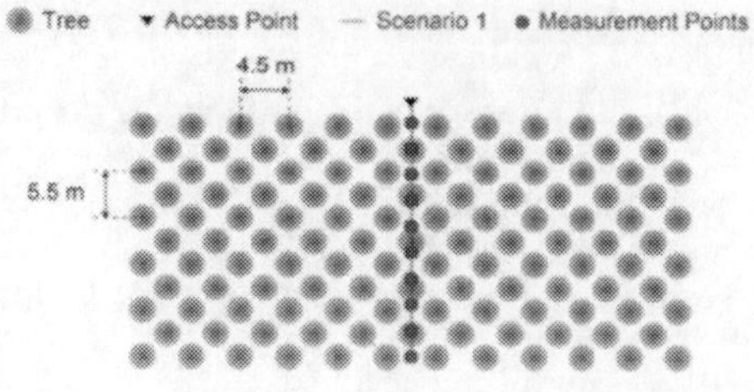

Figure 1. Vegetation geometry and measurement points.

Figure 2. Measurement scenario.

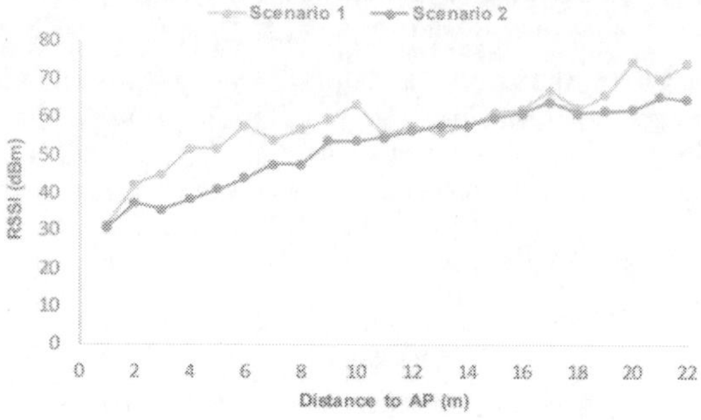

Figure 3. Measured Received Signal Strength Indicator.

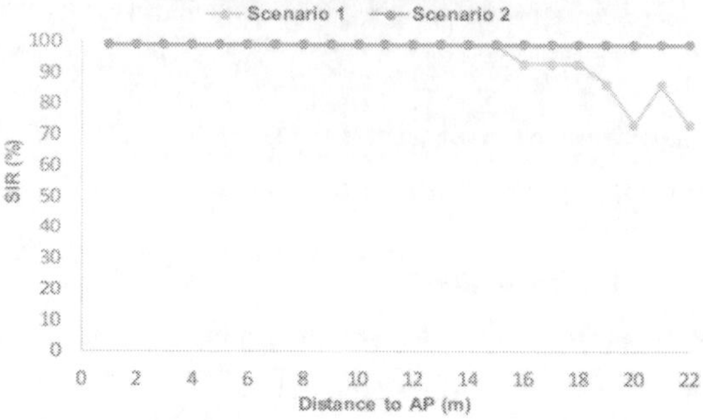

Figure 4. Measured Signal to Interference Ratio.

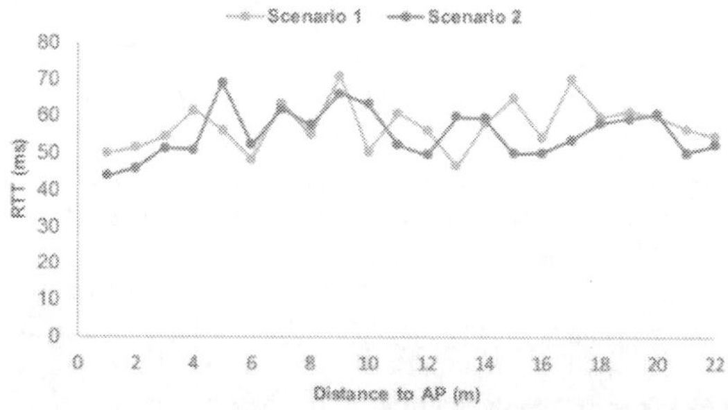

Figure 5. Measured Round Trip Time.

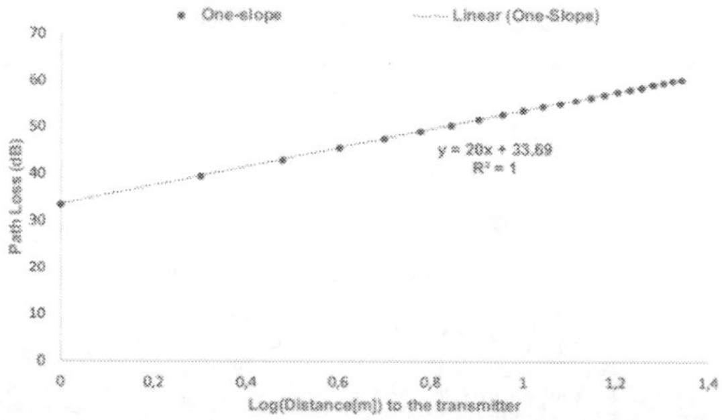

Figure 6. Log-normal Path Loss Model (One-Slope).

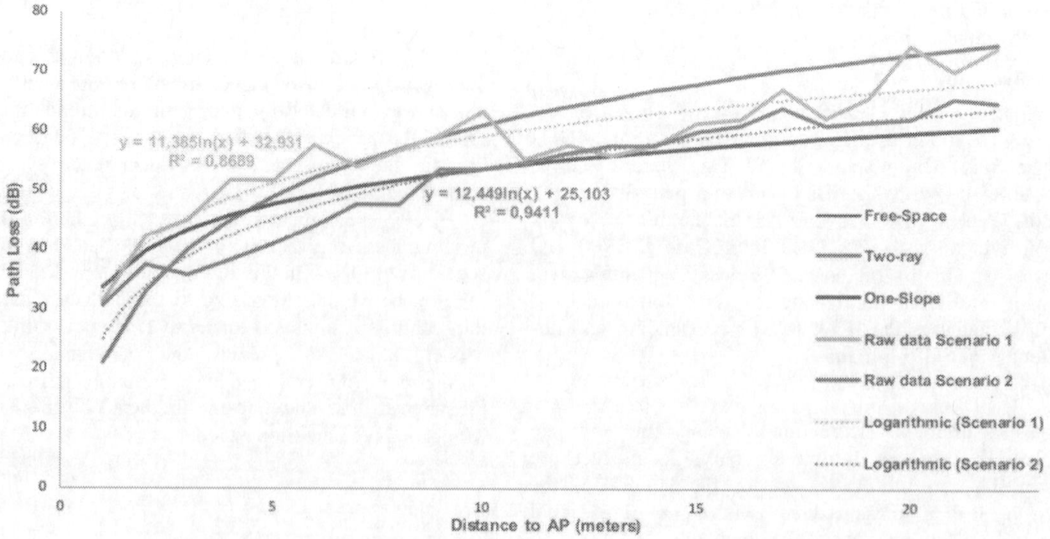

Figure 7. Comparison of path loss models with measured data from Scenario 1 and Scenario 2.

VI. Conclusion and Future Work

In this paper, we attempted to determine how near-ground radio-waves are affected by field components such as grass, soil and, trunks. To this end, we performed an experiment at two different scenarios: one with vegetation and one without vegetation, where measurements were taken 30 cm above the ground.

In this case study, we analysed the signal quality by measuring the RSSI, the SIR and the RTT of a wireless signal and compared the collated data with three different path loss prediction models. The results showed that, in near-ground scenarios, the RSSI tends to fluctuate much more in the presence of vegetation (Scenario 1). In other terms, the geometry of the trees and the presence of grass produced a scattering of energy, as well as a higher number of reflections and refractions. However, the interference was only noticeable from 15 m. As for the selected prediction models, none of them managed to accurately forecast the path loss, though Free-Space Model and One-Slope Model were close to the measured RSSI of Scenario 2.

As future work, we would like to include in the experimental test different types of plantations agriculture environments such as vineyard [9]. Additionally, it could be interesting to perform these practical experiments with other technologies such as LoRa [21], Zigbee and Sigfox which are currently being used in farming activities and compare them with the results of IEEE 802.11 standard.

Acknowledgment

This work has been partially supported by European Union through the ERANETMED project ERANETMED3-227 SMARTWATIR, by the "Ministerio de Economía y Competitividad" in the "Programa Estatal de Fomento de la Investigación Científica y Técnica de Excelencia, Subprograma Estatal de Generación de Conocimiento" within the project under Grant TIN2017-84802-C2-1-P, by the "Ministerio de Ciencia, Innovación y Universidades" through the "Ayudas para la adquisición de equipamiento científico-técnico, Subprograma estatal de infraestructuras de investigación y equipamiento científico-técnico (plan Estatal I+D+i 2017-2020)" (project EQC2018-004988-P), by the Universidad de Granada through the "Programa de Proyectos de Investigación Precompetitivos para Jóvenes Investigadores. Modalidad A jóvenes Doctores" of "Plan Propio de Investigación y Transferencia 2019" (PPJIA2019.10) and by the Campus de Excelencia Internacional Global del Mar (CEI·Mar) through the "Ayudas Proyectos Jóvenes Investigadores CEI·Mar 2019" (Project CEIJ-020).

References

[1] UN DESA | United Nations Department of Economic and Social Affairs (2017), "World population projected to reach 9.8 billion in 2050, and 11.2 billion in 2100" [online] Available at: https://www.un.org/development/desa/en/news/population/world-population-prospects-2017.html (accessed Feb 27, 2020).

[2] H. Bach and W. Mauser, "Sustainable Agriculture and Smart Farming". Earth Observation Open Science and Innovation. ISSI Scientific Report Series, 2018, vol. 15, pp. 261-269.

[3] D. Pivoto, P. D. Waquil, E. Talamini, C. Pauletto, S. Finocchio, V. F. Dalla Corte and G. de Vargas Mores, "Scientific development of smart farming technologies and their application in Brazil". Information Processing in Agriculture, 2018, vol. 5, no. 1, pp. 21-32.

[4] L. Garcia, L. Parra, J. M. Jimenez and J. Lloret, " IoT-Based Smart Irrigation Systems: An Overview on the Recent Trends on Sensors and IoT Systems for Irrigation in Precision Agriculture", Sensors (Basel), 2020, vol. 20, no.4, pp. 1042.

[5] Q. Li and N. Liu, "Monitoring are coverage optimization algorithm based on nodes perceptual mathematical model in wireless sensor networks". Computer Communications, 2019. (In Press). Available at: https://www.sciencedirect.com/science/article/abs/pii/S0140366419315117 (accessed Feb 27, 2020).

[6] S. Sendra, P. Fernandez, C. Turro and J. Lloret. "IEEE 802.11a/b/g/n Indoor Coverage and Performance Comparison". In proc. of the 2010 6th International Conference on Wireless and Mobile Communications, Valencia, Spain, Sept. 23-25, 2010.

[7] M. Bacco, P. Barsocchi, E. Ferro, A. Gotta and M. Ruggeri. "The Digitisation of Agriculture: a Survey of Research Activities on Smart Farming". Array, 2019, vol. 3-4, article 100009.

[8] J. Lindblom, C. Lundström, M. Ljung and A. Jonsson, "Promoting sustainable intensification in precision agriculture: review of decision support systems development and strategies". Precision Agriculture, 2017, vol.18, no.3, pp. 309-331.

[9] J. Lloret, I. Bosch, S. Sendra and A. Serrano, "A Wireless Sensor Network for Vineyard Monitoring That Uses Image Processing". Sensors (Basel), 2011, vol. 11, no.6, pp. 6165-6196.

[10] D. Wand, L. Song, X. Kong and Z. Zhang, "Near-Ground Path Loss Measurements and Modeling for Wireless Sensor Networks at 2.4 GHz". International Journal of Distributed Sensor Networks, 2012, vol. 8, no. 8, 969712.

[11] D. P. Luciani and A. Davis, "RSSI based range analysis of near-ground nodes in Wi-Fi crowded environments," 2013 IEEE International Conference on Technologies for Homeland Security (HST), Waltham, MA, November 12-14, 2013, pp. 693-697.

[12] A. Szajna, M. Athi, A. Rubeck and S. Zekavat, "2.45 GHz near Ground Path Loss and Spatial Correlation for Open Indoor and Snowy Terrain," 2015 IEEE 82nd Vehicular Technology Conference (VTC2015-Fall), Boston, MA, September 6–9, 2015. pp. 1-5.

[13] A. Torabi and S. A. Zekavat, "A Rigorous Model for Predicting the Path Loss in Near-Ground Wireless Sensor Networks," 2015 IEEE 82nd Vehicular Technology Conference (VTC2015-Fall), Boston, MA, September 6–9, 2015, pp. 1-5.

[14] S. Sangodoyin, S. Niranjayan and A. F. Molisch, "A Measurement-Based Model for Outdoor Near-Ground Ultrawideband Channels," IEEE Transactions on Antennas and Propagation, 2016. vol. 64, no. 2, pp. 740-751.

[15] H. Klaina, A. Alejos, O. Aghzout and F. Falcone. "Characterization of Near-Ground Radio Propagation Channel for Wireless Sensor Network with Application in Smart Agriculture", 4th International Electronic Conference on Sensors and Applications (ECSA-4), Online, Nov. 15-30, 2017.

[16] W. Tang, X. Ma, J. Wei and Z. Wang, "Measurement and Analysis of Near-Ground Propagation Models under Different Terrains for Wireless Sensor Networks". Sensors, 2019, vol.19, no.8, pp.1901.

[17] H. U. Yildiz, S. Kurt and B. Tavli, "The Impact of Near-Ground Path Loss Modeling on Wireless Sensor Network Lifetime," 2014 IEEE Military Communications Conference, Baltimore, MD, October 6-8, 2014. pp. 1114-1119.

[18] S. Sun, T. A. Thomas, T. S. Rappaport, H. Nguyen, I. Z. Kovacs and I. Rodriguez, "Path Loss, Shadow Fading, and Line-of-Sight Probability Models for 5G Urban Macro-Cellular Scenarios," 2015 IEEE Globecom Workshops (GC Wkshps), San Diego, CA, December 6-10, 2015. pp. 1-7.

[19] Linksys.com (2020). Linksys WRT320N Dual-Band Wireless-N Gigabit Router Frequently Asked Questions. [online] Available at: https://www.linksys.com/us/support-article?articleNum=137128 (accessed February 27, 2020).

[20] Vistumbler.net. (2020). Vistumbler - Open Source WiFi scanner and channel scanner for windows. [online] Available at: https://www.vistumbler.net/ (accessed February 27, 2020).

[21] R. Vega-Rodríguez, S. Sendra, J. Lloret, P. Romero-Díaz and J. L. Garcia-Navas, "Low Cost LoRa based Network for Forest Fire Detection," 2019 Sixth International Conference on Internet of Things: Systems, Management and Security (IOTSMS), October 22-25, 2019, Granada, Spain, 2019, pp. 177-184.